WHAT THE BIBLE
SAYS ABOUT

LOVE
MARRIAGE
&SEX

The author is represented by Yates & Yates, Attorneys & Literary Agents.

Editorial and Design Services:

Mark Gilroy Creative, LLC with ThinkPen Design, Inc.

www.markgilroy.com

www.thinkpendesign.com

Special thanks to Rob Suggs and William Kruidenier

Unless otherwise indicated, Scripture verses quoted are from *The Holy Bible, New King James Version*, copyright © 1982 by Thomas Nelson, Inc.

Scripture verses marked KJV are taken from *The Holy Bible*, King James Version.

Scripture verses marked NIV are taken from the *Holy Bible, New International Version*® NIV®. Copyright © 1973, 1978, 1984 by International Bible Society. Used by permission of Zondervan Publishing House. All rights reserved.

Scripture quotations from *THE MESSAGE*. Copyright © by Eugene H. Peterson 1993, 1994, 1995, 1996, 2000, 2001, 2002. Used by permission of NavPress Publishing Group.

Scripture quotations taken from the New American Standard Bible® Copyright © 1960, 1962, 1963, 1968, 1971, 1972, 1973, 1975, 1977, 1995 by The Lockman Foundation. Used by permission. (www.Lockman.org)

Scripture quotations marked NLT are taken from the Holy Bible, New Living Translation, copyright 1996, 2004. Used by permission of Tyndale House Publishers, Inc., Wheaton, Illinois 60189. All rights reserved.

Scripture quotations are from The Holy Bible, English Standard Version® (ESV®), copyright © 2001 by Crossway, a publishing ministry of Good News Publishers. Used by permission. All rights reserved.

FaithWords

Hachette Book Group

237 Park Avenue

New York, NY 10017

www.faithwords.com

Printed in the United States of America

RRD-C

First Edition: April 2012

10 9 8 7 6 5 4 3 2 1

FaithWords is a division of Hachette Book Group, Inc.

The FaithWords name and logo are trademarks of Hachette Book Group, Inc.

The Hachette Speakers Bureau provides a wide range of authors for speaking events. To find out more, go to www.hachettespeakersbureau.com or call (866) 376-6591.

The publisher is not responsible for websites (or their content) that are not owned by the publisher.

ISBN 978-1-4555-1142-6

WHAT THE BIBLE
SAYS ABOUT

LOVE
MARRIAGE
&SEX

**THE SONG OF
SOLOMON**

DAVID JEREMIAH

NEW YORK | BOSTON | NASHVILLE

Contents

INTRODUCTION: THE BIBLE TELLS ME *WHAT*?....................... 7

CHAPTER 1: DREAMING OF A PERFECT LOVE...................... 17

CHAPTER 2: THE LANGUAGE OF LOVE 37

CHAPTER 3: LOVESICK AND LOVE-HEALTHY...................... 59

CHAPTER 4: THE QUEST FOR THE PERFECT MATE 81

CHAPTER 5: DREAMING OF SECURITY........................... 101

CHAPTER 6: THE WEDDING PLANNER........................... 125

CHAPTER 7: WHAT GOD THINKS OF SEX 147

CHAPTER 8: LOVE AT LIFE SPEED 169

CHAPTER 9: REKINDLING THE FIRE............................ 189

CHAPTER 10: THE ROMANTIC HUSBAND 213

CHAPTER 11: THE GREAT ESCAPE 235

CHAPTER 12: STAYING IN LOVE FOR LIFE 255

AFTERWORD... 279

Introduction

The Bible Tells Me *What?*

While it seems no subject is off-limits in public conversation today, not that many years ago there were boundaries. Sex, religion, and politics were the big three that were reserved for private discussions—but not always for the right reasons. The Bible doesn't shy away from any topic that is common to human experience and neither should we. The difference between the Bible and our cultural communication is one word: context. The Bible puts every topic in its appropriate context, providing reasons and results from God's perspective.

Can you remember the first time you discovered there was sex in the Bible? More than one young or new Christian has been shocked while perusing the pages of the Old Testament book called Song of Solomon. It says next to nothing about God and seems way too racy to be included in a book about Him. And that shock points out a problem: We've allowed the world to hijack something beautiful and God-given and to turn it into something tawdry. In our reaction to what the world has done with sex and love, we have forgotten a biblical truth: Sex and passionate, romantic love are God's ideas! And in the right setting (there's the context thing), romantic love between a husband and wife is highly charged, amazingly beautiful, and unapologetically physical.

In today's world, you or I might be embarrassed to have a love story like Solomon's—if we had written it about our own love life and broadcast it to the whole world in the Bible. But Solomon wasn't. There's not a thing in the Song of Solomon to be ashamed of. Indeed, you and I can learn a lot about human love and passion from the young king who not only knew how to romance his beloved but how to write about it as well.

That's why I love the Bible. It doesn't dress up for us; it wears the truth just the way we experience it in life. It deals with those topics we're afraid to talk about in public or put into prayer requests. I am so thankful that the Holy Spirit inspired the Bible rather than somebody's proper old great-great-great aunt who lived in Victorian England, as fine a soul as that great aunt might have been. If you or I had written the Bible, we might have taken great pains to make its characters look prim and proper—instead of human. The Bible pulls back the curtain in every area of life, whether sinful or graceful, and sets the stage for God's grace to come in and sanctify the act or correct it. And in Song of Solomon, we get the God-blessed record of marital love in all its glory. I'm glad the Bible is the original no-spin zone.

The fact is that people were created as sexual beings, and the Bible reveals that truth frankly. Throughout the Scriptures we are reminded that "male and female He created them" (Genesis 1:27). And in this short prose poem by Solomon, we get our most extended, gracious, and elegant discourse on how God views love, marriage, and sex between husband and wife.

LOST IN TRANSLATION

There are many common misconceptions about the biblical view of sex, love, and marriage. What God has wanted us to understand from the beginning is profoundly, breathtakingly beautiful. It was the apostle Paul, in the New Testament, who clearly delineated the relationship between earthly love and heavenly love. In Ephesians 5:22-23, he demonstrated that the bond between husband and wife is an earthly picture of a heavenly reality: the bond between Christ and His church. The husband is to love his wife as Christ loves His bride, the church. Can you imagine how lovely our marriages would be if every husband sought to love his wife as Christ loves His church? Can you imagine what a passionate, lovely place the church would be if we brought to it the devotion of a young married couple deeply committed to one another?

Marital love, then, is inherently spiritual, just as true Christian fellowship (and marriage is the pinnacle of Christian fellowship) is intensely passionate and committed. This book is based on Solomon's love poem to his betrothed. Therefore, it is about love, sex, and marriage—lovely gifts of God that bless us and glorify Him.

In teaching the Bible, we should try to say what God says without apology. But too often, as culture and tradition press their dictates upon us, we lose God's voice; we tone down or ramp up His words. For instance, the early church leaders took Paul's teaching about marriage from Ephesians to heart. They enshrined marriage as a spiritual sacrament that ennobles sexual intimacy between husband and wife, particularly for purposes of procreation. But during the later Protestant Reformation (sixteenth-century Europe) church leaders lost or misplaced the idea of marriage as a holy sacrament— though they saw its value for the procreation of families and as a hedge against immorality.

As a result, the church lost that elevated image of sex as a good gift of God, an ongoing symbol of the depth of joy reflecting Christ's powerful love for His church. People began to see marital sex as a matter of satisfying physical desires or procreation which were at best the simple baggage of being human. Sex in marriage became little more than a human means to an end; the notion of its divine heritage seemed to have been lost.

When our teaching about any subject loses its spiritual compass that means people begin to see that topic inadequately—as if there is *any* realm over which Christ is not Lord. Body, soul, mind, and spirit all have their proper place in His kingdom. But we've often treated sexuality so much as a challenge to overcome that many of those venerated as saints, or model Christians, have taken vows of celibacy. I don't point this out to denigrate the lives of those devoted men and women. It's simply to show how we've promoted the idea that sex is somehow an embarrassment to godliness rather than a reflection of it.

Sexuality has become a very confusing subject, laden with anxiety, for Christians today. Hebrews 13:4 captures the two-sided approach to the subject: "Marriage is honorable among all, and the bed undefiled; but fornicators and adulterers God will judge." In his powerful paraphrase of the Bible called *The Message*, Eugene Peterson puts that verse this way: "Honor marriage, and guard the sacredness of sexual intimacy between wife and husband. God draws a firm line against casual and illicit sex." [1]

Here's our question: Have those two views (sacred and sinful) gotten equal time in church? Probably not. Most people I know would agree that it's the second part, the part about casual and illicit sex, with which we've been preoccupied. Preachers (myself included) have done our job proclaiming the dangers of misusing God's gift of sex, and rightfully so. But we've avoided saying all that should have been said about "the sacredness of sexual intimacy between wife and husband." You could say we have thrown out the baby of beautiful, marital sex with the bathwater of immoral, thoughtless sex. In our attempts to guard against the one, we have left people confused about the other.

Could it be that we'd have had to say less about part B if we had done a better job teaching part A? This book is my little effort to do a better job of teaching the sanctity of sexuality.

THE THOUSANDTH SONG

The passage you just read from Hebrews assures us that God blesses sexual love within marriage. And that's not an isolated verse; this message is consistent throughout the Scriptures. Solomon himself wrote in Proverbs—again, in plain language that invites us to do likewise— about the basic goodness of sex:

> *Let your fountain be blessed,*
> *And rejoice with the wife of your youth.*
> *As a loving deer and a graceful doe,*
> *Let her breasts satisfy you at all times;*
> *And always be enraptured with her love.*
> Proverbs 5:18-19

Lots of people who love the Book of Proverbs and have memorized many of its verses are surprised when they come across that passage. It's so . . . well, plain! It's how we might think, but never talk. Yet here's the Bible saying out loud what we might only dare to dream about.

Let's use basic common sense. God is the architect of everything, including sexual intimacy within marriage. It is at the very foundation of human design; where else could it have come from? He made it good, and He made it pleasing for us, and we should not try to cover up or forget that fact. It's like looking at a sunset over the Rocky Mountains and trying to convince ourselves the view is ugly and unworthy. This is something God made, and to be frank about it, one of the most exciting gifts of all! Shame comes only in the misuse of the gift.

Why should we blush over this subject? God devoted a whole book of the Bible to present the context in which sexual love and romance find their fullest expression. That book is the one under our consideration, the Song of Solomon. And the first reason I'm writing this book is that I decided it was high time to add another voice to the few who have spoken out plainly and respectfully about this wonderful book. The Song of Solomon is part of the Bible—the same Bible that houses the Gospels, the Epistles of Paul, the Psalms, and every other inspired portion that we dearly love. It's time to stop the blushing and find the blessing.

The second reason for this book is that our institution of marriage, though endorsed by heaven, is being destroyed by society. You can see it as well as I can; just look around your neighborhood, your community. A 2008 Barna poll revealed that marriages within the church are faring no better than marriages outside it. One-third of the nearly four thousand adult Americans polled have been married and subsequently divorced. When evangelical Christians are grouped with non-evangelical Born Again Christians, their divorce rates mirror those in the general findings of the poll: thirty-two percent. [2] Both the public at large and committed Christians have the same divorce rate.

There's an intriguing little reference in 1 Kings 4:32. It tells us that Solomon wrote a total of one thousand and five songs. From that large field, he selected his chart-topper, his all-time greatest hit. This is why, in Song of Solomon 1:1, Solomon himself refers to this song as "Solomon's Song of Songs." Whatever he found to write about in those other one thousand and four, this love ballad is the one he felt to be his ultimate. More importantly, the Holy Spirit inspired it for all of eternity, intending for hundreds of generations before you, and many yet to be born, to read its words. That makes it a number-one hit on my personal charts.

You might have noticed the variation in title. Is this the Song of Solomon or the Song of Songs? Truthfully, it's both. The Hebrew text of the first verse of the book reads, "The song of songs, which is Solomon's." "Song of Songs" was a Hebrew figure of speech (like Holy of Holies, King of Kings, or Lord of Lords found elsewhere in the Bible) which could also mean "the best of songs." So some English Bible translations take their cue from verse one and call the book Song of Songs. But others call it Song of Solomon because it is, after all, Solomon's song. Either title is justified.

In a previous book I pointed out how Solomon gathered his accumulated wisdom and distilled the best lessons he had learned about the meaning of life.[3] Those lessons he wrote down near the end of his life in the book we know as Ecclesiastes. Song of Solomon, I believe, was written in his younger years when the passion of youth and the desire for love washed over his soul. Completing his literary trilogy is Proverbs—reflective of the most productive period of his life, his middle years as the wisest man on earth.

Readers of world literature have acknowledged Proverbs and Ecclesiastes to be classics on their subjects—practical wisdom and the meaning of life, respectively. And there is no reason for not reading Song of Solomon with the same expectation. All of Solomon's writings pay the diligent reader in spades. I hope that is your expectation as you get to know the world's most beautiful ode to the delights of love and marriage. It is surely the "best of songs" in that regard.

BUT ISN'T IT ALL A METAPHOR?

"Yes, yes," say some. "There is no doubt this is beautiful and inspired poetry. But you're missing the point. It's all symbolism! This isn't really

about sex, but an Old Testament prophetic poem about the relationship
of Christ with His church."

I understand that is what some say—that Song of Solomon is an Old
Testament, metaphorical version of Ephesians 5:22-33, that it's not
about human love and marriage but about divine love and the union
of Christ and His "bride," the church. Various commentators have
espoused this view of the book through the centuries. They've had a
field day going over the imagery in all these verses and matching it up
to New Testament principles. There's something to be said for that, and
I've read some wonderful suggestions about the nature of Christ's love
for His church based on Solomon's love for his bride.

But I'm not prepared to embrace that view of the book myself—to
de-sexualize the Song of Solomon. Our Scriptures work on many levels,
but the presence of symbolism doesn't overrule literal meaning. In
other words, we *can* read the book as a symbolic poem about Christ,
but we *should* primarily read it at face value: as a song of love—romantic and emotional and sexual—between husband and wife. We can read
it as God's benediction and blessing upon marital love—upon the joy
we feel in finding and passionately nurturing the love of a lifetime.

Eugene Peterson has pointed out the two observations we all make as
we read Solomon's book. First, there is beautiful love poetry. Second,
there is explicit sexual detail. It is critical that we see how love and sex
are intertwined. We are tempted to "sanctify" love by speaking of it as
if sex does not exist. Or we make the opposite mistake of stripping sex
of its context of true love. We can no more do either than we can divide
body and soul. Peterson concludes, "The Song proclaims an integrated
wholeness that is at the center of Christian teaching on committed,
wedded love for a world that seems to specialize in loveless sex. The
Song is a convincing witness that men and women were created physically, emotionally, and spiritually to live in love." [4] (By the way, for this

volume I'm borrowing Peterson's convention of referring to Solomon's book as The Song. It's a convenient and pleasing shorthand.)

As always, I entirely place my trust in the Holy Spirit's power to apply these words to the specifics of your life. I must write for as many kinds of readers as possible. You could be at any stage on the love journey. It may be you're eagerly anticipating that ecstatic experience of first love. Or you could be dating, engaged, or a newlywed. You might be thriving in spite of, or merely surviving in the midst of, the tests of marital endurance. You could be in crisis or sitting amidst the rubble of a shattered relationship, praying for God's comfort and guidance. I cannot write to one specific experience, of course, but I know God's Spirit will apply The Song to your life and your heart in a way that is tailor-made for you.

So whether you are 19 or 91, male or female, curious or cultivated in love, let us all look to the same Lord, the one Source of all love and all wisdom, for growth through these stages and in these pages. My prayer is that you'll be as blessed in this reading as I've been in the writing. Once more, I lay down my pen in the realization that we serve a God whose love for us is so powerful, so profound that we can't even capture a glimmer of its totality for an instant. But in the vast array of His many gifts—marital, physical love among them—we grasp tangible signs of His infinite, depthless, and matchless affection for us.

By the time you've finished this study of The Song, I hope you'll be thinking, "If love on earth is this wonderful, what must God have planned for eternity?" May you get glimpses of His eternal love through knowing the gift of His love on earth.

1   Eugene H. Peterson, *The Message: The Bible in Contemporary Language* (Colorado Springs, CO: NavPress, 2002), 2198.

2   "New Marriage and Divorce Statistics Released," *The Barna Update*, 31 March 2008. www.barna.org/FlexPage.aspx?Page=BarnaUpdate&BarnaUpdateID=295, (accessed 31 March 2008.)

3   David Jeremiah, *Searching for Heaven on Earth* (Nashville, TN: Thomas Nelson, 2004).

4   Ibid, Peterson; 1182.

1

DREAMING OF A PERFECT LOVE

Song of Solomon 1:1-8

Here's how it works with love stories: Getting to know the characters makes all the difference.

Take the classic film *Gone With the Wind*. Much of that movie is about
Scarlett O'Hara and the men in her life. But her love story wouldn't
make much sense apart from its background, which happens to be
the Deep South at the time of the American Civil War. Just as in the
real world, even in the movies everyday life has a great impact on one's
love life.

The Song of Solomon works along those lines. If we plunge right in
and read the fervent words of devotion, we're initially taken aback. But
when we know who these people are, the words begin to come to life. So
let's meet the two protagonists in this romance.

First, of course, is Solomon, the lover. He is the second son of David
and Bathsheba, the king of a nation at its historic peak of power. As a
young man he asked God for wisdom, and His wish was granted. We
also remember that it was Solomon who fulfilled his father's dream by

directing the building of Israel's first temple. He was the biblical author of one book of wise sayings, one book of wry reflections, and one passionate song of love. Solomon was a man of terrific wisdom and accomplishment, as well as one with significant flaws that, in the end, brought misfortune to his kingdom.

And the object of his Song? Let's go with tradition and give her the name of Shulamith. Over the years, Bible commentators have latched onto that name for her, based on her identification as "the Shulamite" in Chapter 1. The root word means "the perfect, the peaceful." Compared to Solomon, a dynamic historical figure, Shulamith remains in the shadows. We only know about her what we can gather from the meager scattering of clues in The Song.

We do know that she came from the village of Shunem, located in northeastern Israel, in the territory given to Issachar. She lived and worked among the vineyards there, her skin richly tanned in the manner of those who toil in the sun. We learn that she is Solomon's beloved. This book is a kind of poetic celebration of the couple's courtship, wedding, and even wedding night. It culminates in the later years of their marriage.

Our love story is set ten centuries before Christ. Solomon has already attained tremendous wealth and power, owning vineyards all over Israel. One day the young king happens to be in the vicinity of the Lebanon Mountains, the setting for one of his vineyards. He is there inspecting the vines when a young lady catches his eye. Against the backdrop of the green grapes and the blue sky she is a vision of loveliness, and Solomon is captivated. He knows he will return to these vines more frequently courting this beautiful girl who outshines all the women of Israel.

Inevitably the marriage proposal is made. Considering this is the Son of David offering his love, few women would hesitate a fraction of a second before accepting. Shulamith shows herself to be thoughtful and virtuous by giving the matter some thought. Does she really love him? Can she, a country girl, be happy in the elevated palace of bustling Jerusalem? She concludes that the answer to both questions is yes, though the changes to her simple life will be staggering. Soon the happy couple is traveling to the holy city in an elegant wedding processional.

In the first chapter of the Song, Shulamith is in the midst of her wedding plans, but her heart is already longing for her groom. In lyric poetry, we read about her desire for Solomon, then the wedding, and its night of love. The details are there, captured elegantly rather than crassly. This comprises the first half—we might say the first act—of the Song of Solomon. Act II is all about the joy and tribulation of marriage itself.

Isn't that just the way love is for you and me? Love is terrific, but love is always tested.

INSIDE THE SONG

I don't know how much lyric poetry you've read lately. You might have noticed that genre of writing isn't usually found on the bestseller list. So for most of us, it is necessary to become acclimated to the style of the Song of Solomon. It's not like reading Old Testament history, a Gospel, or an epistle of Paul. It's not even quite like reading a psalm penned by Solomon's father.

The Song of Solomon is a unique hybrid—it combines the elements of a play, a poem, and a song. It is written to be sung, but there is a story being told—something like "John Brown's Body" or some other narrative ballad from our early American heritage. There are different characters who sing their parts—something like a Broadway musical, really. There is figurative and symbolic language, as in the poetry of Shakespeare or Robert Frost. Since the original language was Hebrew, you won't find the rhyme or rhythm you might expect in our own native poetry.

Poetry, play, and song are fused in the Spirit-inspired creativity of Solomon. We also need to get acclimated to the chronology of the story—or the lack thereof. Just as the four Gospels often arrange the stories of Jesus in slightly different order, the action here is not necessarily presented in strict order of occurrence. Think of it as something like a movie with flashbacks as a character recalls the past. At times we may be a little impatient to know what happened when, but that's part of the charm of the Song of Solomon. The lovers are walking a meandering garden path through the history of their relationship, and it is left for us to slowly piece together the picture.

The lovers are not quite alone on that path. The "Daughters of Jerusalem" function in a tradition we often refer to as a "Greek chorus." That is, they're not the principal characters, but they come to the forefront to comment on the action at transitional moments. Sometimes we have to guess who is speaking. Imagine that Solomon and Shulamith are recalling what others have said, and have sprinkled these lines throughout their reminiscences. Don't we all do this when we talk to our spouses? "Solomon, listen to what the other women are saying about us."

To help readers determine who is speaking in The Song, the editors of some Bibles have added headings in the text to identify the speaker. These can be helpful, but keep in mind that they were appended by modern Bible translators, not the Holy Spirit. It's the words of the original text that are inspired, not the headings on which all may not agree.

The Song of Solomon contains eight chapters in our English Bible. Those eight chapters contain fifteen reflections that make up the Song of Solomon. Think of these as fifteen pages from the scrapbook of a woman's love journey, fifteen short movements of a romantic symphony.

I have combined several of the shorter movements, resulting in twelve chapters for this book.

This is a book about love, romance, marriage, and sexual intimacy. The dialogue between Solomon and Shulamith and the mutual love they express for one another provides a lesson for us all; and it is by absorbing the spirit of their loving relationship that our lives can be changed.

THE TRUTH ABOUT SOLOMON

What should every couple do when they become "serious" about a future together? They should sit down and be honest about their individual pasts. We need to do that with Solomon, whose biography we have already looked at in a general way.

Let's not whitewash Solomon's track record, particularly since this is a book about marital love. If you know much about Solomon, you know that marital fidelity wasn't his strong suit. He is a man who began his career in sheer brilliance. He took on the family business, so to speak, and made it a world leader. David had been a wildly popular king, and under Solomon the nation became an empire.

If Solomon exceeded his father's accomplishments, he also exceeded his mistakes. We are told that "when Solomon was old . . . his heart was not loyal to the LORD His God" (1 Kings 11:4). Like his father David, he had a wandering eye and a strong appetite for pleasure. Solomon was especially attracted to foreign women, a vice against which God had warned him. Why? In a time of unprecedented commercial traffic with other nations, the great danger was in the ideas that might drift in along with goods, services, and relationships. False gods were (and are) the greatest danger for God's people. Very gradually, Solomon's vices overcame his virtues and he disobeyed his Lord's commandment about spiritual purity as he built a household of seven hundred wives and three hundred concubines. He pursued not only the women but the gods they served.

Knowing these things, it's reasonable to ask: What can Solomon teach us about the sanctity of the marriage bond; about purity and fidelity? Hasn't he disqualified himself from that discussion? Are we to listen to lessons on monogamy from a man with a thousand women?

Think about the Solomon we meet in Ecclesiastes, the older and sadder, but wiser, man who looks ruefully on the vanity of his mistakes. If we could interview him today, I believe he would come clean about his terrible disobedience, particularly in the way his nation suffered for it. He strayed from the path, but it remains true that he once walked that path with sincere devotion. He walked it with a heart of genuine, selfless commitment. His eventual fall remains as a cautionary lesson for us, but in his best moments he remains a worthy teacher. We also have this divine perspective from the Book of Nehemiah: "Did not Solomon king of Israel sin by these things? Yet among many nations there was no king like him, who was beloved of his God" (Nehemiah 13:26).

Let's remember that David committed a tragic sin with Bathsheba—which doesn't blacken the faith and courage of his earlier confrontation with Goliath. Then there is Moses, whose late act of spiritual arrogance was a disappointment to God; yet his body of work stands, too. I could go on to add your name and mine—none of us perfect, all of us capable of living as a model of obedience if we only submit to walk in the Spirit. In His grace, our Lord bears with our weaknesses. Let us learn from Solomon, in his humanity—negative and positive alike.

DREAM LOVER

What is the key word in the first chapter of The Song? It is *love*. Some form of that four-letter word recurs ten times. And why not? These first words are about first love.

It happens to the best of us, doesn't it? Usually in the age of adolescence we "fall in love" for the first time and it brings the giddiest of life's emotions. We do and say things we might not consider at any other time. For those of us who observe first-time lovers, it can be a bit amusing and delightful to behold. (But we shouldn't forget we were once those starry-eyed lovers ourselves, and maybe still are.)

Look at the first words of Shulamith: "Let him kiss me with the kisses of his mouth—for your love is better than wine" (1:1). The curtain has barely opened and already the passion is pouring forth. Welcome to the Song of Solomon!

The bride-in-waiting doesn't shyly request a polite peck on the cheek. She desires plural kisses right on the mouth. Have you ever thought about a kiss? It's the blending of two senses, taste and touch; stimulating stuff. For Shulamith, the thought of Solomon's kisses is more intoxicating than wine.

One of those landmarks that everyone remembers is the first romantic kiss. For each it is a different experience, but if you and I compared notes we would use words like *awkward, tentative, clumsy,* and *thrilling*— but always *unforgettable.* What we lack in skill, we make up for in sheer emotional electricity.

Little brothers, of course, always seem to be lurking somewhere to spy on the big moment. I heard about a boy who overheard his big sister's cell phone conversation with a friend. Sis said she was expecting her boyfriend to kiss her for the first time on that night's date. At the proper time, little brother climbed the branches of an oak tree near the front door. When the boyfriend walked his sister to the door, he awkwardly asked for a good night kiss. The girl, coming from a devout family, said she wanted to pray first. With just a tad too much drama, she looked into the sky and said, "Father, Father up above, should I kiss the one I love?" To which an answer seemed to come from the branches:

"Sister, sister down below, pucker up and let it go!" Strange and memorable things happen in such moments.

Marriage counselors tell us that kissing is highly underrated. It's the sign of a healthy, romantic marriage. Even more than sex, tender, meaningful kisses are one of the first things to disappear when spouses aren't getting along. Remember this: A kiss is still a kiss, and it still says, "I love you."

Shulamith dreams about expressing love, but she also dreams of experiencing love. The kiss is only the appetizer to the meal of a lifetime. Real love is more than a moment of passion; it is the most comprehensive and inclusive emotion known to man. It may be expressed in a kiss, but Shulamith suggests that love is expressed in several other ways. Let's look at some of them.

THE NOSE KNOWS

Shulamith loves Solomon for his self-respect. Doesn't that always make people more attractive? In verse 3, Shulamith begins her sentence, "Because of the fragrance of your good ointments." She simply refers to Solomon's care in personal grooming. We take that for granted in our culture, but in other places and times the issue has been more significant. In the Israel of three thousand years ago, water and washing weren't readily available. Fresh water was not always accessible and there was no indoor plumbing. Your daily bath or shower would have been far less than daily in Solomon's time. Fragrance came through perfumed ointments (often used to camouflage body odor between bathing). Shulamith is telling us that Solomon's sweet fragrance stays with her.

There will be many lessons in The Song that are difficult to apply in modern terms but this matter of fragrance is not one of them. Men generally think of women as investing "too much time" in their hair, clothes, fragrance—the whole appearance thing. But if Solomon was here, he would tell us men that we ought to pay a bit more attention to sensory things like fragrance. As I counsel with grieving spouses, I often hear about how the lingering fragrance of the absent partner is a poignant reminder of their loved one. A man will encounter her scent among the clothing she has left behind. A woman will climb into his car and it will feel as if he were there not five minutes ago.

When my wife is away from home on a trip, I struggle with her absence. I feel it most when I roll over in bed at night and sniff the fragrance of her hair on her pillow. The scent, of course, is a very pleasant one to me, but it underlines her absence. A man's favorite cologne, worn through the years, can become a powerful stimulus, evoking instant memories in the mind of the one who loves him—just as it did for Shulamith.

THE NAME ENNOBLES

But there is another fragrance that has captured her senses—this time, a figurative one. Shulamith continues, "Your name is ointment poured forth; therefore the virgins love you" (verse 3).

Solomon's grooming was evidence of self-respect; the fragrance of his good name was evidence of others' respect. His fiancée heard the deference and honor with which others treated his name, and it made the word *Solomon* even sweeter to her ear. We've spoken of the senses of taste and touch in the kiss, and of smell in the fragrance. This is the delight of the ear simply to hear her beloved's name and to notice its nobility among others.

Interestingly, it was another young lover who we recall asking, "What's in a name?"—Juliet, in Shakespeare's *Romeo and Juliet*. The two star-crossed lovers agreed that there was nothing of importance in their families' names. But in the Bible, there is much in a name. Names had important meanings, given at birth and maintained through thoughtful living. *Shulamith* had connotations of peace and perfection—goals for which to strive. *Solomon* comes from a similar root and has the same associations. (Note that both *Solomon* and *Shulamith* have the same first three consonants, *s-l-m*, as Hebrew *shalom*, the word for peace.)

We all have literal names and often figurative names that become how we are known to others—our reputation, if you will. Think of names that represent carte blanche in American society, such as Rockefeller, Kennedy, or Vanderbilt. Names can be polished or blackened by the behavior of those who bear them. In Solomon's case, his father David brought a royal pedigree to what was already a good tribal reputation throughout Israel. Jesus Himself would come to bear the honor of the "House of David"—even being known as "Son of David." Names can therefore reach even toward eternity.

Shulamith realized that the sound of *Solomon* was poetry in her hearing, but its ultimate credibility came from the honor it earned more objectively in society. The bride observed that even the young women loved Solomon, increasing her joy that Jerusalem's most eligible bachelor would select her.

Out of deep respect flowed deep love. Throughout this opening of The Song we see how love is built upon this crucial building block of respect. It begins with a man's self-respect, in as small a detail as his grooming; it continues through the evidence of his good name. Respect remains at the very center of a marriage, and it must always be a street that runs two ways. It comes as no surprise that the apostle Paul's admonition to wives is that they "respect" their husband (Ephesians 5:33).

Paige Patterson, President of the Southwestern Baptist Theological Seminary, is a faithful student of the Word of God. He observes that a key theme of the Song of Solomon is introduced here: that sexual intimacy does not emerge from a vacuum. It is bound up in several other factors, the first of which is admiration. Shulamith's adoration of Solomon is reflected in the way she cherishes his name for its sound and its social esteem. These help to flame her love into passion. [1]

Again we realize the foolishness of our world's attempts to separate sex from love as if there can be true and genuine passion apart from soulish intimacy in God's blueprint. Sex doesn't begin in the bedroom or even with a dozen roses. It begins in quiet observations of things like respect, integrity, and character. A wisely observant young lady watches to see how her date treats: the server at a restaurant, or the salesman at the door—or most importantly, his own mother. She watches how he behaves in traffic and what kind of person he is when he thinks no one is looking. Most of all, she looks for his respectful regard of herself. And it works the other way, too.

THE NEED NOURISHES

"Draw me away!" whispers Shulamith in her reverie. "We will run after you. The king has brought me into his chambers. We will be glad and rejoice in you. We will remember your love more than wine. Rightly do they love you" (1:4). Thinking of all these things, including how Solomon is admired by other young women, she can only sigh and wish he would come riding up in a golden chariot to whisk her away forever.

Romantic love expresses itself as an aching need for the beloved. No one else in all the world will do. We glory in who the person is and enjoy the world's shared admiration for him or her. But most of all, we adore what the two of us are together. We *need* to be with one another, to be nourished by one another.

These are the dreams from a young woman's heart, the beginning of the greatest romantic love song ever written. Shulamith dreams of a man whose self-esteem shows in his self-care, whose good name is fragrant among people of repute, and in whose presence life simply feels the best it can possibly feel. If you're reading this book as a single adult, I hope the wisdom of this young woman speaks to you across three thousand years of time. Contemporary television and checkout-lane magazines will never give you this kind of sound advice. Heed the truth of The Song only if you want to build a marriage to last.

And yet these are dreams. In good time, love has a way of bringing us into the real world, doesn't it? Reveries are nice, because we can create our own perfect world within them. The challenge is to make those dreams come true. Beginning in verse five of this first chapter, Shulamith steps out of her dream and begins to contemplate reality.

REAL WORLD LOOKS

The heart's infatuation focuses on the beloved. Then, of course, comes the moment of self-doubt, usually involving a rueful glance in a mirror.

Have you noticed how people who seem to have it all find ways to devalue their "Perfect 10" score? We can be quite certain Shulamith was no wallflower, but notice the way she frets over her reflection in verses 5-6: "I am dark, but lovely, O Daughters of Jerusalem, like the tents of Kedar, like the curtains of Solomon. Do not look upon me, because I am dark, because the sun has tanned me. My mother's sons were angry with me; they made me the keeper of the vineyards, but my own vine-yard I have not kept."

Don't you understand her timidity about moving into a new sphere with different standards? Solomon represents life in the fast lane com-pared to a simple country village. She compares her ruddy complexion to the young women of Jerusalem and wonders again how Solomon could have chosen her. Pale skin was highly valued, a sign of wealth and luxury protected from the sun that vineyards require. She can imagine the other women whispering about her deep tan. How can she fit in when her coloring is so different? She regrets the way her brothers have pushed her out to the fields where her skin was exposed to the Middle Eastern sun.

Yes, Solomon has already spoken. Yes, it was in the fields that he first noticed and loved her. But self-doubt can be irrational. *Will his heart stay constant to someone whose appearance is so different from the usual?* This is a young woman in love, desperately in love. We have all felt as she does.

Even so, hear the words offered almost defiantly to the women of Jerusalem in her imagination: "I am dark, *but I am lovely.*" At the rim of self-doubt, Shulamith reaches back for the assurance of rational reassurance. Dark skin and beauty are in no way incompatible. *I am lovely.* There is no conceit, no vanity in appreciating God's good work in making us. As a matter of fact, we should all see His beauty in ourselves. There is nothing quite so clearly insincere as false modesty. This isn't to say we should be boastful or obsessive about our appearance, but we should regard it as God's work and take pleasure in it.

Just as Solomon has a strong self-regard, we see the same in Shulamith. If she were to give in to poor self-esteem here, it would have negative repercussions on this new relationship. We need to learn to love ourselves before we can fully love each other. Shulamith is comfortable in her own skin. The question is: Are we?

REAL WORLD RESPONSIBILITY

Real world appearance, of course, comes from real world responsibility. It's important for us to care for our health and our personal presentation. At the end of verse six, Shulamith says: "They made me the keeper of the vineyards, but my own vineyard I have not kept." What exactly is she talking about?

You'll remember that vineyards are a crucial point of reference in Shulamith's world. She will use them as metaphors frequently in The

Song, and the meanings will shift according to her subject. The context always gives the clue. Here she refers to her own body. Paraphrase: "I cared for my workplace, but I didn't care for me."

The vineyard in which she labored was a beautiful place, a sunny place, one that required a good bit of maintenance, one that produced fine fruit in the way that a young woman would look forward to giving birth. The analogy is an apt one. Yet even with her God-given beauty, she hadn't the luxury of the "maintenance" her own body needed. She would have realized it as she looked upon the women of Solomon's palatial world: immaculately clothed, perfumed with the most exotic fragrances, their hair gloriously arranged, their skin not bronzed by the sun. Shulamith sees it all, yet no pity parties are in order. We realize from the tone of this passage that she is the kind who steps up to personal responsibility. She will adapt to the new expectations of a princess.

This issue of physical appearance is another confused one for Christians. Early in my ministry, many evangelical churches could be astonishingly legalistic about what women should or should not wear to church. Some were vigilant to make sure that if any lipstick was worn, it wasn't brighter than modern lip gloss—it had a shine but no real color. And rouge? We would have to squint to see it. Conservative churchgoers tolerated "painted women" as well as they did the idea of drums in church. Times change, and as long as we can reasonably see that we're not violating scriptural standards, we have some room to change with the times. Our bodies are like a tasteful frame surrounding a beautiful painting. The frame can detract from the painting by being either shabby or gaudy. And we can draw attention to ourselves and away from Christ by being unkempt or unattractive on the one hand, or too extravagant on the other. Based on the principles in 1 Peter 3:1-6, I believe the apostle would have us to be "appropriate" in appearance—without setting rules which long to be broken. Both Peter and the Old

Testament prophet Samuel call us to give the most attention to the hidden person of the heart (1 Samuel 16:7; 1 Peter 3:4).

Appearance counts. Shulamith knows it, and she wants to be all that she can be for the sake of pleasing her man. The Bible never counsels us to accept mediocrity in anything, but to do everything as to the Lord, including caring for our physical appearance. And it warns us against the folly of comparing ourselves with others (2 Corinthians 10:2). If God is satisfied with our appearance—both physical and in terms of adornment—then we should be as well.

REAL WORLD MATURITY

But there will be other demands on Shulamith. She and Solomon must make their relationship work in a real world with real people—many of whom will stake their own claims on the time of Solomon, who is an important national figure. Shulamith will care for her looks. She will attempt to be all that she can be for the good of the marriage. But sometimes her husband simply won't be present. Like many young wives, she will have to adapt to a lifestyle that often finds her beloved out of reach.

In the seventh verse she confronts this fact. She says: "Tell me, O you whom I love, where you feed your flock, where you make it rest at noon. For why should I be as one who veils herself by the flocks of your companions?"

We'll get to that strange "veil" reference shortly. But let's notice what is really under discussion. As these words are spoken, Solomon is away. He could be involved in any number of royal activities; he isn't free to wander the vineyards of Israel at leisure. Solomon is a type of shepherd, guiding a nation of "sheep." Shulamith wonders why she must wander alongside his flocks, craving a little attention. I need not point out that these thoughts have a very contemporary ring for us. In any time, any place, it is a high-wire balancing act to keep work and family in their proper ratios. Spouses and children are asked to understand, but employers should not abuse the power of being the check-signer: If our families suffer, our society suffers.

Now about that veil: In ancient times, brides wore a veil until the bridegroom removed it in the bridal chamber. In public, veils were worn only by women of ill repute—loose women, prostitutes. They wandered alongside the "shepherds" who might be walking along the avenue going about their work. Shulamith is saying, "You are my man. There is no one else for me but you. Come and remove this veil, free me from following on the heels of your office entourage, and let's be man and wife." It's a touching, plaintive sigh of a woman in love who knows she must make a sacrifice.

This section closes with a very interesting comment from the supporting chorus—the women of the court. As they take the stage of our ancient Broadway musical they hit a sour note. In verse eight, they answer the question Shulamith has just asked, namely, "My love, where do you feed your flocks? Where are you right now?"

No one asked them, but the ladies answer anyway: "If you do not know O fairest among women, follow in the footsteps of the flock, and feed your little goats beside the shepherds' tents" (verse 8). Did you know there was cattiness in the Bible? This may be the first instance of it that I've yet found. Do we detect a note of jealousy? They're saying, "Have you happened to notice that you're marrying a world leader, girl-friend? Get used to the sheep or stay out of the pasture. I think I hear your goats calling you!" Or as they might say in small town America, "If you can't run with the big dogs, stay under the porch."

Even a love story has these petty moments, serving the purpose of showing Shulamith's virtue by contrast. Sadly, there are always those who can't tolerate the supreme happiness and good fortune of others.

SMART LOVE

Let's close this chapter with five observations on love and marriage. If we can get these facts straight, we will be smart about love instead of smarting from it.

You and I Are Wired for Love and Marriage. It's simply in our DNA. Why is it that members of the human race, in all countries, all eras, and all situations reach a certain age and begin to seek a mate? Why is that such a given that we take it completely for granted? Easy. It is because God made us that way. It's a kind of pleasant wake-up call deep inside us, designed to ring at the right time. On the second page of your Bible you'll find these words: "And the LORD God said, 'It is not good that man should be alone; I will make him a helper comparable to him'" (Genesis 2:18). The desire for love and marriage is God-given. He set it lovingly within our hearts amidst many other thoughtful gifts.

Love Is a Full Body Experience. Intimacy is carefully crafted by God to take in the spiritual, emotional, and physical realms of the human experience. In most cases it begins as a physical attraction for us. Time proves to us that this initial bodily impulse is a very small part of the total package. Solomon's Song is going to teach us that everything about us is bound up in our love—and love will change everything about us. That's why it is so powerful in our lives. Intimacy includes sexuality, but it is so much more. Shulamith noticed the fragrance of Solomon's grooming, and then she noticed the fragrance of his popularity. She loved her man with heart, mind, and soul. Love begins with the obvious, physical things and continues to plumb greater depths as long as we share and nurture our relationship. It remains a delightful, profound mystery, but one that educates us in so many ways.

The Marriage Decision Requires Solid Thinking. If you happen to be an unmarried reader, be prepared for that moment when you fall head over heels and want to elope overnight after your first date. Emotions can cloud the intellect. This is one of life's most urgent decisions, one which can bring you incredible joy or unendurable misery. You want to give it some thought, my friend. Shulamith, in these early verses, is doing that. She is still gathering information, pondering, sending her mind into the future and the distance of Jerusalem, considering all the changes that this decision will bring. It is not wrong to be coolly realistic about the secondary considerations that come with hitching one's wagon to that of another. Are you willing to travel where that other wagon takes you?

In premarital counseling, I'm always startled by how many critical issues have not been broached by engaged couples. Will there be children? How many? Who will handle the money? The bride and groom have often had more discussion about the china pattern than they have about the issues that will in large part determine the quality of their relationship.

Looks Shouldn't Be Ignored or Obsessed Over. Like most things, the issue of physical appearance must take its proper place. Some attempt to keep it as the central issue of a relationship, and this is wrong. Others behave just as wrongly, as if they can let themselves go the moment the honeymoon is over. We've seen some mention of physical attributes in The Song, and we'll see more and more graphic ones. Some Christians have the misperception that it's somehow "unspiritual" to attend to the body rather than merely to the soul. The man in his fine suit, the woman with fashionable cosmetics—these must be shallow believers, or so goes the myth.

Yes, it's true that in great marriages we see each other through loving eyes, and we're compassionate about the aging process that impacts us both. But when we make little or no effort to "keep up appearances," what message is being sent to the mate? "I don't care how I look for you." By extension, "I don't care very deeply for you."

I don't particularly enjoy the extra effort of rising early in the morning to go to the gym. But I also don't enjoy the thought of my wife being married to an unattractive old man. I'm working out to keep her husband as well-preserved as possible. I'm working hard on that guy. My personal battles with cancer helped me understand the sheer, often unappreciated gift of optimal physical health. My body is His temple, and it will receive care in accordance with that. Time will take its toll, but that doesn't mean I have to surrender and contribute to the damage.

I am living to maintain the perspective of Job 5:26: "You shall come to the grave at a full age, as a sheaf of grain ripens in its season."

The Fundamental Things Apply. This book is about The Song of Solomon, but you and I realize the real goal is to help Christian couples build strong marriages. It's worth mentioning the basics—God's essentials—before we move on.

First, if you are considering marriage, realize that the Bible forbids Christians from uniting with non-believers (2 Corinthians 6:14). Both God's Word and good common sense give you all the reason you need. But what if you're already married to a non-believing spouse? Philippians 4:11 tells you to stay right where you are, and pray for your spouse. Be the very best mate that you can be, and with God's grace and power your partner may yet come to faith. (See 1 Corinthians 7:12-16.)

And what about you, my friend? If this book has fallen into your hands, you could be realizing just about now that you don't possess the faith we're discussing. The greatest gift you could give yourself, your mate, and your little piece of the world is to find a love deeper than all others: a saving relationship with Jesus Christ. You'll never be a true soul-mate with another human being until your soul finds its home in Him. No, you won't find every human problem solved. It won't immediately cure a bad marriage or the problem of loneliness. But you will begin the process of being transformed toward the destination of an entirely new creature. All the resources of heaven will be available to you, and you will know that the rest of this life, and the one beyond, is a joyful road toward ultimate love, peace, and purpose.

Human love is better than anything in this world with one exception: God's love. His love is outrageously wonderful—precious beyond value, yet totally free. No other words in this book will be more important for you to understand. ◆

1   Paige Patterson, *Song of Solomon* (Chicago, IL: Moody Press, 1986), 34.

2

The Language of Love

Song of Solomon 1:9-14

Maybe love makes the world go 'round, but miscommunication makes marriages go 'round and 'round. Take the case of Vladimir R. and his wife Rosina from Mannheim, Germany.

According to a CNN news report, this older married couple could not see eye-to-eye. What made this couple unique, however, was the creativity used by Vladimir R., 73, in making his point. His side of the story was that his wife would never let him sneak in a word. Once she got warmed up, she simply continued the verbal barrage.

Therefore he brought out the air raid siren.

Who knows where he found it, but it still worked quite well. When Vladimir was ready to do the talking, he turned on the machine and even his wife quickly got the point. "I crank up the siren and let it rip for a few minutes," he said. "It works every time. Afterwards, it's real quiet again."

The neighbors weren't nearly as impressed. They called the police, and soon the 220-volt wartime air-raid siren had been confiscated.

All his wife would say was, "My husband is a stubborn mule, so I have to get loud." [1]

Most marriages aren't quite as bad as that. But even when we try our best we often have problems communicating clearly in our marriages. One good woman, it is told, had to take care of some urgent errands around dinnertime. So she cooked a delicious casserole for her husband, set it in the oven, and set the timer. She quickly scrawled a note and left it on the kitchen table where her husband would see it. The note read, "Dinner in oven." Then she climbed into her car and left to take care of her appointments.

Upon her return, the woman was surprised to find her husband sitting sullenly in the family room eating a peanut butter sandwich and a few stale potato chips from the back of the pantry. He didn't seem very happy. She checked the kitchen and there was her casserole dish, still in the oven untouched. It was his favorite dish!

"Didn't you see my note?" she asked.

"Sure did," he said stiffly. "I got your message. *'Dinner is over!'*"

Suddenly his wife understood that legibility counts in handwriting. [2]

When I say that communication is at the very heart of success or failure in marriage, I'm sure I'm not telling you anything new. It's like saying that bad weather is going to cause you some inconvenience during the year. We all know that, but what can we do about it?

Whether your problem is measured in decibels or "legibles," the issue comes down to the same thing: the challenge of keeping two people on the same page. We find that the longer we allow the disconnection, the greater the number of "pages" that separates us. Soon we're not even in the same book.

That's why we need to keep our marriages in the right Book—the one inspired by God. At the foundation of our identity as His children, we have basic needs, implanted by our Creator that can only be met by the nourishing and unconditional love of an intimate partner. That love is given and received by the medium of clear communication. Let's look at some biblical principles for doing that right, courtesy of Solomon and Shulamith.

1. BE PERSONAL WITH YOUR PRAISE

You simply can't show your love without using the principle of praise. When we are in love we say, "Let me count the ways." It's right here in The Song: the power of magnifying all that is good in your loved one. In the ninth and tenth verses of Chapter 1, we learn to get personal when it comes to praising someone. We also receive a few practical tips on how to do it.

In the previous chapter I'm sure you noticed that we had yet to hear from Solomon himself. Now he speaks. At the beginning of this section, he brings us from the countryside to the palace. You will also recall Shulamith's insecurity about her physical appearance, particularly as measured against the fair-skinned women of the city.

We learn that Solomon is sensitive to her doubts and fears. How does he confront them? By building her up with genuine, heartfelt praise and encouragement.

Tell Her She's Loved. What could be more simple? Love never "goes without saying," nor can it be taken for granted. Many husbands would rather avoid this subject, but they do so at their own risk. Love must find ongoing expression, or it isn't love at all.

Not that you want to say it today as Solomon did in his own time: "I have compared you, my love," he begins, "to my filly among Pharaoh's chariots" (1:9).

I don't know you, but I'm going to go out on a limb and assume your loved one won't appreciate being compared to a horse—even a beautiful horse! Just know that, coming from Solomon's place and time, these are indeed words of praise.

On the other hand, he calls her "my love" ("my darling" in some translations). That one is timeless—one size fits all eras, all situations. We will hear Solomon use this term of endearment eight more times in The Song. Would it be heard eight times in your marriage, say, this week? This month? This year?

Remember also that Shulamith has been treated poorly by her brothers. Why? We know that they grew angry and sentenced her to some period of hard labor in the vineyards. We can draw our own conclusions about this family relationship by the way she refers to her siblings, not as "my brothers" but as "my mother's sons." That's the kind of ambivalence we use when we say about our children, "Guess what *your* son did today?"

Our feelings are revealed in the way we phrase things, aren't they? That is why praise is so important. Solomon looks at his bride and sees the damage of strained family relationships, and his love seeks to repair the damage. He affirms to her that in his home she will be comfortable and well treated. She will be honored and protected, provided for and loved.

At this point it's not unreasonable to ask, "That sounds well and good, but how do you derive all of that from one phrase about a chariot horse?" Solomon's words sound strange to our ears, but we have to understand what he intended to convey. In the days of Solomon, a horse was a symbol of royalty. The king had the best in the land, none of them served as simple beasts of burden.

In 1 Kings 10:26-29 we find Solomon gathering chariots and horsemen—1,400 of the former, 12,000 of the latter. This was no small operation. The king had discerning taste in his stallions that were bought at great price from Egypt. A fine horse brought one hundred fifty shekels, a considerable sum. The art of the chariot worked this way. A team of stallions pulled the cart. They were sleek, powerful, and strong, but (if you know much about horses) not natural leaders. Therefore a harnessed team would be led by what we might call a "boss mare." [3] You can guess why. The stallions had an eye for the fine-looking filly front and center and when she took off, they willingly followed. Now think back to what the king says to his beloved. He compares her to the beautiful mare that runs with the stallions. Shulamith is a lovely woman in a world of men. She is special, worthy of pursuit. This is an elegant metaphor perfect for building up a woman of the time, one who was uncertain and a little bruised.

All of this simply helps us to understand the importance of saying "I love you" in the most powerful terms we can employ—with words spoken and unspoken. We don't need to be told such a thing at the beginning of a love relationship, do we? We are our most eloquent, energetic, and creative selves when we fall in love. We devote ourselves fully to pursuing this person by saying "I love you" in every conceivable fashion. The romantic eloquence peaks at the time of engagement and, in the days after marriage, sadly begins to subside for a thousand trifling reasons.

Marriage must be about things other than romance—things not always romantic: taking out the garbage, paying the bills, dealing with bickering children. It's a great challenge to keep the fire of marital love going. How sad it would be if we saw a comparison graph of the statements we use with each other. For example, what would be the ratio of times when we said, "I love you," to times when we said, "Did you run those errands?" or "What's for supper?" As our marriage talk necessarily becomes more task-centric, we forget the language that makes it so pleasurable. It is so easy to lift the other's heart, and yet is so often forgotten.

Howard Hendricks, one of my professors at Dallas Seminary, used to talk about leading a Bible study with the Dallas Cowboys during their days of regular Super Bowl appearances. When Dr. Hendricks visited the locker room, it was impossible to miss the presence of an offensive guard—a six-foot-eight, 350-pound mountain of a man. Dr. Hendricks got word that the player was having problems in his marriage, and he took him aside for counseling. One of the first questions he asked the player was, "Do you ever tell your wife that you love her?"

The giant replied, "I told her I loved her on our wedding day. That stands until I revoke it!" [4] We laugh at that line because we understand his problem; we've been there ourselves. "I love you" is not a contractual agreement. You need to sign the wedding license only once, but you need to say those three little words thousands of times. Please believe me when I say that they never become redundant. Unlike those who utter them, the words grow richer, not older. As a matter of fact, you might say they keep us young. Love is life-giving.

As a popular song put it back in the 1980s, find ten thousand ways to say it. Be as creative, as Solomon was. Suit the style to the situation. In what way does your spouse need to hear it? Solomon's example suggests several keys.

Tell Her She's Lovely. Have you ever noticed how much more believable a story is when you give details? You make a statement, and when you fill in the blanks you establish credibility. It's wonderful to say the three words we've just discussed, but it's even better to add *why* we love someone. What do you love about your spouse? Yes, "Everything" is an easy answer. But it's far more effective to be specific.

Here is Solomon's example: "Your cheeks are lovely with ornaments, your neck with chains of gold" (verse 10). He focuses on her beauty. Doesn't everyone want to hear that they look nice? Shulamith's cheeks are lovely and beautiful, Solomon observes. They are enhanced by the gentle dance of dangling earrings that catch the rays of a setting sun.

Now having heard those more pleasing words, you might be surprised to hear that Solomon is still thinking about horses! Chariot horses, you see, were dressed accordingly for the transportation of royalty. Their bridles were decorated with jewels, spangles, and feathers. Their manes were braided with jewelry, and all of it complemented the artistry of the carving on the side of the chariot itself. When royal figures made their way through the streets, everyone hurried to watch. It was quite a spectacle of art, pageantry, and power.

How natural it is, then, that Solomon seizes upon the richest imagery of his personal world and pulls his beloved into it, implying that she is worthy of any king.

Notice, however, that it is "your cheeks" and "your neck" that are lovely—not the priceless ornamentation upon them. Youth is a beauty unto itself, and less needful of embellishment than at later stages of life. In any case, it wouldn't mean much for Solomon to say, "Your accessories are the most expensive in the boutique." No, it is Shulamith herself who is lovely, just as the fine mare created by God and trained in the Pharaoh's stable is more inspiring in her own right than a few feathers and ornaments.

As I read Solomon's poetry, I can only wish I had such a gift for eloquence. I would love to be capable of laying such lovely words before my wife on a regular basis, building her up, and honoring her. But we don't need to be poets to find ways to speak our love or declare the other's beauty. Just a humble attempt will create an environment of romance in your home.

Husbands, if you aren't overly confident in your mastery of words, take Gary Chapman's suggestion from his book *The Five Love Languages*. Try writing your expression down on paper, taking your very best shot, and then giving it to your wife. We've lost the enduring art of letter-writing that our great-grandparents enjoyed, and we've forgotten that written expressions can be saved and cherished. Even the best-spoken words fade from memory. Aren't you glad William Shakespeare happened to have a pen in his hand? Put one in yours and write words of loving praise.

I can share that suggestion, but I can't give you the actual script. I can't suggest any Web sites that have the perfect words for your marriage or any books. It has to come from your own heart, and it must be genuine. Believe me, God has given you sufficient creativity to find new ways to say and to show your love. He will inspire you.

Telling our spouse we love her or him can be meaningful as we head out the door to work or prepare to hang up the phone. But there also needs to be quiet, extended moments. And for us men, that means putting down the TV remote or the newspaper and focusing solely on our beloved, just as Solomon did—with words of adoration, admiration, and appreciation. Words of love that reflect thought and conviction born out of an awareness of who she is specifically. What is she wearing? Is it colorful or pleasing? What has she done with her hair? Since God made her, she is lovely—that's a lasting truth. Your job is to keep a running account of the various aspects of that beauty.

2. GO PUBLIC WITH YOUR PRAISE

Now it gets a little more difficult—but hang in there.

Have you ever seen that guy at the office who is surrounded by co-workers when his wife calls on the phone—the guy who at the end of the conversation says, "Me, too"? It's obvious that his wife has just said, "I love you," and he has replied with a shorthand substitute: "Me, too." He may actually say "I love you" at home, but he's not quite secure enough to say it in front of the guys in the office.

Yet here's the next principle we learn from The Song. Go public! Put it out there. In the eleventh verse, Solomon continues, "We will make you ornaments of gold with studs of silver." Note the change in pronouns from verse nine ("I") to verse eleven ("we"). Solomon has gone public with his love; he is involving other people ("we") in professing his love for Shulamith through the creation of gifts of gold and silver.

As you socialize with other couples, how do you notice them speaking of each other? What clues are dropped about their mutual respect, or lack thereof?

Gary Chapman has a great idea. He suggests praising your spouse to a third party, out of the spouse's hearing. Why would we do that? Because powerful words always find their way back to their object. The spouse will find out what you said, and the words will have even greater power, greater credibility—a compliment unearthed like buried treasure. Call it indirect praise filtered through someone else. Chapman even points out that if a husband praises his wife to her mother, the mother will amplify his words when she passes them on, and the husband will get extra credit! He also recommends that we give the praise when our spouses are there to bask in it. Also, we can share any praise that comes our way: "Thank you, but I never could have done that without the help of (spouse)." [5]

I read a book about John Newton, the composer of "Amazing Grace," that is filled with the wonderful remarks he made about his wife. An example: "Every room where Mary is not present looks unfurnished." [6] Again, the point is not whether you or I could ever turn a phrase like a gifted hymn-writer. The point is that as you read about that man's life you observe marital praise frequently, and Newton made his praise public. Talking up our spouses should be an entrenched habit as natural as breathing.

These are all ways to magnify the power of speaking our love. Winston Churchill certainly found a way to get it done. At a banquet, he was sitting next to his wife when asked to field this question: If he could not be himself but had to be someone else, who would he choose to be? He took his wife's hand as he answered," If I couldn't be who I am, I would most like to be Lady Churchill's second husband." James Humes, the prime minister's biographer, concluded, "That night, Churchill scored some points." [7]

Need I tell you that the opposite approach can be devastating? Make it a steadfast rule never to air out a grievance about your spouse in the presence of others—no matter how slight. I've seen the pain too many times in my work as a pastor. On one occasion, Donna and I were on our way to a capital campaign to raise money for a building project. This was a formal dinner at a country club in Fort Wayne, Indiana, and our church leaders and committee members were present. After a fine dinner, we were standing around talking when one of the wives approached us. She said to her husband, "We have a babysitter. We need to leave pretty soon." Her husband turned around and replied, for everyone to hear: "Well, if you want to go home, why don't you just walk?"

It was as if someone had let the air out of the room. Everyone was shocked, and I can tell you that after thirty years, I can still see it and hear it vividly in my memory—particularly the injured expression on the woman's face. Nothing will destroy a marriage more quickly than public insult. If there's an issue, you need to attend to it. But do it in the privacy of your home. In public, only loving support is appropriate.

3. BE PASSIONATE WITH YOUR PRAISE

We need to be personal and public, but we must also be passionate. That's the carbonation that puts the "fizz" in the cola. There is, "I love you," and then there is, "I *love* you!" The italics and the exclamation mark may be invisible in conversation, but we recognize the difference in how the words are said. One spouse says it with real meaning, the other bats the words back where they came from with no discernible emotion. Sometimes it's worse to say "I love you" the wrong way, than not to say it at all.

In our biblical passage, Solomon has been speaking words of love to Shulamith. But now the speaker changes again; Shulamith begins to address praises to Solomon. The effect is something like a contest in which the two try to "outdo one another in showing honor" (Romans 12:10, *English Standard Version*). It's a nice idea, isn't it? Solomon has spoken his love, and Shulamith tries to top him.

Gordon McDonald has written of this passage:

> *These are two people whose emotions are so swelled that words are inadequate to express what they are feeling. They must resort to other images like the strength and the beauty of trees, or the taste of fruit. Suddenly I realized why a man may call his wife "Honey" or "Baby." A loving couple began early in their relationship to develop a private vocabulary, some of which they would never disclose to the outside world. These words have significance which only the two understand.* [8]

Nearly every couple develops a private love vocabulary. Shortly after Donna and I were married, we went off to seminary where I began studying the biblical Greek language. One day I came home and told Donna that I loved her—using *koiné* Greek, the biblical language which all New Testament students learn. Fascinated, Donna immediately wanted to learn how to say it herself. I had fun teaching her to pronounce the phrase. And to this very day, the *koiné* Greek words for "I love you" are special and personal for us. It's an ancient language that isn't used in any culture, but it's very active in the culture of our home. It's fun to be able to say something to each other that is "our little secret," so that no one around us understands. Even our kids never caught on! I hope you have a special language in your marriage.

Let's discover how Shulamith shows her passion.

Passionate About His Dignity. Be forewarned: In this section, when we use the word *passionate*, we mean it. A biblical display of affection follows.

Verse 12 reads, "While the king is at his table, my spikenard sends forth its fragrance." The word *spikenard* doesn't quite carry the music of poetry, does it? Nor does it sound like a name we would assign to a perfume. Yet in the Bible, this is the name of a very precious fragrance. Shulamith will describe her love for Solomon by referring to three different kinds of perfume.

Spikenard is derived from a plant native to the Himalayan region of India and grown between 11,000 and 17,000 feet above sea level. In ancient times, only the very rich could afford it. For one thing, it couldn't exactly be grown in one's backyard—the conditions had to be just so. Even today, spikenard is available and costly, pungent with its warm, earthy aroma. [9] A little of it goes a long way, or so I'm told. You might recall the Gospel story of Mary of Bethany, who poured an alabaster container of spikenard perfume on Jesus in an act of extravagant worship. The Bible tells us that the fragrance quickly permeated the house (Luke 7:36-50). Back in the Old Testament, a dab of the scent on Shulamith would be certain to attract Solomon's attention, even as he presided at a royal banquet table spread with rich-smelling culinary delights.

Shulamith is passionate about her man's dignity. Royalty deserves royal fragrance, and the aroma of spikenard sends that message.

Passionate About His Devotion. Shulamith says, "A bundle of myrrh is my beloved to me, that lies all night between my breasts" (verse 13). Not only is Shulamith passionate about his dignity, but also his devotion. She feels the love of Solomon like a sachet of myrrh resting between her breasts.

And now for a word about myrrh, that strange substance we hear about at Christmas time—a gift to the Christ child from the wise men who followed the star. (See Matthew 2:11.) Myrrh is a resinous gum gathered from a species of South Arabian trees. As a liquid, it was carried in small bottles like a perfume. But it could also be found in solid form, in which case it might be carried in a small pouch or sachet worn about a woman's neck. The myrrh would be mixed with a bit of fat that would melt from the heat of the sun releasing the fragrance of resin to fill the room. [10] It tasted bitter, but it smelled rich and lovely. Worth its weight in gold, this was to be the primary ingredient in the anointing oil that God directed Moses to prepare in Exodus 30:23-33.

Shulamith's words are sensual but not particularly sexual. The idea is that the fragrance of the myrrh was another rich, fragrant reminder of Solomon, who held a royal place in her nation and her heart. The sachet, worn close to the heart day and night, was a symbol of his devotion to her that was permanent and unchanging. The constant love of a spouse is like that—we close our eyes at night knowing that same head will be on the other pillow for this night and every night to come. With so many transient, untrustworthy things in this world, we hold the love of our marriage close to our heart, fragrant and precious.

Passionate About His Distinction. Finally, Shulamith is passionate about the qualities that set Solomon apart from other men. In the following verse she says, "My beloved is to me a cluster of henna blooms in the vineyards of En Gedi" (verse 14).

En Gedi lies along the western shore of the Dead Sea. Vineyards are there, but the name means "The Spring of Kid" because of the wild mountain goats nearby. Known as ibexes, these goats find their way down the mountain to the oasis of En Gedi to drink from its cool springs. The vicinity is surrounded by arid desert, and it's also the region where David once hid in the rock caves from King Saul. So, like so much of Israel, this is an intriguing area: beauty surrounded by desolation, tranquility tinged with danger—a place where God's hand has moved in profound ways.

In this climate and with the many watering holes all around, henna sprung up across the hillsides. It has a blue-black berry and a white flower with a sweet, clean, fragrance that lingers in the air. [11]

Isn't it delightful how Solomon's Song must be read with the five senses at full attention? Smell, taste, touch, sight, and sound are all vessels of human and godly love. Genuine love has that effect on us. Our devotion overflows through every human channel.

Archeologists have excavated shops where perfume was formulated at En Gedi.[12] In these very markets, the fine henna perfume that Shulamith describes was sold. For her, of course, it's all about Solomon, of whom all these tastes and aromatic delights are only a reminder. She sees her man as a wonderful oasis in a desert of unremarkable men.

For many of our single men and women, the great quest of life is that one person who stands out, that man or woman of distinction in a seemingly arid landscape of humanity. Some people say, "When you meet the right one, you'll just know." It sounds too trite, too Hollywood, and yet sometimes it works out like that after all. Years ago our youngest daughter, Jennifer, was getting ready to go to seminary.

One of her friends from the school called her on the phone to fill her in on what to expect when she got there. She said, "Jennifer, as a female seminary student, you're going to be in the minority up here. Let me tell you about that: The odds are good, but the goods are odd." In her opinion, more quantity than quality. Yet Jennifer found the love of her life there.

We want to "just know." We need love to be as clear as a bright, vivid oasis in the middle of a desert. In this day of broken relationships, we want to be rock-solid certain that we've found the one and only life partner that God has reserved for us. We have a full chapter on this subject a little later; for the time being, our point is that there was no doubt in Shulamith's mind. Her man was outstanding in his field—an oasis in the desert.

If you're married, have you recently told your partner what distinguishes him or her? You might need to give that some thought, and thank God that He found the right one for you. Then, after expressing your gratitude to Him, let your spouse know. Build up your life mate with praise. This first chapter of The Song has given us a terrific example of how a couple can creatively express their love for one another. You can only imagine how these words inflamed their mutual passion. Is there any doubt that such a loving exchange, using more contemporary terms, would do the same for you?

FOUR SECRETS OF LOVING CONVERSATION

Just as fragrant perfume was extracted from some of the plants we've discussed, real wisdom can be extracted from the verses of the biblical chapter we are studying. Let's think about four of these.

1. Speak Sweet Words to One Another. Elsewhere, Solomon has written: "Pleasant words are like a honeycomb, sweetness to the soul and the health of the bones" (Proverb 16:24). What could be sweeter or more refreshing than words of praise and love?

In his book, *A Couples Guide to Communication,* John Gottman tells us that what sets married couples apart from strangers is that married couples are far less polite with each other. With his or her own spouse, tragically enough, someone is much more likely to interrupt and to criticize, and far less likely to offer a compliment. [13] A courtship begins, it has been said, when a man whispers sweet nothings. It ends when he says nothing sweet.

Such is the way of the world, but is there any law that says we have to live that way? God's law says not only that we do not, but that we must not. Peter writes: "Husbands, likewise, dwell with them with understanding, giving honor to the wife . . ." (1 Peter 3:7). One of the truths of that verse is that marriage is a learning experience that never ends. The relationship must keep growing, and we must continue finding new ways to renew our love and help each other become the people God has called us to be.

Marriage must be kept alive and filled with delight and surprise. The best way to get that started is to sweeten our language. Nothing could be simpler for us to do than to offer words of praise and encouragement. Nothing could reap greater rewards for both of us.

2. Speak Soft Words to One Another. Again, look to Solomon for the right guideline: "A soft answer turns away wrath, but a harsh word stirs up anger" (Proverbs 15:1). Why must we be so harsh so frequently in marriage? There's never any genuine excuse, considering that a husband is to love his wife as Christ loves the church, and a wife is to honor her husband as the church honors Christ. Mean-spirited words are the slowest and most venomous of weapons, a poison that ultimately brings down two lives. And it is nearly always the tone of voice that makes the difference. This is why Solomon so wisely counsels us to offer a *soft* answer to someone else's wrath. It defuses the bomb. A much more recent poet, Ogden Nash, has it exactly right:

> *To keep your marriage brimming*
> *With love in the loving cup,*
> *Whenever you're wrong admit it;*
> *Whenever you're right; shut up.* [14]

Watch that tone, and temper those words. As for your home, there should be a sweet, sweet spirit there—and your words are the leading indicator.

3. Speak Sensitive Words to One Another. Try this one: "He who gives a right answer kisses the lips" (Proverbs 24:26). You'll have to admit, that's a compelling Bible verse (though I wouldn't recommend it for a classroom policy!) What does this mean? Soft, sensitive words are as pleasing as a tender kiss. When we say just the right words at just the right time, it feels very good to both people.

It's not just *what* you say, but *how* you say it. In other words, when it comes to communication, style points apply. The wife asks, "Do you think this dress looks okay on me?" It's possible to give a good, honest answer but to give it with love and sensitivity. Instead of saying, "No way! It makes you look overweight!" you could give her a little hug and say, "Anything you wear looks nice because you're the one wearing it. But since you asked—you know I've always loved how you look in the blue dress. But I'm fine with whatever you choose."

That's what Solomon calls "the right answer." And you might even try giving it *with* a kiss on the lips!

4. Speak Strengthening Words to One Another. Sweet, soft, sensitive—and finally, strengthening. "Anxiety in the heart of man causes depression, but a good word makes it glad" (Proverbs 12:25).

Here is a thought for the ladies. Your husband comes home after a terrible day. He's beset by the anxieties of the workplace, and he's had to put up with little irritations from co-workers and disrespectful treatment from the boss. In this business climate, it's not as if he can simply pack his briefcase and go take a less stressful job. There are so many pressures in the corporate world of today. As he walks in the door, try to put yourself in his shoes. Sense his mood, and act accordingly. The Bible says that even when anxieties burden his heart, a good word will gladden him.

Here's a suggestion, an old chestnut that never grows old: "Honey, I'm so thankful for the way you are strong for our family. The way you can hang tough in a tough world, simply in order to provide for us." Respect and admiration mean a lot to a man. He can be stronger when he knows it is appreciated.

In the New Testament, there are fifteen different passages detailing how to respond to one another in the family of God. Five of those fifteen specify *encouragement*. (See 1 Thessalonians 4:18 and 5:11, for example.) Paul was all about encouragement, sending various young men to encourage the discouraged even as he himself sat in prison. The church is continually to revitalize and renew itself through the encouragement that we provide for each other. How many of your words perform that function in a given day? How many in your marriage? How many as a parent? How many as a worker?

CREATE THE PERFECT MATE

Joe is a character in a story told by the late Ted Engstrom, former leader of Youth for Christ International and World Vision International. Joe is thoroughly sick of his wife after only three years of marriage. She has gained weight, so he isn't attracted to her anymore. He doesn't even find her very likeable; and now he wants to express his resentment in some way that will pay her back for his misery. He meets with a divorce lawyer, but takes one more step before the papers can be served—a *coup de grace* as a parting gesture. He meets with an old buddy who is a psychiatrist and asks for advice on how to make his wife's life as difficult as possible in the final days of their marriage.

The psychiatrist listens carefully, then says, "Okay, Joe, here's what you do. I want you to go home tonight and treat her as if she were a goddess. That's right—a goddess. I want you to veer 180 degrees from how you've been feeling and how you've been treating her. Make every moment a mission dedicated to her deepest pleasure. Listen carefully to everything she says as if it's the most important thing in the world at that instant. When you see her doing any housework, leap up and out-work her. Then you're going to take her out to dinner—no diner either, but the best place in town. She's going to be a *goddess*, got that? I want you to do this for two months."

Joe attends to all this rather dubiously. "Yeah? And what comes next?"

"Just when she's on Cloud Nine," says the psychiatrist, "Walk out. Pack your bags, tell her it's over, and hit the road."

"Man," says Joe, catching his breath. "That's . . . that's *ruthless*. It will be devastating!"

With great relish, Joe put his devious plan into action. He treats her as if the moon, sun, and stars revolve around her. There's breakfast in bed, a dozen roses at unexpected moments, gourmet restaurants, trips to the theater, and Joe has dishpan hands. She drifts off to sleep at night as he reads to her from her favorite novel. There is one romantic getaway weekend for each of the two months. Best of all from her perspective, Joe is listening to her. She has never felt such attentiveness, such empathy. She has absolutely no idea what lightning bolt has struck her husband, but she hopes it keeps doing its thing.

Inevitably, of course, the two months are over. The psychiatrist, curious to find out how the plan has worked, calls Joe on the phone. "Well?" he asks. "Are you a bachelor yet? Have you gotten the divorce?"

"Divorce?" Joe asks, as if the idea is brand new to him. "Are you crazy? Why would I file for divorce, when I'm married to a goddess?" [15]

The truth is that we respond positively when we are treated with love. We are shaping one another every day in slow sculpture. C. S. Lewis once gave an address entitled "The Weight of Glory" that asks whether we are ready for the challenge of carrying the burden of each other's final glory, our spiritual destination. We are constantly helping one another, small act by small act, toward becoming the godly creature—the image of Christ—that God intends. Or, tragically, we are tearing each other down, making the distance to ultimate glory farther by increments. Nowhere is this more true than in the daily life of marriage.

Today you might speak little words that never get a second thought from you—words of slight blessing or curse. Yet those words can contribute toward your spouse's personal dignity and self-love; or they can subtly weaken and discourage that precious, beloved life mate that God has provided you. When we counsel young people contemplating marriage, we need to ask them C. S. Lewis's question: Are you willing to bear the weight of this person's glory, to shoulder the burden of his or her spiritual destiny? Are you prepared to carry such a load for someone's journey toward heaven?

We can all tell certain things about couples. We can spend just a few moments around them and see the nature of their relationship. Sometimes we see unholy deadlock. And every now and then we see holy wedlock: two souls who, by virtue of their combined love, are becoming stronger and wiser every single day, transformed to the image of Christ. They even start to look like one another, but they act like Someone else.

SPIRITUALLY KNIT

The greatest goal for your marriage is one of spiritual intimacy—simply getting on the same page in your pursuit of God. Let me give you an example of how that may work.

Let's consider a newly married couple. The wife, through one of her close friends, becomes a new Christian, but the husband is still a non-believer. As she begins to grow in her new faith, the husband observes the change with great interest. He sees her becoming more patient, more kind and attentive; and she tells him how she is praying and working toward applying the Scripture that she is now studying daily. She is a better wife; it can't be denied. He watches her leave for church on Sunday, and finds himself wanting to go along, to see what it's all about.

The husband finds that he is becoming a spiritual seeker himself. He seeks the Lord his wife has been serving—and as he approaches Christ, he grows closer to his wife. There is a new depth, a new maturity in their marriage. Both are aware of it. The happy day comes when both of them have accepted Christ as Lord and Savior, and they can begin serving Him together.

The most intimate place any couple can be is a state of unity in Christ—entwined in His love, which empowers their own affection. This is the highest goal of marriage, and without it, any marriage is frankly handicapped.

Take two different pianos and tune them to the same tuning fork. You will find that the pianos will naturally be in tune with each other. Christ is the source of our music in marriage and in life. If your marriage has grown discordant, if it is out of tune, or even if you're only beginning the first verse—make it your greatest goal to find spiritual harmony by loving and serving Christ together.

Will you avoid all future problems and live in some state of ecstatic bliss? Of course not. But will you experience far more joy, far more peace and contentment, and far more comfort in the arms of each other? Absolutely. There is a reason this is The Song of Solomon rather than the Dry Lecture of Solomon or the Marriage Counseling of Solomon. After a while, it's no longer such hard work, such drudgery to keep a marriage going.

After a while, it's just like a song—perfectly in tune; two contented souls singing to the glory of God and the sheer pleasure of one another. ◆

1   ABC News, April 20, 2003, at http://www.abc.net.au/news/stories/2003/04/20/836126.htm (accessed at 22 December 2008).
2   Evelyn Shetter, Abilene, Kansas, "Lite Fare," *Christian Reader* (May/June 2000), quoted at http://www.preachingtoday.com (accessed 5 January 2009).
3   "Stallion," http://en.wikipedia.org/wiki/Stallion (accessed 13 November 2008).
4   Gary Smalley and John Trent, *The Blessing* (Nashville: Thomas Nelson, 1993), 54.
5   Gary Chapman, *The Five Love Languages: How to Express Your Heartfelt Commitment to Your Mate* (Chicago, IL: Northfield Publishing, 1995), 49-50.
6   Steve Turner, *Amazing Grace: The Story of American's Most Beloved Song* (New York: HarperCollins, 2003), 105.
7   James Humes, *Churchill, Speaker of the Century* (Briarcliff Manor, NY: Stein and Day/Scarborough House, 1980), 29.
8   Gordon MacDonald, *Magnificent Marriage* (Wheaton, IL: Tyndale House, 1976), 23.
9   [http://en.wikipedia.org/wiki/Spikenard]
10 G. Lloyd Carr, *The Song of Solomon: An Introduction and Commentary* (Downers Grove, IL: InterVarsity Press, 1984), 84-85.
11 "Henna" http://www.tigerflag.com/madini_henna.html (accessed 13 November 2008).
12 "En Gedi," http://www.bibleplaces.com/engedi.htm (accessed 13 November 2008).
13 John Gottman, *A Couple's Guide to Communication* (Champaign, IL: Research Press, 1976), 45.
14 Douglas M. Parker, *Ogden Nash: The Life and Work of America's Laureate of Light Verse* (Chicago, IL: Ivan R. Dee, Publisher, 2005), 106.
15 Ted W. Engstrom, *The Fine Art of Friendship* (Nashville: Thomas Nelson, 1985), 128-129.

3

Lovesick and Love-Healthy

Song of Solomon 1:15-2:7

"I've fallen and I can't get up!"

Those words were originally part of a health service commercial, but Solomon could have been saying them about himself—fallen in love, that is. Has it ever happened to you? Have you fallen "head over heels," as we say, so that you can't seem to focus on anything else?

It's certainly nothing new. The Greek philosopher Plato called this passionate, romantic love *theia mania*, or "madness from the gods," characterized by the sudden absence of rational thinking and the wild emotional ups and downs that accompany the experience. [1] Many people become lovesick, but the question remains: Is it a sickness at all, and if so, do we want to be cured?

Science has tried to get a grip on the mysteries of falling in love for centuries. The psychologist Dorothy Tennov decided we needed an entirely new word, something that sounded more scholarly than *lovesick*. The word she chose was *limerence*, and she devoted her professional life to carefully interviewing thousands of people who were truly, madly, deeply in love. A few of the inevitable signs of *limerence*, she said, were these:

- A literal "heartache"—a pressure in the chest, relieved by sighing.
- A longing to have one's love reciprocated.
- An intense fear of rejection.
- Drastic, almost bipolar mood swings.
- A passion that resistance or adversity only served to increase.
- Intrusive thinking about the one we love: 30 percent of one's time at first, then, in the "second wave" of limerence, something approaching 100 percent of our thinking. [2]

It sounds as if the psychologists have been listening to too many show tunes, but Dr. Tennov's enormous research was consistent in its findings of how we behave when we're truly lovesick. When obsessive love meets its match, the results can be extraordinary. Some years ago, Sheldon Vanauken wrote a classic memoir about the love of his life. It was called *A Severe Mercy,* and it told the moving story of a remarkable love between man and wife that endured until the death of Davy, Vanauken's beloved. In the beginning, the two made a covenant together that everything in life must be shared to the full—if one person couldn't have an experience, the other shouldn't either. Their love must be all-inclusive.

Therefore they actually decided not to have children, because a man could not have the experience of childbirth. Remember, they were young and starry-eyed, more than a bit irrational, and at this point nonbelievers. Nonetheless, even if they took their relationship to extremes, their powerful sense of romantic love and devotion is inspiring to read. In time, the couple found a love even greater than they could share together. Through their journey, and through correspondence with their friend C. S. Lewis, the Vanaukens ultimately came to a saving faith in Christ.[3]

Human love can be something like a force of nature—powerful, irresistible. It can take over all our thoughts and feelings. So many things happen inside us: body, mind, and spirit are all working overtime. Should we be surprised to find that Solomon was thousands of years ahead of the curve? In his Song, he eloquently describes lovesickness, *limerence*, or whatever you may choose to call it. His book is somewhat of a travel guide to the entire journey of love, for it is divided into three sections: courtship, wedding, and marriage. We are still moving through the first chapter, and therefore we're in the early stages of the romance of Solomon and Shulamith.

A MUTUAL ADMIRATION SOCIETY

We find ourselves in the midst of a series of dialogues between lovers. Solomon speaks his feelings, Shulamith responds, and Solomon replies—a kind of "tennis match" of love. (Remember, the word "love" is used in scoring tennis!)

One thing we must do, particularly as we isolate each verse for our discussion, is to keep in mind who is doing the talking and what idea is being answered. We also need to step back occasionally and get the whole picture, in which case we discover that every exchange is a bit more intimate, a bit more passionate than the one it follows.

In short, the heat rises, and all that passion is here for our delight and edification for those who are married and for those who plan to be so. We can simply grab a box of popcorn and sit back to enjoy a couple in their competition to out-love one another. That, by the way, is the only competition I can endorse for marriage.

Let's pick up the action.

Solomon Admires the Sensuality of Her Eyes. We begin, as always, with verbal affirmation. Solomon leads off by admiring the sensuality of Shulamith's eyes: "Behold, you are fair, my love! Behold, you are fair! You have dove's eyes" (verse 15).

Again Solomon addresses Shulamith as "My love." Some translations render this phrase, "How beautiful you are, my darling" (NIV, NASB). Twice he says she is fair, and he uses a word that indicates a beauty that is more than skin deep.

Then, having declared that beauty, Solomon sets out to describe it. Shulamith's eyes are like those of a dove, meaning soft and gentle— filled with innocence. Then as now, the eyes are a focal point of a woman's beauty. It has been said that the eyes are windows to the soul. We feel somehow that when we look into those deep pools, we see into the depth of the soul itself. Whatever we may be, the eyes have it; they serve as the body's most definitive barometer of what we are thinking and feeling. You can listen to someone's words, but the eyes seem to provide a far more accurate reading.

Solomon, then, sees the loveliness of Shulamith's inner being reflected through those two prisms of the soul. Rabbinic tradition identifies beautiful eyes with a beautiful personality. Long after Solomon and Shulamith are married, we will observe that the king still adores the eyes of his love. In Song of Solomon 4:9 we read his words to her: "You have ravished my heart, my sister, my spouse; you have ravished my heart with one look of your eyes . . ."

Have you ever noticed how adeptly a married couple can speak through the eyes? The song says, "Just one look—that's all it took." Without a word we can say, "Change the subject; I don't want to talk about this right now." We can say, "You're stepping on my last nerve right now, dear one." But we can also say, "Meet me in the bedroom." The eyes pick up where language leaves off.

For women in particular, eyes are lovely and expressive. Maybe that's why so much of the cosmetic industry attends to them, accentuating the place we look most often when we regard someone. Solomon loves the eyes of Shulamith.

Shulamith Admires the Sensitivity of His Charm. Solomon has gotten the dialogue rolling, and he's going to be a hard act to follow. Shulamith addresses what we might call his sensitive charm. "Behold, you are handsome, my beloved!" she says. "Yes, pleasant!" (verse 16).

In our language today, we like to use the word *handsome*, as we translate it here, to compliment a man's looks. The actual Hebrew word means *beautiful*. It is used fourteen times in this biblical book, but only on this one occasion for Solomon. When she adds the descriptive word *pleasant*, we know she refers to his charm. Solomon has a need to be affirmed, and his lover receives those signals and responds to him in just the right way.

They Admire the Security of Their Home. He loves her eyes. She adores his charm. And suddenly, first person singular becomes first person plural. We come across the word *our*: "Also our bed is green. The beams of our houses are cedar and our rafters of fir" (verses 16b-17). Isn't this shift from *me* to *us* the sign of a deepening relationship? Me + Me = We. He says, she says, and then the two begin to merge so that separate souls see themselves as one couple.

Marriage may be the "urge to merge," but mergers often take a while to finalize. Many newlyweds continue to keep separate checkbooks and to think of their possessions and their lives individually. But more and more, particularly with the arrival of children, husband and wife are, in fact, joined as one flesh, just as the wedding ceremony decrees.

Shulamith, for her part, has come from the country vineyards to the city palace. She sees that it is a good thing to be king, and in particular she praises the careful preparation the groom has made for their home together. As we read the phrase "our bed is green," we need to understand that the reference is to a piece of furniture in the home—not the sexual bed of husband and wife. A better translation for this word would be *couch*. But the main point is the greenness of everything, which perhaps Solomon has chosen to make a country girl feel at home. Again, he is sensitive and thoughtful.

In that part of the world, we learn, the choicest cedar grows in the mountains of Lebanon, the very area Shulamith had called home. Pine green would have set her at ease, made her feel right at home. Solomon has met his true love, and then returned to the palace to establish a new and personal lodging, a country place in the midst of the city.

Have you made those loving adjustments to make the life of your loved one as comfortable as possible? Think of Solomon, described by God Himself as the wisest man and greatest king of Israel's history. Think of Shulamith, a dark-skinned girl of the countryside whose hands have become calloused from servant labor. This is an amazing love story, but particularly remarkable for the way a man of power and prominence would do the little, humble things to make a girl feel good about herself and her life. How much more should we be doing the same thing?

AN AFFIRMATION SITUATION

Perhaps the most notable characteristic of the Song of Solomon—as well as the most practical for our lives—is the power of simple affirmation. Love, for Solomon and Shulamith, is an affirmation situation.

Solomon Affirms His Devotion to Her Strong Spirit. This is a woman who can say, "I am the rose of Sharon, and the lily of the valleys" (2:1). Strong words, wouldn't you agree? You might be tempted to read a bit of conceit or pride into them, but the context tells us otherwise. This is a woman who has come to the palace, elevated to the side of a monarch. It has all come through Solomon's love for her. We've seen her self-doubts, and now we see the strengthened self-concept he has given her through his devotion. There was a time in recent memory when she labored bitterly under a baking sun, pruning an endless field of vinery at the order of her brothers. Now, she is the rose who has emerged from those vines. Solomon has carried her home. He has ministered with his words, nourished her with his love. How could anything but a strong spirit result?

An old gospel song, "The Lily of the Valley," adapts this verse and tells us that Jesus is the Rose of Sharon, and "the fairest of ten thousand." We assume this rose must be something magnificent, a rare flower of unparalleled color and fragrance on a long stem. That's actually not what Shulamith has in mind. The Rose of Sharon is a wild autumn flower of the valley, and this is how she sees herself—a flower out of season and out of place, a country girl among the elite of the nation. Yet the "lily of the valleys," according to Paige Patterson, is something else: a beautiful, delicate white blossom with six leaves and six petals. It is closely associated with wedding celebrations. [4] It's even possible that Shulamith might have been dropping a hint about the wedding she hoped for!

In these two floral images, we see the complex self-image of Shulamith, who feels her humble origin, yet knows she has been found worthy to be that autumn flower that springs up in an unexpected time and place. She is from the country, but why can't she live in the city? Her skin is darker than that of others, but why shouldn't that fact underscore her beauty? Love is an adventure that takes us on a journey of self-discovery. It shows us our past in a new light, and gives us unbounded hope for the future.

Solomon responds in kind, in keeping with this competition of mutual affirmation. "Like a lily among the thorns, so is my love among the daughters," he answers (2:2). He transforms the lily imagery to something new: not just a flower in the field, but one among thorns. He is saying that in her presence, other women seem unattractive and forbidding. Thus a husband listens carefully to his wife's words, takes them and turns them to something that will delight her with unexpected affirmation.

Shulamith Affirms Her Delight in Him. Solomon's strategy works; she is delighted, and her words reflect it: "Like an apple tree among the trees of the woods, so is my beloved among the sons. I sat down in his shade with great delight . . ." (2:3). You have to admit one thing: The Song of Solomon is a gardener's delight.

It is also a delight from a woman's perspective. Most often we hear from a man's perspective in the Bible. Out of The Song's one hundred seventeen verses, fifty-five come from the lips of Shulamith. Another nineteen verses are attributed to her. Then there are the palace women, "the Daughters of Jerusalem," a collective who receive credit for many of the remaining verses.

We know that in ancient love poetry, women often take the lead. In that respect, The Song is representative of its genre. Even when it comes to issues of frank sexuality, Shulamith speaks most frequently. Is that somehow wrong on Solomon's part? Is he the typical non-responsive male? We already know that would be an unfair charge based upon Shulamith's characterization of him. But if he lacks quantity of words, he shines in the quality department, wouldn't you agree? He does quite well in terms of creativity and affirmation. He is, of course (and like his father), a poet inspired by God, with an ear for the sheer music of language.

So she is a lily among thorns in his eyes; he, an apple tree in a dark forest. There are plenty of trees, of course, but few that supply delicious nourishment. Shulamith finds her beloved to be like that, and she sits in the shade of his stature and prominence. The first Psalm says that the man who delights in God's Word is like a tree by the river, "that brings forth its fruit in its season, whose leaf also shall not wither; and whatever he does shall prosper" (Psalm 1:3). There are so many wonderful aspects to the word picture of a fruit tree; Shulamith chooses well.

There is so much we can say to one another through the medium of comparison: you are like a flower, you are like an apple tree. In our day, we compare ourselves to each other, and we seem to compete in every way we can find to keep score. We compare jobs, cars, incomes, homes, and spouses. We are relentlessly, selfishly trying to declare ourselves the best. In this book, we find two lovers telling each other, "*You* are the best. You compare to the very best in life, the best of God's creation. In my eyes, no one can compare to you." In a way, this is a whole book about two lovers telling each other, "You are the one and only" with every metaphor conceivable, and every color in the rainbow, and every note of the musical scale.

The other great message is, "You are set apart." That means, "You and me, together, we are a God thing." When we use the term *holy matrimony,* the first word (holy) means "to set apart." In the Old Testament tabernacle every element of worship was called holy and set apart for use in worshipping an awesome God. Everything had to be pure; everything had to be the best. Marriage is established for the same purpose. It isn't just a human thing, but a holy thing. Not only are we set apart by God as individuals, a holy priesthood; our marriages are specially set apart to accomplish things that we could never do as individuals.

We are set apart by God. We set one another apart as holy elements of worship. And we set apart our marriage as something directly from heaven, something touched by God Himself.

This is a very serious question. Have you looked at your marriage that way? It could be that you did so at the time of the wedding when you dressed in the fine clothing of the ceremony, uttered the special vows, and heard the minister read from the Bible. Those vows were sacred, and witnesses were present to affirm the sanctity of this marital tie. Let me tell you that the moment you eat your breakfast together, half-awake, is just as sacred a moment within your marriage. The moment you have an argument, the moment you are away from one another, the moment you pay bills together—all of these are sacred moments, set-apart moments of a marriage made in heaven. We all know we are wed "in the presence of God," but we never for a moment leave that presence.

We must understand marriage precisely that way—first in our own mind, and then in the understanding we share as a couple. Solomon and Shulamith are building something holy and sacred. They are using their sanctified imaginations to affirm and praise one another, so that they can build a foundation of viewing each other with absolute love— the love only God can provide.

It's something every one of us should likewise emulate in our marriage.

AN ATTRACTION REACTION

The Setting of Love. How do we react to sharing our admiration and affirmation? The result is passionate mutual attraction.

Shulamith says, "He brought me to the banqueting house" (2:4). That table was quite a large one in an expansive room geared to seat a large delegation of guests. What point is Shulamith making as she turns to us, her listeners, and tells us what Solomon has done? He is showing off his Lebanese country girl to the entire world. It's one thing to fall in love with someone from a different side of life; it's another to parade her proudly before one's peers.

Imagine a single United States President, the leader of the free world, who falls in love with a simple young lady from a rural setting. He could avoid all the media, all the gossip, and all the press conference questions by keeping the relationship discreet. Instead, he ushers her into the White House where all the cameras and microphones await. He smiles broadly as he introduces her to reporters and visiting heads of state. What would this tell her—and everyone else—about his love?

The Safety of Love. We've seen what matters about the setting for Solomon's love. In the latter portion of verse 3, Shulamith speaks of the safety and security she feels: "His banner over me was love" (2:4b). Again, we recognize the words from a popular church chorus that is fun to sing, but that frankly has little to do with the biblical text. Let's find out what Shulamith really has in mind.

A banner marked someone's territory, just as a flag does. It flew over the troops in battle to show that they fought for this king or that nation. Shulamith may have seen proud banners of Israel decorating the banquet hall; her message here is that Solomon's love hovers around her like a striking flag of conquest telling the world he has claimed her.

It is tradition in the United Kingdom to see a certain banner outside the palace telling whether the queen is in residence or not. That banner flew over the British Embassy in Washington, D.C. during her American visit declaring her presence among us. This same custom was observed in Bible times. A banner told everyone the king was home, and they'd better be on their best behavior. As Shulamith entered the great room, all eyes would rest upon this attractive stranger. Everyone would know she was with the king, because his love could no more be missed than a great, colorful banner of state. Just as we can go to a restaurant and easily recognize a couple in the throes of love, dignitaries could take in the story of Solomon and Shulamith at a glance. "They were with each other, present to each other. Any person who might intrude into their relationship was only a temporary visitor, not a resident of their relationship."[5]

A banner was also a canopy of special blessing. Today in Jewish weddings, a prayer shawl is suspended like a banner above the couple. This is a sign of God's presence in the match. He blesses it and makes them one flesh.[6]

Solomon's love is Shulamith's home. It tells her, "Your place is with me, and it is a special place where there can be no other residents, only temporary guests. You are safe and secure here—just as if you were at home in the hills." How comforting a feeling in such a time of transition for her.

I like the title of a book by Greg and Erin Smalley: *Before You Plan Your Wedding, Plan Your Marriage*. That sounds like a good idea to me. In their book, the couple describes the importance of feeling truly safe within a marriage. How do we behave when we are safe and comfortable? We let our hair down; we relax our inhibitions and feel that we can be ourselves. Isn't that a pretty good definition of intimacy? When we're young, single, and dating someone new, we try to be our "best selves," not our real selves. Our guard is up, we are cautious in our speech, and afterward we actually feel tired from the work of trying to be perfect.

Intimacy means being 100 percent real. It refreshes rather than tires us. We know that if we stumble in some small way it will make no difference to the other person. If we have some area of vulnerability, we need not hide it. If we are hurting, we can share it. We say, "Here is my heart and soul, just as they are. I'm trusting them to you, because I feel safe with you."[7]

The Satisfaction of Love. There is love and a sense of security in a new home. The result is deep satisfaction. In the context of marriage a passionate response likely follows; in the context of courtship we must show restraint. "Sustain me with cakes of raisins," says Shulamith. "Refresh me with apples, for I am lovesick. His left hand is under my head, and his right hand embraces me" (2:5-6).

Here is that word *lovesick*. Even standing in the banquet hall with this magnificent king, this architect of temples, this wise and poetic prince, Shulamith swoons with desire for him. Perhaps she looks at the admiring crowds and wishes they would disappear so that she could be alone with her beloved. Her stomach feels a little funny, and she wonders if a few apples and raisins might settle her down.

It might seem strange, particularly, to find *lovesick* in the Bible. But people in love always strike us as a little eccentric. As we read through these first two chapters of The Song, we read an accumulation of romantic details, a mass of affirmation, praise, and words of love. It's like paging through the scrapbook of thrilling courtship. Every now and then the compiler of the scrapbook stops, takes all of it in, and feels that surge of adoration again. This is the emotional adrenaline rush of what Dr. Tennov calls *limerence*. A recent news item, by the way, tells us that researchers are finding that there are couples who still experience that powerful rush after many years of marriage. [8] Yes, it's possible to nurture this kind of love and keep it alive indefinitely.

Could anything feel more intensely satisfying than the feeling of being truly loved?

The Sanctity of Love. And now, from Shulamith, a cautionary note: This love is powerful stuff! It's not made for everyone. As we reach the seventh verse, it's as if she feels her stomach has turned upside down.

She experiences that dizziness and hears one of the other women sigh and say, "I wish I were in love like that."

To which Shulamith wants to reply, "No you don't—not unless all the conditions are right."

The idea is not to fall head over heels until we are ready to manage the tumble.

What she actually says is this: "By the gazelles or by the does of the field, do not stir up nor awaken love until it pleases" (2:7). Again, it takes a little thinking about country living to understand her points of reference. Gazelles and does are graceful yet powerful animals. Once stirred, they can bound with ease across the landscape. A hunter coming upon a sleeping gazelle would need to have his bow loaded in position before making any sudden move that would startle his prey.

Love, gracious and powerful itself, is like that. Don't get it in your sights until you're sure you're ready to take your shot. As Shulamith puts it, "Do not stir up or awaken love." Genuine, passionate love is an adult thing. It is reserved for the right time, like getting a driver's license.

We can almost see the blush on Shulamith's cheeks as the palace women laugh and tell her how obvious her emotional state is. Solomon's beloved is nearly overwhelmed with desire, but that impulse can't be given free rein until a wedding seals the union. The flesh is willing, but the spirit is waiting.

This is a problematic issue in our world, as I hope you will agree. If we take these words seriously, suggesting that physical love should not be awakened until the right time, we will observe that certain kinds of expressions and intimacies don't belong in the dating process. Sex is an important part of marriage, but as in the Song of Solomon, there are many other aspects. So much of this book is simply a dialogue between the lover and his beloved. That's how marriage is: we spend a lot more time communicating together than we do having sex. Sometimes young people don't understand that until they actually marry and discover that sex is a wonderful gift from God, but a small part of that vastly larger gift called marriage. Conversation, oneness, fellowship, security, shared mission and even fun all play significant and satisfying roles. Frankly, marriage would be disappointing if it were nothing but a large, waiting-bed.

Therefore Shulamith looks at those giggling maidens around her and says, "Trust me; you don't want to come down with what I have until you find the right man at the right time and the right place." And how right she is! We don't teach this enough today—the truth that the Bible never condones premarital sex. As a matter of fact, God forbids it.

The movies, of course, condone it. So do television shows and popular songs. What a tragedy when those media have more influence as spiritual guides than the eternal Word of God. Hollywood wants us to believe that an attractive couple meets, has intercourse almost immediately, and experiences satisfying intimacy. In truth, that is impossible; all they can experience is a physical sensation. Intimacy requires so much more—body, mind, and spirit. The biblical term for intimate sex is "to know" (Genesis 4:17, 25).

Shulamith stands with the wide, consistent arc of Scriptural teaching in saying "Do not awaken that impulse until the proper time." We provide premarital counseling in our church, and we constantly observe that there would be far less heartbreak, far less social confusion, and thousands of fewer divorces if people would simply understand what the Bible has said all along. Wait on God. Wait for the right one to come along. Then wait until you truly know one another; and finally, allow godly, passionate marriage to bring that final piece to the puzzle.

Some of you may be convicted by these words about "waiting." Perhaps you are all too aware of your past and regret that you've failed to live up to God's design. The good news is that you are freely and fully forgiven—that is a binding promise of God. It's never too late to begin to live in obedience to Him, nor can any past sin have any future power over you—not if you experience the cleansing forgiveness of Christ. As for your future, whether you are married, single, or single again, you can live in the daily power of the Holy Spirit and the constant blessing of Christ beginning this very instant.

If you seek to begin anew, you might want to mark this covenant with a prayer:

> *Almighty God, I have not always lived as I should. Forgive me for what I've done; renew in me a clean heart and a new opportunity to walk with You. By the grace of God, I will walk with You in my sexuality from this moment on.*

God will honor that prayer every single time.

Some might make the mistake of saying, "Well, there's no reason to close the barn door once the cows have gotten out. I have messed up, and there's no reason to try changing now."

Do you understand who tells you that? The enemy of your soul. The devil is all about binding you to your past. God is all about the unbounded possibilities of your future. The enemy wants to keep convicting you for your past transgressions; God wants to forgive you and transform you into a new creature. As we say at our church, when the devil wants to tell you about your past, you tell him about his future—which is one of eternal punishment. You, on the other hand, look forward to eternal life in God's loving presence.

In premarital counseling, we often encounter couples who are already living together. We deal with them gently and non-judgmentally, but we tell them that what they are doing is wrong in the eyes of God as well as harmful to the marital relationship that will take up the rest of their lives. We say, "If you want to be married here, we would ask you to live in separate locations beginning immediately. Live apart and practice the discipline of abstinence that will honor God." "That will be difficult," they often say. But we encourage them to do it out of respect for each other and for their Lord. And when they've done so, we help them begin a healthy, God-centered marriage relationship.

Isn't it wonderful that we can read Shulamith's endorsement of this policy from thousands of years ago and from the reality of her own human longings? It was difficult for her, too. But she loved God and she loved Solomon enough to live in obedience.

LEARNING FROM LOVESICKNESS

What are the most practical truths we can retain from these verses?

The Priority of Conversation. It's so wonderfully simple: Just talk to one another! As we've seen, that's what the bulk of Solomon's Song really is: a couple sharing a delightful conversation. Don't you love to see a married couple together for years that can sit out on the back porch at the end of the day and simply enjoy each other's company rather than anchor their schedules to the television set? Too many couples forget how to carry on a satisfying conversation. They go to a restaurant and find they have nothing to discuss, nothing to share without a widescreen television in front of them.

As your conversations go, so will go your marriage.

The Pleasure of Compliments. If you like crunching the numbers, consider these that concern our study of The Song:

Verses studied thus far: 24
Compliments encountered: 18

How would you like to receive eighteen different compliments for every twenty-four sentences your spouse dispatched in your direction? Do you think it might help the two of you get along? Yes, you can sit on that back porch. You can go to the restaurant. You can talk. But what's the very best subject to discuss? Each other.

I guarantee you that if you meet someone and wonder what his interests are, you can be absolutely certain of one of them. We're all interested in ourselves. We all need affirmation. We want to know that we look nice or that we're going about things the right way. Never will a compliment be poorly received. It's fun to watch Solomon and Shulamith engage in a duel of high praise, isn't it? Just imagine how much fun it would be in your own life.

The Purpose of Courtship. From conversation, to compliments, to courtship we can see the progression with the biblical couple under discussion. We can also see the emotional progression. We start out by liking someone, we become intrigued by them, and suddenly we desire them passionately. If you're in a "serious relationship" as we describe courtship today, know that it's not only an enjoyable time but a dangerous one. Be on your guard and ask God's Spirit to watch over you and strengthen you against temptation.

The Power of Consecration. Writer Patricia McGerr told a true and wonderful story a number of years ago in a magazine for women. She had heard about a man named Johnny Lingo who lived on an island in the South Pacific. Johnny Lingo was a wealthy trader respected for his ability to strike a hard bargain. You don't build a fine estate without being a shrewd negotiator—except in the case of one particular commodity for which he insisted upon paying a high price.

In this part of the world, a man bought his wife from her father through the currency of livestock. Everyone understood the going rate. If you were willing to offer one to three cows, you could get a decent wife, if not the most popular choice. For four or five cows, you could make a prestigious selection for a wife. If the bargaining grew intense, the price for the most desirable wife could rise to seven cows—quite a sacrifice for even a well-to-do farmer in these islands.

Johnny Lingo was no longer shopping for a wife. He had already made his firm choice, and no other woman would do. Her name was Sarita. She was a simple but very shy young lady from the island of Kiniwata. Johnny fell in love with her, and Sarita's retiring nature only made her more desirable to him. He went to her father with an opening offer of eight cows. This was unprecedented, and—in the eyes of the village folk—unnecessary for an established businessman. Surely he could get a girl like Sarita for half the price. People decided Johnny must be a chump when it came to matters of the heart.

Patricia McGerr, the author, was intrigued enough to make a visit to the household of Johnny Lingo. Sarita, she found, glowed with a striking beauty. The author asked, "Why did you pay a price higher than anyone might ask?"

Johnny patiently explained how things were in the islands. "Do you ever think what it must mean to a woman to know that her husband has settled on the lowest price for what she could be bought?" he asked. The women, he said, would gather to boast of their respective market prices. One might be a four-cow woman, another a six. This would establish their social values as wives and as people.

Johnny continued, "How does the woman feel, the woman who was sold for one or two? This could never happen to my Sarita!"

Patricia McGerr asked, "You just did this to make her happy?"

"Oh," he said, "I wanted Sarita to be happy all right. But I wanted more than that. You say she is different? Oh yes—much different than when I married her, and that is true. Many things change a woman. But the one thing that matters most is what she thinks about herself. In Kiniwata, Sarita believed she was worth nothing. Now she knows she is worth more than any other woman in the islands."[9]

Johnny Lingo found a way to show his love with what he possessed—cows—and his wife was unlikely to ever forget the message. For him, she was the pearl of great price and she would only shine more brightly if she knew it. He paid sacrificially to transform the woman he loved, and she would never be the same.

Do you understand that Christ has done the very same for you? He made a sacrifice that could never be accomplished with livestock. He gave Himself completely and without reservation to let you know just how deeply and perfectly He loves you, and to transform you from someone lost and lonely to someone who is an heir of the kingdom of God—someone who can now live beside the King's throne even as Shulamith could.

Christ made that ultimate sacrifice out of deep and abiding love for you. It is a matter of fact and of history. But have you taken it in? Have you come to a realization of the vast scope of His love? As we learn the truth about the ultimate in marital love, it's worthwhile to stop and think about the heavenly model for this subject. Whether you are married in this world or not, you have been chosen, bought, and paid for by God—only to be set free. You can enjoy the deepest delight, the fullest peace that life has to offer. The great joy of Shulamith is yours, but on an eternal level.

That's not lovesick—that's just love, period. ◆

1   "Phaedrus," in Plato, *Plato's Phaedrus* (Cambridge, England: Cambridge, 1952), p. 97.
2   HP-Time Inc., "Let's Fall in Limerence," *Time* Magazine, 1 January 1980, at http://www.time.com/
    time/magazine/article/0,9171,952554,00.html (accessed 7 January 2009).
3   Sheldon Vanauken, *A Severe Mercy* (New York: Harper & Row, 1977).
4   Paige Patterson; 45.
5   Adapted from Tommy Nelson, *The Book of Romance: What Solomon Says About Love, Sex, and Intimacy*
    (Nashville, TN: Thomas Nelson, 1998), 35-36.
6   Tommy Nelson, 36.
7   Smalley, 11.
8   John Harlow and Brendan Montague, "Scientists discover true love," *The London Times*, 4 January
    2009, at http://women.timesonline.co.uk/tol/life_and_style/women/relationships/article5439805.
    ece (accessed 8 January 2009).
9   Adapted from Joe L. Wheeler, editor, *Heart to Heart: Stories of Love* (Colorado Springs: Focus on the
    Family/Tyndale, 2000), 153-158. Originally published: Patricia McGerr, "Johnny Lingo's Eight-Cow
    Wife," *Woman's Day*, November 1965.

4

The Quest for the Perfect Mate

Song of Solomon 2:8-17

All her life Gail had dreamed about her wedding day. She'd been the bridesmaid many times, but never the bride. She awaited that day when Mr. Right would come riding up on his white horse so she could begin living happily ever after. But wherever she looked, the perfect man never seemed to turn up. In the wisdom of time, she stopped looking for perfection, found a good man who truly loved her, and the two became engaged.

Even so, Gail's friends wondered about her high standards. Could any groom be capable of living up to all of Gail's dreams and goals for an ideal marriage? Yet the wedding itself loomed large in her mind. She found herself growing extremely nervous about the big day and the elaborate ceremony. She'd spent so many years thinking about, praying about, and dreaming about this day that now she was feeling extra pressure.

While meeting with the wedding planner, she confessed her anxiety. "I'm afraid that, come Zero Hour," she said, "I'll be so high-strung that I'll say or do something embarrassing."

The compassionate planner smiled in a motherly way and told her, "That's completely normal, Gail. Everyone gets nervous about a wedding day. Just take it one baby step at a time, my dear, and you'll coast right through it. Try this: When you're in the narthex before the processional, focus just ahead of you, on the aisle you're about to walk. It's the same old aisle you've grown up with here at church.

"Then, while you're walking down the aisle, look just ahead to the altar at the front of the sanctuary. It's the same altar that's been there all your life. Then, as you reach the front of the church, focus on your groom. He's the entire reason you're getting married. Focus on those three things, take them one at a time and you'll do beautifully."

The bride sighed and said, "That sounds like a good plan. Still, I just *know* I'll say or do something embarrassing."

The big day in June came, and Gail fixated on her three focal points. As her friends watched her walk down the aisle—Gail the perfectionist, finally accepting a mate—they were surprised to see her staring ahead with a fixed expression and muttering, "Aisle . . . altar . . . him. Aisle . . . altar . . . him . . ." [1]

Finding Mister or Miss "Right" is central when it comes to marriage, isn't it? Is the perfect person waiting out there, tailor-made for our particular needs? Or will we have to "settle"?

It's not just a female thing, either. It works both ways, with men and women wondering what marriage is really going to be like when all is said and done. After a generation too characterized by troubled marriages, our young adults rightfully want some assurance that it will be possible to establish a strong, positive household. They've seen the heartache and pain that families must encounter when marriages break up.

Thus it has been intriguing to see our culture revert to an old idea—that of the matchmaker. If you've seen either of the musicals *Hello Dolly* or *Fiddler on the Roof*, you know about this third party who plays the match game in certain cultures. In India, to this very day, as many as ninety-five percent of all marriages are arranged. [2] The Russians have a proverb: "Choose a matchmaker, not a bride." The idea is that some objective specialist might keep you from tripping over your own skewed judgment on the way to the altar. After all, they say, love is blind; why not hire someone with a telescope?

The new spin, of course, is to use the Internet rather than Dolly Levi or Yente from their respective Broadway roles. *Time* magazine claims that nearly one thousand online matchmaking sites are in operation, with a combined total annual revenue of six hundred forty-nine million dollars. Pew Research Center reported that of ninety-two million unmarried Americans, eighteen years old and older who were counted in the most recent census, sixteen million of them confess to having tried online dating. [3] Now, keep in mind that this is true even as sixty-six percent of Internet users admit they believe that online dating is dangerous. [4]

Call it what you will, love is a lucrative, recession-proof business. So many are searching for it, and so many will attempt nearly any strategy to find it.

Solomon and Shulamith were forced to face the vicissitudes of life without broadband Internet service. They had to woo each other with means other than e-mail or text messages. But the Song of Solomon seems to testify that they did strikingly well without the aid of technology. As the story continues, Solomon and Shulamith are still in the courtship phase of their relationship. We've had a nice scene at the royal palace where Shulamith took in the pageantry of the royal scene. Now, however, we shift back to the country, to the home of Shulamith.

The wedding is a few days away, and the two lovers are still learning new and fascinating facts about each other.

Those of us who are married have done this: size up every new piece of information about the other person, contemplating what this will mean about a life spent together. It's a time of questions, and Shulamith has a number of them. Even in something of a fairy-tale romance like this one, it's always good to ask questions. This section of The Song serves as our tutorial for marriage planning, suggesting to us what kinds of questions we should ask. Some of them, we'll find, are questions we should continually ask throughout the life of a marriage.

Let's discover four central questions we might ask about a potential life partner.

1. DOES HE SPEND TIME WITH YOU?

This is a big one, and it suggests two related questions:

Is He Excited About You? Shulamith says, "The voice of my beloved! Behold, he comes leaping upon the mountains, skipping upon the hills. My beloved is like a gazelle or a young stag" (2:8-9a).

Five times in verses eight through seventeen, Shulamith refers to Solomon as "my lover." What does that tell you about her own feelings? The attachment has been growing deeper between these two as God knits their hearts together. And now, in verse 8, Shulamith hears her man's voice in the distance echoing across the hills. In her excitement, she imagines him leaping and bounding like a gazelle or a young stag. These animals are admired for strength, grace, and beauty.

Awaiting a lover's arrival is a time of joy. The heartbeat speeds up as time slows down. Shulamith knows that Solomon is coming for her, and she listens with anticipation for the sound of his voice. Then he calls out for her (2:14-15), not caring who hears him. Her words, by the way, are significant—her last words to her beloved are nearly identical (see 8:14).

Yes, it's true that we're talking about a couple at the peak of their romantic attraction. Today's cynical types might roll their eyes and call all this corny or cheesy. But this is love as we experience it. There's a certain excitement about being near the one we love. As time passes, we may be calmer on the outside, but the essential yearning remains solid and powerful over time. Is there still an excitement in your relationship? Do you miss each other bitterly when separated? Do you feel at least a quiet joy and satisfaction when you are reunited at the end of a work day?

Let's admit that we all navigate marriage through our own personality types. There are men and women alike who aren't prone to showing their emotions even at home. Others wear their feelings on their sleeve, as the saying goes. But even the calm and unflappable get excited about the prospect of marriage. We all know it's a Day of Days in this life. I can remember being incapable of eating the week before our wedding. I was somehow nervous and thrilled at the same time.

While there should always remain a certain excitement about marriage, there should definitely be some jump on the emotional barometer in the days leading up to the wedding. If you're facing that day without much emotion, it may serve as a warning sign concerning a lack of emotion or passion in later married life.

Is He Enchanted by You? There should also be the presence of a feeling we might identify as enchantment. That's a fairy tale word, so what is it we're getting at here? There is a kind of captivation—a fascination—with the one we love. Shulamith says, "Behold, he stands behind our wall; he is looking through the windows, gazing through the lattice" (2:9).

Solomon has seen Shulamith before, probably a number of times. Yet here he is, returned from his travels, so eager to see his beloved that he can't even wait to enter the house. He stops and peers through the window like a boy hurrying to the toy store stops to gaze in the window with awe at the electric train he has come to purchase. Can you think of a time when you scanned a crowd eagerly for someone, trying to pick them out at the airport or a train station? You couldn't wait to see that particular face.

Commentator Paige Patterson detects a bit of playfulness in Solomon in this verse. Solomon peeks in through a window, disappears, moves stealthily along the wall, and then is quickly revealed through the lattice work.[5] People in love are playful, aren't they? Lovers seem to experience a kind of second childhood. It's part of the enchantment that makes the whole experience so wonderful.

We need to see that from time to time, because we tend to make marriage too business-like. For the prospective groom, perhaps it's a little depressing to find himself immersed in china patterns and choices of upholstery for the new home. Before now it was all about love and courting, but now it's getting down to business. A lot of this is necessary, of course, but love should never lose its wonder. Even "date night," which some couples observe, shouldn't dissolve into a ritual of the same restaurant, the same movie theater, the same old same-old. We all need surprise and fun in our central life relationship. God made us for joy, and he established marriage as an ideal forum for enchantment.

Does he or she spend time with you? Is there excitement? Enchantment? If you're not too sure about the answers as you prepare for a wedding day—for example, if he frequently prefers activities other than spending time with you—you can know that things won't get any better after the ceremony. In courtship, we're seeing each other at our best. If we're not eager to be together even then—if there are other things more thrilling to either one of us—there is a problem that must be confronted. Love-struck people often think they can change their beloved once they've exchanged vows—spiritually, emotionally, or in other ways. Trust me: It rarely happens. If there is little enchantment before the wedding, the chances of finding more after the ceremony are very slim.

2. DOES HE SPEAK TENDERLY TO YOU?

What is the quality of your communication? It should be something different than the tone he uses with co-workers or buddies. Between husband and wife, there must be an established tone of tenderness.

I think we can all agree that this one area can be a special challenge for the male. Many representatives of that gender lack the gift of gab. We say, "He's a man of few words." The "woman of few words" is also out there, but we don't hear about her as frequently. Sometimes men don't have a clue about what to say. One guy expressed it this way: "When my daughters call, I only say three things: How's the weather? Need any money? and Here's your mother." [6]

Meanwhile, *Mrs.* Man of Few Words can chat effortlessly on the phone for thirty-minutes—even to a stranger. After she hangs up, her husband asks to whom she was talking. She says, "I don't know, it was a wrong number." [7] God made many women who can talk to anyone in any situation. They are sensitive and capable of excelling at communication.

Ask a man about his inexpressiveness and all he can do is reply, "I don't know what to say about that."

Even so, a guy's gotta do what a guy's gotta do—and one of those things he's gotta do is to learn to speak tenderly. Here is his checklist toward that goal.

Does He Speak of His Loyalty? Shulamith reports, "My beloved spoke, and said to me: 'Rise up, my love, my fair one, and come away'"

(2:10). Three verses later, he repeats the admonition with more force: "'Rise up, my love, my fair one, and come away!'" (2:13).

Twice Solomon speaks tenderly of his love for Shulamith calling her "my love" ("my darling" in NIV and NASB). He calls her "my fair one" twice. Solomon didn't expect Shulamith to take his love for granted. He let it overflow in all of his conversations with her. One endearment was not enough; she had to be "my love, my fair one."

Loving couples have their own versions of this declaration. One says, "I love you." The other says, "I love you more!" It's a playful competition of expression not much different from our two biblical lovers here. Who cares if it sounds a bit saccharine to bystanders? This isn't their marriage, it's yours. I've never heard of a woman telling her husband at the end of the day, "You have been way too sweet to me today. You told me you loved me too many times. I'm frankly a little tired of hearing it."

Some things can't be said too frequently. But they can certainly be said too rarely, can't they? Men in particular need to make an extra effort to err on the side of extravagance. When we continue to speak of our love, we communicate our loyalty—our steadfast devotion.

Does He Speak of His Life? This is a subtle component of our Bible passage, and we need to be careful not to miss it. "For lo, the winter is past, the rain is over and gone. The flowers appear on the earth; the time of singing has come, and the voice of the turtledove is heard in our land. The fig tree puts forth her green figs, and the vines with the tender grapes give a good smell" (2:11-13b).

Unless you've examined the life of Solomon in detail, you're likely to miss this point entirely. I made that study a few years ago, being fascinated by this man who was Israel's most successful king. He was so wealthy, so wise—the builder of the first temple and author of three different books of wisdom, a great military leader, and a financial genius. These facts are well known. But did you realize he was also a scientist? We read that "also he spoke of trees, from the cedar tree of Lebanon even to the hyssop that springs out of the wall; he spoke also of animals, of birds, of creeping things, and of fish" (1 Kings 4:33).

Centuries later, Solomon would have been identified as a naturalist. He was one of the first in history—a man supremely educated in the fields of natural history, zoology, ornithology, and botany. He had not only the wisdom he had requested of God as a young man; he also had wide-ranging knowledge about the world around him. Read through his three books—Ecclesiastes, Proverbs, and Song of Solomon—and you'll notice references to nature everywhere. I'm certain you've already seen it in our study of this book—herbs, rare perfumes, doves, deer, and goats. He is a man who loves the flowers, the seasons, the rain, and everything connected to God's creation. He weaves a tapestry of creation through his love talk to Shulamith.

As a country girl, that approach would have delighted her. But it also drew her in an intimate way into the personal life of a man with a passion for the outdoors. He had one of the world's great palaces and built the Temple of Almighty God—but it was in nature where he felt God's presence most joyously amidst tree and beast and stone.

"These things," he is saying, "make up my world. They are beautiful as you are beautiful." Danny Akin writes:

> Solomon . . . understood that the way to a woman's heart is often in the details, the little things. In verses 11-13 Solomon invites Shulamith to take a walk in the countryside. No doubt she would have found this romantic. Furthermore, the poetic description of the passing of winter and coming of spring is startling, especially for a man.[8]

Akin goes on to point out the parallel between the lovers' walk and springtime. The natural green renewal of the season always reminds us of new love. The winter is forgotten, the birds are singing, and the world itself seems to share the joy that a man and woman feel together.[9] Solomon is experiencing the next thing to heaven—surrounded by nature and his Shulamith at their best. He, in turn, is sharing with her what he loves in life.

What a great way to help someone love you more: show them the things in life you're passionate about. Share yourself. As I counsel married couples, I'm always sad to hear someone say, "He had this whole part of his life I had never heard about." How can couples joined in marriage, made one flesh, keep secrets from each other? It's a mystery to me. If we want our relationships to be the best they can be, we must lay out all that we are. We must share ourselves in totality.

Again, we find that the men tend to be most private. We need to open up and be transparent, giving our loved ones an all-access pass to our world.

Does He Speak of His Love? Having learned what you just did about Solomon, you won't be surprised to read the next verse: "Oh my dove, in the clefts of the rock, in the secret places of the cliff, let me see your face, let me hear your voice; for your voice is sweet, and your face is lovely" (2:14).

Here again are birds and features of the landscape. However, it should be pointed out that most scholars actually assign this verse to Shulamith rather than Solomon. The fact that we can't be certain underlines the fact that two lovers can become almost indistinguishable in their expressions of love. They find a common language and personal symbolism. It would be fitting for Shulamith to adopt Solomon's personal vocabulary just as he used the language of vineyards. In this way they show that they're already beginning to become one.

If these are truly Shulamith's words, she is replying to him as he peers through the lattice of her home. She wants to see him more clearly: "Let me see your face!" And she compares him to a dove, as he has done with her. Literally the reference here is to a rock pigeon, a bird that seems less familiar. The rock pigeon builds its nest in the towering, craggy places of the rocks in safe isolation. Shulamith wants to be alone with Solomon where no one can intrude on their relationship. Think of the people who have been hovering around them at the palace. Perhaps she saw a flock of birds through the palace window and wished that she and her lover could simply fly away like that. When we're truly in love, the world shrinks to a small place—a planet with a population of two.

Even as we're amazed by the amount of passion in these verses, we again see that the real key is communication—the way these two talk to one another. So much is wrapped up in the qualities of the words they choose for their beloved. People often associate the Song of Solomon with sex, and of course it's here. But it's here in the same ratio to ordinary life and talk that we find in life. In short, physical sexuality does not steer the course—true, intimate communication does. It's what makes the physical part possible and makes it even better.

As Craig Glickman has written in his commentary on this passage, real love renders fascinating every single detail about the beloved. Nothing is trivial. "That which would be insignificant or boring to even a good friend is eagerly received with genuine interest by the one who loves you . . . The mere voice of the one loved is enchantingly special just in itself. One could read from the telephone book and the other would raptly listen simply for the sound of the voice."[10]

A member of our church lost a loved one recently, and we learned that she could not bring herself to erase the voicemail greeting he left behind. It was *his* voice preserved in a machine, and to her it was more precious than gold. For anyone else it would be another recording of a man saying nothing particularly important—just a disposable thing. Being loved by one other human being transforms every one of us to someone fascinating and special in every single respect. This is why we crave to be loved.

It was the summer before my engagement to Donna when I traveled across the Eastern United States with a vocal ensemble. Five of us represented Cedarville College, and we sang in different churches every night. What a memorable tour—it earned tuition money and offered the kind of great fun and fellowship we all want to enjoy during those student years. As much of a pleasure as it was, it meant seeing almost nothing of Donna for a summer; she was working in Cleveland. We made a serious commitment to shorten the distance by writing each other every single day. I had her address, and she had our itinerary. Whenever we pulled into the next town, the pastor would come and ask, "Are you David? I have a letter for you."

I would smile with satisfaction, never surprised but always delighted; I looked forward to every single installment of Donna's ongoing account of her life. Occasionally there would be two or three letters because they'd miss me and be forwarded. I'll own up to the fact that the *second* thing I would do when handed a letter would be my actual duty: setting up for the concert, unloading the trailer, and meeting the host family. My *first* action was to find a quiet corner of the church and hungrily consume every word of the new letter. I read each one several times, and I still have the whole set to this very day. Let me tell you that I still pull them out to read occasionally, and the pleasure has not worn off; it comes right off the page like still-fresh perfume. What I see in those letters is a wonderful girl who wanted to know every detail of every concert while giving me all the details I asked about from her daily life. We were caught up in each other's worlds.

That's love: it glories in the little things because those are matters that concern the one we love.

3. DOES HE SHARE TRIALS WITH YOU?

There is a third central question that applies to the worthiness of a life mate.

"Catch us the foxes, the little foxes that spoil the vines, for our vines have tender grapes" (verse 15). This verse provided the title for a famous play and subsequent film starring Bette Davis, *The Little Foxes*. In the movie, Bette Davis's character is a kind of "little fox" who is spoiling the tender grapes of the family around her.

The foxes of Bible times were closely related to jackals. In the Book of Judges, we recall Samson tying a number of these together, lighting their tails, and sending them out to spoil the fields of the Philistines. Foxes and crops simply didn't go together. Shulamith would have known about their danger to her vineyards, because they loved grapes and other fruit. The little foxes were the worst. They worked in large groups that would descend on a field or orchard and lay waste to it. In this text, the animals are used as metaphors for the clusters of little problems that creep into marriages and destroy the sweetness there. Shulamith is saying, "*Do* sweat the small stuff—it can add up to big problems."

Chuck Swindoll observes that the "large stuff," paradoxically enough, will actually strengthen a marriage in many instances: the loss of a job, a sudden illness, a long absence. It's those "little foxes"—often minor irritations that don't get discussed—that add up. "It's the slow leaks, not the blow outs; the insidious pests we seldom even consider that cut away at the heart of a home until it crumbles and two people end up walking away."[11]

We joke about how he squeezes the toothpaste from the center while she squeezes it from the end, but the little annoyances drip, drip, drip away until a flood finally ensues. Given enough time, the peaceful flow of a river can wear away solid rock. Bigger challenges catch our attention in marriage. We're more likely to rise and face them in strength. But the little foxes creep in with stealth and spoil the fruit of a beautiful relationship.

The New Testament speaks of "looking carefully lest anyone fall short of the grace of God; lest any root of bitterness springing up cause trouble, and by this many become defiled" (Hebrews 12:15).

Let's keep our marriages from becoming defiled by those deadly roots. They spring up from the underground to choke away all that we have together. Prune them before it's too late.

One final word about the ringleader of the foxes. Peter describes him as a prowling lion (1 Peter 5:8), but he can appear as a fox, too. He hates a powerful marriage, and he is the one who will find those points of vulnerability and exploit them. Whatever it takes to sow discord, whether it's a tube of toothpaste or the way he slurps his cereal—that fox will take advantage of whatever you give him. So watch out for the little things. If your spouse is irritated over something minor, take care of it. Don't give the devil a foothold; just a small one is all he needs.

4. DOES HE SOLIDIFY TRUST IN YOU?

There is one final question to consider. Do you experience genuine unity together? Have you simply found someone you can live with—or have you actually found someone you can't live without? That's the key idea of these next verses: the feeling of absolute trust that comes through oneness with another human being.

"My beloved is mine, and I am his. He feeds his flock among the lilies. Until the day breaks and the shadows flee away, turn, my beloved, and be like a gazelle or a young stag upon the mountains of Bether" (2:16-17).

Those first words say it all: "My beloved is mine, and I am his." That's as perfect a statement of unity and completeness as I can imagine. We'll encounter this idea again in Song of Solomon 6:3 and 7:10. You could say it's the chorus of The Song, the message of this book in eight words.

This mutuality is the center of any successful marriage. Look around at couples you know who have created dynamic marriages and you'll see the truth of this every time. Paul wrote: "Let the husband render to his wife the affection due her, and likewise also the wife to her husband. The wife does not have authority over her own body, but the husband does. And likewise the husband does not have authority over his own body, but the wife does" (1 Corinthians 7:3-4). This is true mutuality: the surrendering of all that we are, even our bodies, to each other. Marriage defies mathematics because $1 + 1 = 2$, then the two become one—a new and more powerful one.

Your willingness to share your deepest self with your mate is at the foundation of your marriage. We go to the very beginning of the Bible to the story of our original creation by God, and we find this principle: "Therefore a man shall leave his father and mother and be joined to his wife, and they shall become one flesh" (Genesis 2:24). Oneness in marriage is unity that comes out of relinquished singleness.

Daniel Webster is a towering figure from American history, a lawyer and statesman who lived in the nineteenth century. You might be familiar with the American folklore of "The Devil and Daniel Webster" in which he was so good in the courtroom that he won an argument with the devil! As for the real-life Webster, as a young man he courted his true love, Grace Fletcher. One evening when he was calling upon her, he held a shiny skein of silk thread for her as the young lady quietly went about her knitting. "Grace," he said. "We've been engaged in untying knots; let us see if we can tie a knot which will not untie for a lifetime." Immediately, Grace put down her work. The two of them proceeded to tie a silk knot so tight, so complex that it would be almost impossible to disentangle.

Webster proposed, and Grace accepted.

Many years passed, and both had passed from this world to the next. When their children were going through some of their parents' personal effects from a long life together, they found a little box marked "Precious Documents." Among the letters of courtship and cherished miscellanea, there was a tiny silk knot—still tight, forever to be untied. [12]

Can you tie a knot so perfect that it can't be untied by the most skilled sailor? In marriage, it is possible—by the grace of God and the love of Jesus Christ. Two of you together can tie one so perfect that the devil himself can't untie it. Believe me, he will give it his best effort, but that effort will never approach the strength of the Lord through a sanctified marriage knot.

MY OLD FLAME

There is a mystery about the power of oneness in marriage, because God Himself is at the center. I have always felt that this mystery is best illustrated by the unity candle ceremony that we see incorporated into many weddings today. I've officiated at more weddings than I can count over these decades, and though I've seen any number of variations of the symbolic ritual, three candles are almost invariably used. These candles are prominently placed in the sight of the family and guests, all of whom bear witness to the commitments made in the ceremony. The two shorter candles, one on either side, symbolize the bride and the groom prior to their union. They are individuals, single adults. The large candle in the center, of course, represents their marriage.

The imagery is so simple, yet so visual and powerful. In that one picture, everyone at the ceremony, even children, can understand why this wedding is being held and why we count it as such a solemn *and* celebratory occasion. My friend Gary Smalley has written a whole book about the unity candle ceremony. He does a beautiful job explaining the symbol of the candles, the "winds" from outside that threaten the gentle and fragile flame, and the power of that candle to light a dark world.

In the ceremony, husband and wife approach the three candles. They take the individual candles from their holders, and together they bring them to the candle in the middle. After they have blended their individual flames into the one new light symbolizing their marriage, they then snuff out the candles representing their singleness. Once extinguished, those single candles belong to the past. Their work is done, and now there is one bold flame where once there were two. "The moment the bride and groom say their vows before God," writes Smalley, "they're not single anymore. They're married people. They're united."[13]

Smalley continues, "The symbolism is beautiful and obvious. No longer will their lights burn for themselves alone. No longer will they live as two single people. Instead, they will enjoy one brighter light, a light that represents the oneness of marriage. . . Oneness is the strength of marriage. . . It is the place where the couple is stronger than either partner is separately." [14]

Marriage has been around since the beginning of humanity, so we tend to take it for granted. Have you ever stopped to consider what a breathtakingly beautiful, mysterious, and profound gift of God it is? Have you ever thanked Him for placing such a wonderful, supernatural miracle in this world, and giving you the opportunity to receive its blessing? We begin life as children, and as we grow taller we become wiser. But in marriage, we can become something entirely new; we give up our solitude for unity with another person who completes us. Then we partake of wonderful joy every single day for the rest of our lives.

I certainly believe every single word in that preceding paragraph, and I hope you do, too. But if you are presently engaged and I've gotten you excited and eager, I want to temper just a bit of that emotion with a reality check. (Don't you hate reality checks?)

Wonderful as marriage is, it opens with the most challenging adjustment you will ever make in life. You and your spouse will be encountering the thousands of little habits and ideas and details that make up each of your backgrounds. Life for you is based on certain assumptions, many of them different from the assumptions of your spouse. The best thing you can do is to anticipate that adjustment, and perform as much preventive maintenance in advance as you can. You do that by asking the kinds of questions we have posed in this chapter. Those are the "big ones."

As for the little ones, the "foxes in the grapes," expect those, too— and face them with love and determination. Decree that nothing is going to place any crack in the foundation of the union you're forging. No root of bitterness will be allowed. Find out which of you rolls up the toothpaste and who squeezes the middle of the tube. Then have a good laugh and discover a compromise. The big secret is for you, personally, to give in as much as you can. "In lowliness of mind let each esteem others better than himself" (Philippians 2:3).

Those little sacrifices, you will find, actually give you more joy than annoyance. It feels good to serve, to be humble for a moment, and especially to make someone else happy— particularly when that someone is the person you love more than anyone else in this crowded world. Cheerfully deferring to your spouse is one of the quickest ways to truly become one.

ULTIMATE UNITY

Then, my friend, in that moment when you realize you've become one flesh—you will feel such a deep sense of peace and gratitude toward God. You will realize you have reached a precious goal He has cherished for your life. His desire has been for you to knit your heart with another's for whom each of you was made. As in Genesis, He looked at you and said, "It is not good that he (or she) is alone," and He decreed a union just for you.

Of course, this is profoundly more true if your union together comes through the love and power of Christ. I have said that $1 + 1 = 1$ when we do it right. But there is another way of looking at it, another alternative of spiritual mathematics. When you come together in marriage, you are ideally the denominator—the bottom of the equation 1/1 (one over one), because Christ is over your marriage at all times, the head of your union. It is He who holds you together, He who makes you a complete number never to be divided. Solomon reminds us "A triple-braided cord is not easily broken" (Ecclesiastes 4:12, NLT).

Looking at it another way, where do you think the light comes from in that unity candle? Jesus said, "I am the light of the world" (John 8:12). He is eternal, and His light never wavers. Darkness flees before His light. If you are married, or you're contemplating marriage, don't you want to know that the source of your power is someone perfect, wise, loving, and eternal? Don't you want your unity to be based on His unwavering love for you?

Here is a final thought on the oneness we were meant to experience. On His final night with His disciples, Jesus prayed for them. Then He added a prayer for you and me:

> *"I do not pray for these alone, but also for those who will believe in Me through their word; that they all may be one, as You, Father, are in Me, and I in You; that they also may be one in Us, that the world may believe that You sent Me. And the glory which You gave Me I have given them, that they may be one just as We are one: I in them, and You in Me; that they may be made perfect in one, and that the world may know that You have sent Me, and have loved them as You have loved Me."* John 17:20-23

That's a lot of words, of course, and these verses carry one of the deepest thoughts Jesus ever offered us. But the gist of them is this: Christ wants us to enjoy the same unity with each other that He enjoys with His Father. That includes the special unity of marriage, and the unity we have with fellow believers. When I read that such a blessing is available to me, I become very excited—much as I have always become when I think about seeing my wife after a long trip somewhere. This life offers me the wonderful thrill of marriage—and, even deeper than that, the joy and peace and fulfillment of both of us, as one unit, being reconciled with God.

As you think about the meaning of earthly family, be sure you also consider the meaning of heavenly family. You have a Father, a Lord, a Savior, who loves you (Christ loving His Church) as the groom loves the bride.

Therefore, if you're waiting for the perfect mate, take heart. There is one perfect love that every single one of us can enjoy—at any moment, at any time. I hope that's a knot you've already tied. ◆

1   Entry under "Love and marriage," http://www.preachingtoday.com; submitted by J. R. Love, Rushton, Louisiana.
2   Yelena Antonova "Arranged Marriages in India," at http://www.geocities.com/justalenka/arranged/index.htm (accessed 10 January 2009).
3   Lisa Takeuchi and Coco Master, "We Just Clicked," *Time*, 28 January 2008, 84-89.
4   "Mary Madden and Amanda Lenhart, Reports: Online Activities and Pursuits," 5 March 2006, www.pewinternet.org/PPF/r/177/report_display.asp *and* www.pewinternet.org/pdfs/PIP_Online_Dating.pdf, 5 March 2006 (accessed 29 January 2008).
5   Paige Patterson; 51.
6   Charles Lowery, *Cosmic Belief* (Irving, TX: Acts Press, 2004), 19.
7   Ibid.
8   Daniel L. Akin, *God on Sex* (Nashville: B & H Publishing Group, 2003), 85-86.
9   Ibid.
10 S. Craig Glickman, *A Song for Lovers* (Downers Grove: IL: InterVarsity Press, 1976), 47-48.
11 Charles Swindoll, *Strike the Original Match*, (Portland, OR: Multnomah Press, 1980), 87.
12 Clifton Fadiman, *The Little Brown Book of Anecdotes* (Boston: Little, Brown & Co, 1985). 575.
13 Gary Smalley, *One Flame* (Carol Stream, IL: Tyndale House Publishers, 2002), 16.
14 Ibid; 16, 3.

5

Dreaming of Security

Song of Solomon 3:1-5

Most adults of a certain age remember George Burns, the popular comedian with a cigar who died just after his one hundredth birthday in 1996. He was a wry wit and a study in graceful aging. Many of his younger fans weren't even aware that he had labored for three decades without half of his comedy team. His wife Gracie had died in 1964.

George Burns and Gracie Allen met on the old Vaudeville circuit, a network of song-and-dance and comedy stages from a bygone era. Burns was a failed comedian whose act was missing that certain something—and Gracie held the missing piece to the puzzle. In those days, boy-and-girl acts were a dime a dozen. But in most of them, the female played the "straight" role, while the male got all the laugh lines. George Burns had the finely tuned instincts to reverse that formula.

Though quite articulate in real life, Gracie Allen played what today we'd call an "air-head"—someone who gets little things wrong in a comical way. But there was brilliance in her delivery, and George Burns kept feeding her the best lines. The couple became a radio sensation as that medium took off in the 1930s. In the 1940s they added Hollywood films to their résumé. And in the 1950s, their television show was a ratings hit. George and Gracie were one of America's favorite couples. In 1940, Gracie even ran for President of the United States on her radio show, losing by more than a few votes to someone named Roosevelt. Only Gracie's health slowed them down. By the late fifties, she was becoming ill more frequently.

After Gracie's death, when George Burns reluctantly became a solo act, people were startled to discover the comedian's personal comic genius. For forty years of marriage, he had deferred to his wife, giving her the spotlight and public adoration as he played the straight man, the irritated husband.

Burns stayed busy acting, joking, and appearing on talk shows until he was 99 years old. But he never quite got over the loss of his beloved wife. In 1987, when the spotlight was finally all his own, this was the name of the book he wrote: *Gracie: A Love Story*. In that volume he wrote the following about his wife: "I go to Forest Lawn Cemetery once a month to see her and I tell her everything that's going on. I told her I was writing this book about her. Evidently she approves—she didn't say anything. I don't know if she hears me, but I do know that every time I talk to her, I feel better."[1]

There is a wonderful thing called security that comes from every good marriage. We have seen how true oneness is a product of that bond. That oneness, in turn, brings the most secure feeling we know other than the knowledge of eternal salvation. In marriage there is one person who will always be there. And married couples know each other so perfectly, so intimately, that they can work together with the timing and perfection that George Burns and Gracie Allen brought to their act. Burns could give away all the best lines because he was secure in their identity as a married couple and in their mutual strengths. Why should he be insecure? He gloried in his wife's triumphs just as if they were his own. They were, of course.

In marriage, we are not our own. We give ourselves completely to one another. To some that idea could be threatening; in truth, genuine freedom comes from giving ourselves away. As in the spiritual life, so it is in marriage.

Young single people dream of marriage, and one of the things about it that most appeals to them is the idea of the security it brings—the destiny of "settling down." For one thing, there is an end to the restless merry-go-round of dating, the superficial games, and the ups and downs of looking for the right one. The future becomes an established certainty, and there is power and freedom in knowing it has been secured. Before we have met our soul-mate, the future can't even begin to come into focus. Nothing else can truly be settled. So much will depend upon that one with whom we share it.

Shulamith had those dreams, much as men and women today have them. As a matter of fact, as we begin the third chapter of the Song of Solomon, we find five verses that make up a dream of Shulamith's just prior to marriage—at least so the scholars have come to believe. Dreams play a large part in this book, and that's as it should be; love, in the beginning, is a "dreamy" kind of thing, isn't it? Falling in love often feels more like something from the fantasy world of sleep than the tedium of daily life. Song of Solomon begins with a dream, then a dream sequence in its third chapter, and shows us several more reveries before we are finished.

My own dreams are quite strange and surprising; I'm sure yours are the same. Some of them mix and match various stages of my life, places, and emotions. Dreams are the graffiti of a playful imagination while the more businesslike mind is off duty. We need to be very cautious about drawing conclusions or directions from our dreams. But they do provide interesting entertainment, don't they? A different movie every night projected on the backs of our eyelids. And sometimes dreams can suggest the truth about our basic feelings in life.

Let's find out what Shulamith sees in her dreams of several key aspects of the security in her future.

THE SECURITY TO DENY INDEPENDENCE

How do we begin to feel secure in any particular setting? It takes a basic trust and a willingness to be open. When parents leave their two-year-old daughter in the nursery at church, she cries desperately. We call that "separation anxiety." At first she will keep to herself sullenly. Yet within a few minutes, the child usually looks around, sees friendly faces and nice toys, and makes a decision to trust her environment. She feels enough basic security to relax and enjoy herself, so she gives up her independence and gets involved.

In marriage, we must also deny the independence that was a way of life in single living. We can't sit sullenly in a corner and say, "These toys are mine!" We realize that the only working system is one of *inter*dependence, relying upon each other. Life is better when we "play well with others." Biblical interdependence is an act of faith. It's letting down the barriers and declaring a state of unity in marriage, "one flesh" unity.

How can we see it in Shulamith and Solomon? In her dream, Shulamith looks for Solomon and she cannot find him. This is actually a common dream for many people when we have a deep connection to someone. In the dream, she is feeling lonely and she begins to search in earnest for the one she loves. In the first chapter, Shulamith was looking for Solomon when the other women told her, "Listen, Girl, if you can't handle a traveling husband, you're not ready for the big city. So go find yourself a nice farmer boy back in the fields, why don't you?"

But people in love can have a gnawing fear of losing the one they love and an aching sense of aloneness when that person is gone. Here is what we realize:

We Are Incomplete Without Each Other. In this first section of the third chapter, two important facts emerge. First of all, Shulamith is learning that she feels incomplete without Solomon. She says: "By night on my bed I sought the one I love; I sought him, but I did not find him" (3:1).

In her dream, the couple is already married. (Dreaming has its advantages, doesn't it?) That's the good news; the bad news is that her husband is absent. It's certainly reasonable to assume Shulamith had been thinking of Solomon before she fell asleep, because this is how the imagination often chooses a subject for the night's fantasy. In the dream marriage, the two should be in the same bed as they can't be in real life.

The theme of seeking and finding occurs four times in these verses. It's interesting to discover that the Hebrew word *baqash* has alternate meanings of *seek* or *desire*.[2] It can also mean *yearn* or *long for*.[3] When we desire something, we seek it out in our imagination—or in our dreams. In her sleep, Shulamith is reaching out to Solomon with heart and soul. The part of her mind that modern psychologists would call her subconscious is playing on a deep feeling that she is incomplete without her man. Uncomfortable dreams are usually the ones that explore what we fear or doubt. Shulamith has reached a point in her life when she needs her mate to feel whole.

We Are Insecure Without Each Other. In the latter portion of this first verse, we see that Shulamith is frankly insecure without Solomon. In marriage, we frequently feel uncomfortable without our spouse. We'll be on some trip to another city standing at a reception or sitting in a meeting thinking, "This would go so much better if both of us were here." Socially, we are a functioning unit that is at half-strength when we're apart. We feel what George Burns did as he tried comedy as a solo act.

She recounts, "'I will rise now,' I said, 'and go about the city; in the streets and in the squares I will seek the one I love.' I sought him, but I did not find him" (3:2).

Have you ever dreamed of searching for someone, going everywhere and asking, yet never catching up with that person? In her reverie, Shulamith rises from her empty bed and begins to seek her missing man. She is asleep at home in the country, and perhaps she begins her search in the open fields and green vineyards. Then she does what no young lady would do in the waking world: she walks into the city at night. Decorum would forbid this, but in dreams, all things are possible. Shulamith looks everywhere for "the one my heart loves" (NIV). But Solomon is nowhere to be found.

We can imagine Shulamith waking later and realizing that her dreams have her pegged: Without Solomon, she is a mess! She is incomplete and insecure, and what that adds up to is a full willingness to trade her single independence for the interdependence of a loving marriage that will end this painful separation.

THE SECURITY TO DEAL WITH ISSUES

Shulamith's dream involves seeking and finding. The second part, obviously, is far more satisfying. Back in the dream, the action shifts to the streets and squares of the city. There Shulamith encounters the night watchmen who are making their rounds. Remember, dreams lack interior logic. She is in Solomon's hometown, Jerusalem, rather than her own town of Shunem. She dreams that she climbs out of her bed and puts her feet down in a distant city. But in a way it makes sense. Thinking of Solomon reminds her of Jerusalem. Dreams are mosaics in which one thing puts us in mind of another, and that thing then becomes another ingredient in the tossed-salad world of the dreamscape.

Shulamith is searching, but she is the one who is found: "The watchmen who go about the city found me; I said, 'Have you seen the one I love?'" (3:3)

In real life, she might be polite enough to identify herself as well as the object of her search. In the big city, she wouldn't have been immediately recognized, especially by night. But of course, this is not the real world but the world of Shulamith's imagination. She gets right to the point: Where is he?

The image of this young lady walking the night streets by herself is one that emphasizes her solitude, her loneliness without Solomon. Marriage provides the security to deal with issues, and to do so as a team. The dream is helping her understand how much she needs that security.

Taking Initiative. What can we learn from the "finding" portion of her dream? First, she is proactive. That's a good thing in general, and an essential thing in marriage. A country girl might be someone who was raised to take the initiative. We know that she didn't lead a pampered life; she had been sent to the fields to work. She doesn't send a servant to find Solomon in her dream, but she is on the case herself, even if that means patrolling the streets at night.

We remember earlier passages where it was Solomon who was searching for her. In a healthy relationship, both parties take the initiative at various times. This is what it means to function as a team.

This is a preview of the marriage of Solomon and Shulamith—two active and proactive people who desperately want to be together. As never before, we live in an age of travel where one of us might rise in the morning from home in California and do business that evening in New York

City. The modern world requires us to be apart in marriage. The message
of this passage is not that we should try to turn back the clock, refusing
to work in any industry requiring travel—but that we should never grow
comfortable in having a long-distance marriage. It's an up-close-and-
personal kind of thing like parenting. We need to protect our time
together to the best of our ability; and when we have to, allow absence
to make the heart grow fonder. The one good thing about being apart is
being reunited, and at least we can make a grand occasion out of that.

My call to the ministry has required me to travel frequently in the
United States and on quite a few occasions internationally. If at all possible, I have Donna by my side. If not, then we will talk on the phone
every single day, and not necessarily just one call. It all began with
daily letters during my summertime tour in college. And after all these
years we are fortunate enough to be able to talk by phone, even when
continents and oceans separate us. I don't like being away from my
home, but I absolutely hate being apart from my wife. And when I'm at
home and she's the one on the road, I like that even less. We yearn to be
together, we take the initiative through communication technology or
by traveling together, and our security in marriage increases.

Seeking Information. Shulamith was capable of taking the initiative,
but also receiving the right information. That's a more important item
than it might appear. Some people are great at being proactive, but not
so good at stopping to listen. Have you ever known someone like this?
Others listen well, process all the facts, but won't make the move when
necessary. Every coin needs two sides.

Even if we're bold and confident, ready to walk the streets and seek
what we want, we need to settle down and listen when it's time to do
so. Today, we're often "seeking" behind the wheel of a car. Men are
active; we like to be the one behind the steering wheel. But where do we

struggle? Stopping and asking for directions, of course. Men have been known to be reluctant to do that (so I'm told!).

Shulamith does the equivalent of pulling into the filling station and asking which highway to take. It is so simple, yet such a problem for many people. How does this relate to marriage other than the wife's frustration when her husband grits his teeth and keeps driving? Well, consider the fact that marriages often hit rough spots, and there are wonderful resources to help us through them. Will we be willing to ask the "night watchmen" of marriage's darker streets? Shulamith's helpers initiated the conversation, but that will rarely happen in the secrecy of marriage problems. The pastor or Christian counselor is unlikely to come to your door and ask if he can help put your relationship back together. How will he even know there's a problem? You need to be proactive and go for help.

I've counseled couples who have struggled and suffered for years before seeking help. No one knows how many couples are out there who never asked for assistance at all. How many people go straight to divorce court without seeing if a third party can help solve the problem? It's like being on the way to a wonderful destination, getting lost, and refusing to stop and get a map. You could be within half a block of finding what you need. Don't give up! But sadly, too many husbands and wives place pride before their happiness.

If you find yourself in such a crisis, I humbly beg you to ask yourself this question: "If I look the other way and let my marriage continue to crumble until it collapses, how will I feel about my efforts for the rest of my life? Will I be okay with hurrying right by the watchmen, smiling artificially, and telling them everything is all right? Or will I regret my pride from here into eternity?"

It's true; the counselor may not be able to put all the pieces back together. One of you may be too angry or confused to receive help.

But why make that assumption? Why not exhaust every last option in trying to save what God has joined together?

What Shulamith does in her dream seems deceptively simple, and so it is. Nothing in the world is simpler than saying, "Excuse me. Can you help me get where I'm going?"

THE SECURITY TO DISCOVER INTIMACY

Our third essential is the security to discover intimacy. In the first part of verse four, we read these words: "Scarcely had I passed by them, when I found the one I love. I held him and would not let him go."

Isn't it nice when a nightmare suddenly turns a corner and becomes a pleasant dream? Shulamith's persistence through the nightscape of her imagination pays off, perhaps as God breaks through to comfort her sleeping anxiety. The watchmen have moved along, and the darkness and despair surround her again. Then comes the wonderful surprise of Solomon emerging from the night and into her arms. It's so easy to see this scene in the mind's eye that it's as if we're right there inside her dream—or perhaps in a wonderful old black-and-white movie.

What a satisfying moment when two lovers find one another in their dreams. It sounds like Hollywood, but it's right here in the Bible. What can we learn from this illustration?

Intimacy Means Desire: Wanting Each Other. As we think about this moment in Shulamith's dream, we conclude that it's all about intimacy. The reason her imagination is creating such an intense melodrama inside her is this: she wants one particular person so powerfully that the desire won't shut down even when she shuts her eyes. And she knows he wants her, too. "Scarcely had I passed by them," she said, "when I found the one I love. I held him and would not let him go" (3:4).

Obviously we're not dealing with a half-hearted, glad-to-see-you hug here, but one of the knock-you-down/squeeze-you-flat varieties.

This, too, is a way of showing initiative, is it not? Shulamith grabs her man without delay and swallows him in an embrace. Considering the object of this dream is a man of Solomon's stature demonstrates a bit of audacity. We're even told that she won't let him go (as if he wants her to).

I think we've all held someone like that. It's the way we hold our children after briefly losing them in a crowd; the way we hug a son in the military who is home from a long stint overseas; the way children clutch their parents when they've been awakened by a bad dream. This is the "don't you ever leave me again" hug. No gesture in the human vernacular so clearly says, "I want you; I need you." This is intimacy.

Intimacy Means Discipline: Waiting. Shulamith continues in verse four, "I held him and would not let him go, until I had brought him to the house of my mother, and into the chamber of her who conceived me." She now brings Solomon to her maternal home, a place that, in the simple symbolism of dreams, means safety and security for her. We often dream of our parents even after they've left this life. Mothers and fathers are at the center of who we are and never too far from our thoughts. Therefore the sleeping mind pulls them into the story.

More important, however, is the traditional meaning of bringing a potential mate home to meet the parents. Solomon was clearly the man for her future, and a young lady would be thinking about how her fiancée and her mother—the two most important people in her universe—would get along.

This is always the signal that things are "getting serious." If we're dating a viable prospect, we know this meeting will happen at some point, and that it's absolutely vital that both sides get along well and eventually bond as family. But all of this will take some time. Parents need more than one encounter with a potential son-in-law. Marriage is too important to happen on the spur of the moment. Real intimacy requires waiting.

THE SECURITY TO DENOUNCE IMPATIENCE

Waiting is difficult, isn't it? This dream is all about Shulamith's desperation to be with the one she loves. Desperation and patience don't go together well. As much as Shulamith yearns to be in the arms of Solomon, she is willing to be patient. In verse five we find familiar words, used already in the first chapter and destined to make a further appearance:

"'I charge you, O Daughters of Jerusalem, by the gazelles or by the does of the field, do not stir up nor awaken love until it pleases.'" In the first instance, she has used these words as a cautionary note for the other women. "Don't be so eager to feel what I feel, because it's difficult to control the emotions and desires that come with it." Perhaps now, in the scattered sequence of her dream, she feels the wave of desire again and revisits the occasion in the palace.

The only remedy for impulsiveness is the patience that comes with maturity. All of us have a human side that wants what it wants, when it wants it. The difference between children and adults of integrity is the discipline of deferred gratification—or, to put it more simply, patience is a virtue.

But virtues tend to require sacrifice. They don't come easy, nor is patience any exception. What are some characteristics of this strength known as patience?

Patience Waits for the Right Person. This refrain is in the form of an oath or a vow to wait. It teaches us, first of all, that patience focuses on the one and only person for us. Sure, we're not always certain about determining that. But we can get good counsel on how to walk in obedience to God's will and select the one He provides.

Once we've made that commitment, we must wait. Impatience will delude us into being hasty, rationalizing the wrong one into the right one. God gives His best to those who wait.

A side observation here: As I talk with single people, I'm pleased to see how they're waiting patiently for just the right person. But I want to tell them not to neglect *becoming* the right person during that season of watching. The more they grow in wisdom, in stature, and in favor with God and humanity, the easier it will become to find that right one. God is pleased when His child says, "I trust You to fill my need for a companion on Your own schedule rather than my short-sighted one. Meanwhile, I'm going to do all I can every single day to become more like Your Son." It's far more important to become the right one than to discover the right one—and we have more control over the matter with the Spirit's guidance.

Again, take the initiative in becoming; watch patiently in waiting.

Patience Waits for the Right Time. It's not only about waiting for the right person, but the right time. Some Christian couples find their soul mates realizing that if they had met at an earlier time, they would never have ended up together. By letting God's timetable play out, they found the right one with the right timing.

My friend Rob Morgan found an amusing little poem. It's written in a dialect we can't quite place, but it describes an emotion we can understand:

> *Nice night in June; stars shine, big moon,*
> *In park with girl; heart pound, head swirl*
> *Me say love; she coo like dove*
> *Me smart, me fast; me don't let chance pass*
> *"Get hitched," me say; she say "okay"*

Wedding bells ring; honeymoon, everything
Settle down, happy life; happy man, happy wife
Another night in June; stars shine, big moon
Me not happy anymore; carry baby, walk the floor
Wife mad, she stew; me mad, stew too
Life one big spat; nagging wife, bawling brat
We realized at last we moved too fast.[4]

It's possible to find the right one at the wrong time. Not knowing the future, how can we possibly handle the timing? The short answer is that we can't. It's a good thing God never sleeps. He has His plans for us, to give us a future and a hope. "But, beloved, do not forget this one thing, that with the Lord one day is as a thousand years, and a thousand years as one day" (2 Peter 3:8). Time for us is so pressing, so urgent, yet God sees past, present, and future in one tapestry. If we can only trust Him, we will discover the beauty of heaven's machinery working things out for His glory and our delight. It's as true of marriage as it is of career, of having children, or of anything else.

Psalm 37:9 tells us that those who wait upon the Lord will inherit the earth. Isaiah 40:31 tells us that those who wait upon the Lord will renew their strength. To me, it's as plain as day that we can hope to be both strong and successful simply by waiting upon the Lord. The impatient need not apply.

We all know the result of this impatience when it comes to finding a mate. Many today are trying to reverse the age-old, God-honored commitment process by living together first and deciding later. From the spiritual standpoint, of course, this is clear disobedience. From the merely practical standpoint, the evidence is clear that it doesn't work.

Modern couples often believe they're being smart, doing their research. It seems to them that if there are going to be problems in marriage, why not find out on a trial basis with "no commitment to buy anything"? If not completely satisfied, just return your mate and shop elsewhere. But a recent report indicates that the non-commitment of living together leads only to a non-commitment after marriage. In other words, the couple continues to look at their marriage as a disposable option rather than a living covenant; they've set that mood by living together. As Bill Hybels puts it,

> *The world outside of Christ has a view of marriage that emphasizes maximum pleasure with minimum sacrifice. It does not take into account possibilities such as incapacitating illnesses, emotional disturbance, or financial reversals. That is why this view of marriage is not working, why the divorce rate has soared. Love has never been able to operate for long without sacrifice.*[5]

The way of Christ is the way of sacrifice, the abandonment of self-absorption. The patience of Shulamith is a victory over selfishness and immaturity. Patience says, "I believe God knows what is best for me, and I will wait for the right time and the right one, even if it requires a lot from me to do so right now."

Another poem I've held onto for years:

Love
I love you,
Not only for what you are,
But for what I am
When I am with you.

I love you,
Not only for what
You have made of yourself,

But for what
You are making of me.

I love you
For the part of me
That you bring out.

I love you
For putting your hand
Into my heaped-up heart
And passing over
All the foolish, weak things
That you can't help
Dimly seeing there,
And for drawing out
Into the light
All the beautiful, radiant belongings
That no one else had looked
Quite far enough to find.

I love you because you
Are helping me to make
Of the lumber of my life
Not a tavern
But a temple;
And of the words
Of my every day
Not a reproach
But a song.

I love you
Because you have done

More than any creed
Could have done
To make me good,
And more than any fate
Could have done
To make me happy.

You have done it
Without a touch,
Without a word,
Without a sign.
You have done it
By being yourself.
Perhaps that is what
Being a friend means,
After all.

© Roy Croft (1907–1973) [6]

THE SECRET OF SELFLESSNESS

Marriage, then, isn't about taking, but about giving—which ultimately means that we take away more than we ever need. Only in abandoning our basic self-driven nature, paradoxically, will we find what we need and crave. Commit yourself to having your needs met, and you'll come up empty. Commit yourself to meeting needs, and all your needs will be met.

The great author and scholar C. S. Lewis was married late in life, long after he wrote the apologetic work *Mere Christianity*, which is the finest primer on the Christian life you will ever read. Single as he was, he was wise enough to understand marriage thoroughly. He wrote that a man and wife, as Christians, are a "single organism." Jesus said, "So then, they are no longer two but one flesh. Therefore what God has joined together, let not man separate" (Matthew 19:6).

C. S. Lewis took those words literally, not figuratively, and offered the example of a violin. You can pluck it *pizzicato*, one string at a time, and make simple music. But you'll never hear the richness and power of true violin music unless you apply a bow to the strings. The real instrument, then, is the combination of two separate and very different elements: the violin and the bow working in concert if you will.

Lewis continues that the experience of being in love is ecstatic, wonderful, and healthy. But feelings are transient; we can't base our lives on them. If we did, we'd never get anywhere in life. Remember when you fell head over heels, how generally useless you were for other things? Lewis asks, "Who could bear to live in that excitement for even five years?" He's right; you know it and I know it; we'd simply burn out.

But we can love without being love-struck. In fact, we can experience the deeper, fuller life of loving with body, mind, soul, and spirit in selfless dedication. C. S. Lewis calls it "a deep unity, maintained by the will and deliberately strengthened by habit."[7]

What about the hard times? There come moments when we actually don't feel as if we like each other, much less love each other the way we did at first. Yes, even then, it's possible to act in genuine love. We actually strengthen our love by continuing to keep the covenant of devotion regardless of transient feelings. And let's be honest, as far as those emotions are concerned, they could lead us to dangerous places. In the course of marriage, we all meet other people with whom we could "fall in love." What is it that separates us from the animals who simply act on every impulse? Human practicality mixed with spiritual wisdom. The first says we would hurt ourselves to act on that desire; the second says we would hurt our mate and displease our loving Father.

In the end, love is much less about feelings than wisdom and commitment. Men are commanded to honor their wives as Christ loves the church. When Jesus prayed at Gethsemane, his feelings told him that some other option than crucifixion would be more pleasant. There was nothing about the experience of the cross that He "felt" like taking on. (See Matthew 26:36-46.) He wanted to live. But commitment to His mission kept Him focused and obedient to the will of the Father. He loves us—that is, the Church—and we are to love our spouses with the same brand of devotion.

AFTER THE HONEYMOON

We all know that the early throes of love don't last. Every romantic relationship begins with a fireworks display, but what happens when the show is over? What are we going to do when the honeymoon ends?

If we model ourselves on the lifestyles of the rich and famous, we'll just move out and move on—watch the sky for the next fireworks display, and thus go from emotional high to emotional high. Many people actually live this way today.

In the end, of course, love without commitment becomes one more prison, and a dreadfully cold and empty one. Here is a secret the rich and famous haven't figured out: The quieter time after the fireworks is actually far more wonderful, far more fulfilling. The serial monogamy crowd moves nomadically from one superficial relationship to the next, and in the end it's like eating a diet of nothing but ice cream. After a while, I'm sure they crave something more substantial and nutritious— particularly as they grow older, and as looks fade, and options narrow.

On the other hand, in my own experience I've seen what happens after the honeymoon. The aging process is rewarding rather than threatening. From the experience of marriage to a wonderful and godly woman, I receive the fulfillment of a love that continues after several decades to grow in proportion to our willingness to serve one another. It was a wonderful thing when we fell head-over-heels in love as young people; I wouldn't give anything for the memory of it. But what we have now is so much more than hearts and flowers. In a well-seasoned marriage, deep calls to deep. (See Psalm 42:7.) As one grows wiser, that wisdom is shared between us.

Joys and sorrows alike are common property so that when we are happy we have someone to share it with. When we are sad, there is someone to help shoulder the burden. The world goes on changing, friends come and go, but we always have each other; we always have someone who has been on the identical journey, right by our side. Sometimes words aren't even necessary, because we have enjoyed the level of intimacy that tells each of us what the other is thinking. There is nothing in this world quite like it, and I feel truly sorry for those who surf the rising and breaking waves of one partner after another.

The crazy emotions are great, and everyone needs to go through them. But this, the full journey of love, is true intimacy. It is what God wants for every one of us. To use an analogy that doesn't do justice to the subject, it is as if your parents left you a million dollars and you didn't access it but kept borrowing their pocket change. Yet real, godly marriage is better than a million dollars, and empty relationships are less than pocket change. Here is an incredible gift of grace, and it comes at the price of your acceptance and lifelong commitment.

You might let out a sigh at this point. You may be thinking, "Ah, but I don't need to be convinced. I would give all that I have for that experience, but my marriage is too far gone. We never had the things you're talking about."

I don't want to sell the fantasy of a perfect relationship. No marriage is without its flaws, including my own. But maybe you've lost the feeling. That's okay, because feelings aren't the starting place in repairing a damaged marriage. Maybe you've even lost the will. I believe I can help you with that one, too. Keep reading.

MAKEOVER: FIRST LOVE

At the end of the Bible in the Book of Revelation, the Lord Jesus is speaking to seven prominent churches from the first century world. He describes each one, commends them for what they've done right, and then tells them what needs to be fixed. The first church on His list is the one at Ephesus. This is a fellowship that has accomplished great things; they have been fruitful, no question about it. Except . . .

"Nevertheless I have this against you, that you have left your first love" (Revelation 2:4).

Left your first love. That church keeps on keeping on, but they've lost that loving feeling. Is that a description of your marriage? It's interesting that we avoid responsibility by speaking of *losing* a feeling, or saying, "The feeling just left us." The feeling hasn't gone anywhere; we are the ones who leave. Jesus gives the prescription for getting that loving feeling back. He says, "Remember therefore from where you have fallen" (Revelation 2:5).

He isn't talking about sin here. The idea is for the church to remember how it used to be in its love relationship with Christ. Can you do this? Go through the album of memories in your mind, and relive what your marriage used to be like—the way you'd like it to be once again.

That puts you in position to take the next step. Jesus says, "Repent. And do the first works."

Repent. That word is associated, of course, with tough sin. Actually, we all have areas in which we need to repent. It can be something very small, something we don't even think much about. Relationships wither because of a thousand little things we ignore. (Remember the little foxes from the last chapter?) Repentance means speaking sincerely to God and saying, "I've done the wrong thing, which was _____. Forgive me and strengthen me to turn one hundred eighty degrees and walk away from that failure." Maybe you and your spouse can list the obstacles and have that prayer together.

Step three is the second part of the verse: Do the "first works." What was it like when you were truly in love? Did you listen better? Did you take greater pains to be pleasant when you were together? Perhaps you took more pride in your appearance? What about issues of serving one another and counting each other more important than yourself? Repentance happens in the mind and spirit; this part happens through action. Set things right.

Notice that feelings have nothing to do with it. In these steps, you look to God and then to each other, and you begin to work. And the great thing is that if only one of you does this, there is hope for your marriage. If both of you do it, there is a one hundred percent chance of success. Then you will find the feelings "mysteriously" come back.

Don't forget that there are also watchmen and watchwomen walking the streets just outside the window of your marriage. There are those who would love to help you, encourage you, pray for you. People are ready to gather around you and cheer you on to a rejuvenated relationship that shows just how powerful our God is—He brings dead things back to life.

I haven't lived the other way—that of discarding relationships like used tissues. I have never counted myself as part of the jet set of our times. But I know the deep joy of God's way. So does Nancy Kennedy, who described her "(Not So) Terrible, Horrible, No Good, Very Bad Year" on a blog called "Walk With Me," sponsored by *Today's Christian Woman* magazine.

Sitting in yet another hospital waiting room, Nancy reflects upon the fifteen months since her husband Barry underwent open heart and quadruple bypass surgery. For her, much of that time has been spent in waiting rooms. It's been educational; she's added new terminology to her vocabulary such as aneurysm and atrial fibrillation. For her, the less technical meanings are that she must put on a cheerful face for Barry and promise him she won't forget to eat lunch again.

Borrowing from the title of a famous children's book, she says it's been a terrible, horrible, no-good, very bad year—one of the worst of a thirty-two year marriage, and simultaneously one of the *best*.

How can that be? "I learned just how deeply Barry loves me," Nancy writes. She has seen her husband in the moments just prior to serious surgery turning to tell a friend, "Make sure Nancy takes care of herself. Promise me." Knife-bearing doctors were no worry. His wife fretting and failing to take care of herself—that was his sole concern.

Nancy had come to faith in Christ three years after the wedding, then spent nearly three decades praying for her husband's salvation. The day of his open-heart surgery, Barry took her hand and told her that death would not separate the couple; he had come to know Christ as His Savior. He prayed with everyone—Nancy, a friend, even the surgeon. From then on, prayer became the thing that joined Nancy and Barry in the most intimate way.

What had been taken away in spiritual health, God had far more restored in the gift of a shared faith. The Lord had "performed heart surgery on us both, ripping us apart and knitting us back together." And so the couple talked about the eventful year, both awful and awfully good. Only in the deep fullness of a marriage can such a paradox be experienced.

Nancy concludes, "We thank God for the good days and the bad, because in all our days, God has held us both securely in His grip. We've known His incredible kindness to us. Our hearts are in his hands. We've had a terrible, horrible, no-good, very bad year—and I praise God for it."[8]

I would call that security in marriage—the kind too strong to be threatened even by death itself. Don't you think God wants that for you, too? ◆

1 "Gracie Allen," at http://www.encyclopedia.com (accessed 13 January 2009).
2 www.blueletterbible.org/lang/lexicon/lexicon.cfm?Strongs=H1245&t=KJV
3 Daniel Akin, *God on Sex*, 105.
4 Quoted in Robert J. Morgan, "Compassion: How to Pull the Plug on the Reservoir of Resentment," http://www.donelson.org/pocket/pp-down02.html (accessed 19 November 2008).
5 Bill Hybels, *Homemade*, vol. 15, no.10, October 1991.
6 Roy Croft in Albert Lewis Alexander, *Poems that Touch the Heart* (New York: Doubleday, 1962), 5.
7 Adapted from, C.S. Lewis, *The Complete C.S. Lewis Signature Classics* (New York: HarperCollins, 2002), 90, 93-94.
8 Nancy Kennedy, "The (Not So) Terrible, Horrible, No Good, Very Bad Year," from *Walk with Me, a Today's Christian Woman Blog* (12-507) at http://blog.todayschristianwoman.com/walkwithme/2007/12/the_not_so_terrible_horrible_n.html (accessed 14 January 2009).

6

The Wedding Planner

Song of Solomon 3:6-11

I've officiated at enough weddings to know that someone "gives away the bride," usually her father. But I just saw a statistic that has me rethinking that: Apparently, the average wedding now costs $26,000.[1]

Considering who gets the bill, I wouldn't say the bride is being "given away." Would you?

Then again, it's been reported that the recent wedding of Vanisha Mittal and Amit Bhatia cost a cool sixty million dollars.[2] I can think through all that goes into a nice wedding ceremony at our church, including the rehearsal dinner and the reception, and I still can't get the numbers to add up to anything in that neighborhood.

Nor have I seen or tasted a wedding cake worth twenty million dollars like one created in Beverly Hills. (Studded with diamonds, it was never even eaten.)[3] Finally, I haven't seen a wedding gown that is worth twelve million dollars, but you guessed it—there's a precedent.[4] If we had a Guinness Book of Wedding Records, I suppose all of the above would be listed. And I doubt the field will fill up with folks eager to challenge them.

A fine wedding may be pricey, but a fine marriage is priceless. What should we think about our time in history when it's so costly to walk down the aisle at a wedding, and so easy to walk out the door on a marriage? For example (here we go again), *Forbes* magazine listed the most expensive celebrity weddings, and the top spot went to the marriage between Liza Minnelli and David Gest whose big event came in at $3.5 million. Yet after a year of marriage, the two were already separated and eventually divorced.[5] That was one expensive year of matrimony.

I took another look at the *Forbes* list, and at the time of that article, eight of the twenty most expensive weddings had already ended in divorce; who knows how many of the remaining twelve will survive? It can truly be said that when it comes to marriage, we don't always get what we pay for.

Meanwhile, back in the tenth century BC, Solomon and Shulamith were still anticipating their own nuptials. As we rejoin them in the third chapter, they've both, in all probability, adjourned to their own homes—Solomon to the Jerusalem palace, Shulamith to the hills of Lebanon. Hebrew tradition would have Solomon preparing for a royal wedding, a grand occasion on the national calendar. The bride's family plans the wedding in our culture, but it was the groom's family who played that role in Israel, so Solomon's people were hard at work. First in the order of business would be a formal procession that would bring the bride from her home in Shunem to her wedding and new home in Jerusalem.

This portion of Song of Solomon offers us four principles about weddings, and today's families would be wise to follow them closely.

If you're currently planning to be married, you'll have plenty to think about as we explore these verses. If you've ever been married, you have your memories. Pull them out, dust them off, and relive how it felt on that day of days in your life. Reflect upon the vows you made to one another. This section has something for every one of us.

A TIME OF CELEBRATION

Song of Solomon 3:6

We all know that a wedding is a time of celebration, though we love to kid the young couple about what they're getting themselves into. I'll admit to chuckling over the old story about a groom asking the pastor, "Why does the bride wear white?" The pastor replied that white signified the brightest day in her life. The groom then asked, "So what does it mean for the groom to wear black?"

White, of course, actually signifies purity, and I suppose the black just makes a nice contrast for the wedding photographer. The truth is that this is a celebration for everyone, from the couple to their attendants to the families and guests. When two become one, we are actually celebrating a new birth—a new spiritual unit has entered the world in the prime of life and ready to serve God and humanity.

This section begins with a curious question: "Who is this coming out in the wilderness like pillars of smoke, perfumed with myrrh and frankincense, with all the merchant's fragrant powders?" (3:6). This is obviously the wedding procession. The Hebrew word for *comes* means "to go up, to ascend or to climb." And the term *wilderness* probably refers to a rural, more pastoral region.

If you're paying close attention, you might point out that Solomon lived in Jerusalem, not the wilderness. True. But the processional path from Shunem to Jerusalem would have moved on the road along the Jordan River. Even today, you can follow that road and arrive at an oasis on the ancient site of Jericho, just north of the Dead Sea.

The Dead Sea is the lowest point on the face of the earth, an amazing thirteen hundred feet below sea level. So imagine this journey: Solomon and entourage starting from the lowest point on the planet and climbing to the top of the Judean Mountains. We're only talking about fifteen miles from Jericho to Jerusalem, so that's a steep uphill journey. On a clear day, you could stand by the Dead Sea and look upward toward Jerusalem perched atop those mountains. It would seem like a royal crown set by God atop His chosen people, Israel.

This would be a dignified and festive procession worthy of an anointed king, the event of a lifetime for families of that era. As you read this with your own wedding in mind perhaps you're thinking, "What am I supposed to learn from this? I can't afford a massive camel procession!"

We can't all be part of a royal family, but we can bring the same wealth of joy and celebration to the simplest of weddings. There is no day like this one—ever. There are people who experience more than one wedding, after divorce or the death of a spouse. The second wedding may be a wonderful experience, but it will never quite match the anticipation and wonder of that wedding day of youth, a central rite of passage into adulthood, a time of innocence and optimism—a true storybook day that everyone should be able to enjoy and celebrate to its fullest.

The Pageantry of the Wedding. Let's make two observations about the celebration of a wedding. First, think of the pageantry involved. That word makes us think of bright color, multiple sights and sounds, respectful tradition. In the Near East of ancient times, weddings were actually more about civil union than spiritual marriage. The bridal procession was a favorite tradition filled with appropriate symbolism. The groom would travel to the home of the bride, gather her to himself, and escort her to her new home. There the wedding would take place with the groom publicly pledging himself to his bride. Then it would be time for a party.

And what a celebration it would be. The wedding feast might last a full week. People would have traveled many miles for this occasion, and they were in no hurry to turn the camels around and head for home.

In our narrative, Solomon has come to Shulamith's home. The pageantry of the procession is intended for her honor. It marks the day as a special one that belonged to an exceptional young woman. In our time as well, the wedding day should never be a casual affair. Too many items of eternal significance are occurring, and it is right that we wear our best, behave our best, and give our best to the young couple. It's a time to gather around a new family unit and launch it on its life and mission with love and encouragement.

A wedding could rival the day of Solomon and Shulamith, or it could be simple and lovely, an intimate gathering. The point is not the money spent or the total attendance, but the joy and devotion expressed. It's a time for pageantry and celebration.

The Purpose of the Wedding. Now let's look beyond the pomp and ceremony to the purpose and significance. What's it all about? Solomon wants to publish to the world his love for this woman. He is going public with his devotion through the procession and the celebration. She emerges from the obscurity of the wilderness and debuts in a new identity among the throngs of the city. As the procession moves along, there are columns of smoke that result from the burning of frankincense and myrrh.

Frankincense is another name we recognize from the gifts to the Christ child. It is the harvested sap of scraggly, medium-sized trees in southern Arabian areas. This gummy resin hardens into hard, brittle amber drops called tears. In fact, the most fragrant frankincense comes from trees that grow in very inhospitable regions. Their deep roots keep the trees grounded in the highest gales.

Upon burning, frankincense ignites quickly and produces a hot, clear white flame.[6] The resulting fire can be recognized by its distinctive flame, calming fragrance, and copious smoke. Used in the temple, it was a visual symbol of prayers ascending to God.[7] By the way, another name for frankincense is Oil of Lebanon.[8] That land, of course, is Shulamith's home.

Onward and upward travel the celebrants, Shunem behind them and Jerusalem ahead. During night travel smoking torches can be seen from a distance. By the pungent aroma that hangs in the air, the crowd realizes that myrrh is burning along with the frankincense.[9] It's all a feast for the senses, with colors for the eyes, joyful singing for the ears, and even plenty for the nose to enjoy! It's the most well-perfumed parade anyone could imagine, and altogether a tour de force for the five senses.

Just as the great entourage is intended to make a statement to the world, the great outlay of wealth makes a statement of how deeply Solomon values his bride. Smoke from the frankincense is a reminder of the spiritual nature of the wedding, because people see it rising to heaven, and they remember the prayers of the priests. There are several public prayers in a wedding even today (at least in church), along with the private prayers of the bride, the groom, and their family and friends. We all realize the significance of the occasion and we beseech God to give the marriage His blessing, to bind these hearts and bring wonderful children. Hopefully there will be no decline in the habit of prayer after the wedding ends and the marriage begins.

The wedding is among the most ancient traditions of human history, yet it changes with the times like everything else. Even during the period of my ministry, I've seen a relatively new tradition such as the unity candle, a beautiful symbol, come into vogue. It was a rarity when I began tying connubial knots. We've seen the music go through various fads and phases, and even the introduction of multimedia elements such as slide shows depicting the couple from their respective infancies to their bonding as a couple.

There are more variations in the traditional vows these days, some of them a little unsettling. A recent study cited by *USA Today* indicates the Bible is losing its foothold in the wedding vows, and such things as the Apache Blessing are taking its place. Some couples omit the word "forever" when they recite their vows, because they don't believe the marriage will last that long. Twenty-six percent of couples apparently write their own vows now, and an increasing trend is to have no vows at all—some don't desire to make any promises at all.[10]

For many, however, the wedding is what it has been for so long: a formal and highly significant ceremony to symbolize to all the world a new and loving marriage.

A TIME OF CERTIFICATION

Song of Solomon 3:7-8

The Queen of England brought a retinue of thirty-five people when she last toured America. This included ladies-in-waiting and equerries (personal attendants) of the royal family, to say nothing of the reported three tons of luggage.[11] Kings and queens do not travel alone. No exception to the rule, Solomon brings his entourage when he comes for his bride. We read, "Behold, it is Solomon's couch, with sixty valiant men around it, of the valiant of Israel" (3:7).

The finest soldiers in his army were invited to make the trip. We can imagine that gawkers from every surrounding village came to take in the spectacle, and what they saw was a show of military pride and power at the very height of Israel's brief period of empire—one of the world's greatest fighting forces coming to a small town.

What is the real message here? In bringing the infantry, it's not that Solomon is expecting resistance or some kind of skirmish. It's all about

the wedding as a time of certification. Call out the army—this is offi-
cial business!

You Will Be Safe With Me. The message for Shulamith (as well as the
observant family and friends) is, "You will be safe with me." A citizen
who commands a following of sixty highly-trained soldiers makes a big
impression. No one is likely to ask, "Can he protect her in dangerous
times like these?"

If Solomon followed the example of the first king of Israel, Saul, and
his father, David (see 1 Samuel 13:15, 14:2, 27:2, 30:9), these warriors represented one-tenth of Solomon's secret service brigade. They were highly
trained and trusted men who served as his bodyguards. They were with
Solomon everywhere he went. The chosen sixty may have been the ones
he considered personal friends, individuals he would like to have at his
wedding even beyond their military symbolism. Solomon wants everyone
to see that his superb personal protection now extends to Shulamith.

Few of us bring a brigade with us to the wedding these days, yet the
message of safety is still there. Poet Tian Dayton says it well in her
poem, "Holding a Place."

> *I will hold a space*
> *for you in which to be:*
> *My gift to you.*
> *A place*
> *in the world*
> *beside me.*
> *I will honor that space*
> *and I will protect it,*
> *and if you hold*
> *a place for me*

I will accept and value it.
We two
can do one another
a great service
here
on earth
while we are alive.
We can give
one another
shelter.
We cannot change the wind
or the rain or the devastation
of storms.
We cannot make what will
happen
not happen
but we can provide
a feeling of safety
in each other's
arms.[12]

It is still natural for the parents of a bride to wonder if their daughter is going to be in good hands. They've cared for her since birth, and, like any good parents, they would give their lives for their child without even stopping to consider. What if the new son-in-law is going to be doing business overseas and will be gone frequently? The parents have to pray and seek God's will on such a matter. Still, part of the wedding experience speaks to the safety and security of the bride in her new life.

What about the groom? The bride will care for and protect him in a certain sense, too. There will be difficulties both in life and in his career.

His happiness and self-esteem may be damaged by the harshness of the world; and she will be there to bolster him and protect his ego, to provide sanctuary from a cruel world. Through the wedding, both parties say to each other—and to the families, "We will keep each other safe."

You Will Be Secure With Me. The Bible now describes Solomon's return from Shunem with his bride. They are in a *mittah*, a Hebrew word variously translated as a bed (KJV), a couch (NKJV), a traveling couch (NASB), a carriage (NIV), or a bridal car (Amplified). Verse nine adds that Solomon had a special carriage or palanquin built. This is usually an enclosed conveyance carried on the shoulders of men by means of poles—some form of royal carriage.

The vehicle is surrounded by the entourage of sixty valiant men of Israel: "They all hold swords, being expert in war. Every man has his sword on his thigh because of fear in the night" (3:8).

I would love to see a picture of this procession, wouldn't you? There is the *mittah*, impressive and elegant in itself, flanked on every side by elite shoulders with weapons drawn and ready. It would take quite a battalion of bandits to hold up this stagecoach. No one in the vicinity, of course, would dare. These men would be the equivalent of the cream of the U. S. Army Rangers, Navy SEALS, and U. S. Marine Special Forces, with the dedication of the Secret Service to stand between their king and death, even if it meant dying for his safety—and now her safety as well.

Notice the term "fear in the night." The journey proceeds by sun and moon, the latter being the best time for an ambush. A young lady would certainly experience fear in the night if she weren't surrounded by such a show of power. Shulamith is both safe and secure.

She is also a country girl from the hills of Lebanon, now at the center of one of the most auspicious and impressive delegations in the ancient world. Imagine how the whole picture must have appeared to her.

Just watching from the side of the road with everyone else would be the sight of a lifetime. But she is the star of the show, the focal point in whose honor the parade is being held. Every friend of her childhood, every aunt, uncle, and cousin stands by the side of that road and watches with envy. The brothers who sent her out to the fields, possibly trying to make her feel small, now feel three inches tall themselves. The colors of the banners and the *mittah* are brilliantly lit by torches, which cause provocative shadows to dance exotically along the road. The horses are the finest and proudest anyone has ever seen. The incredible, evocative smells of frankincense and myrrh are nearly intoxicating. The moon glints off the long swords of the soldiers, who stand at attention without moving a muscle. Stately anthems are played by the court musicians, in all probability.

Shulamith's heart is racing. She is wondering if all of this could really be true—if her life could, after all, turn out like something from the old stories and legends she has heard around the cooking fire. Perhaps one of the "fears of the night" is that of such an intimidating, fantasy-world procession bearing her away forever. She catches glimpses of her girlfriends in the crowd and wonders if she will ever see them again. There is always something bittersweet in a wedding— the end of childhood.

But security? She could be in no more secure place in all the Mediterranean world. She need only look to her side where the man of her dreams sits: the elegant, laughing groom who has sponsored this incredible event on her behalf, and who delights in her wide eyes at the moment. Would he go to all this trouble if he had no plans to care for her? If anything befell her now it would reflect all the more on him.

Shulamith feels safe and secure, more so than at any time in her life. She need only sit back, clutch the arm of her beloved, and revel in a moment that will never come again—not for her, not in this precise way for anyone.

Tommy Nelson's wonderful book on the Song of Solomon, *The Book of Romance*, makes a very interesting application for today's bride and groom. He points to those individuals on the fringe of our wedding photography: the best man, maid or matron of honor, groomsmen and bridesmaids. These are the "elite army," the "Daughters of Jerusalem" that flank us at our own wedding, so we should choose accordingly. They should be godly men and women who will help to protect our marriage in every way "like a holy hedge of protection around you, keeping you focused toward each other inside the circle of matrimony, and keeping out anybody who might try to destroy your marriage." Nelson warns us that uncommitted "soldiers" will be of no use when the tough times come for us. "And they may embarrass you at the rehearsal dinner!"[13]

The wedding certifies to all witnesses that the bride has chosen the right man. He obviously loves her, and he will keep her safe and secure. Any young man who becomes engaged needs to realize that the world is looking to him to demonstrate that he will be worthy of the one he is marrying. He needs to show that he will forge his place in this world, that he will protect her from every kind of challenge, and that she will flourish as the center of his world.

A TIME OF CONSECRATION

Song of Solomon 3:9-10

Third, a wedding is a moment of consecration. There was a time when that word was common in our language. But like all words that embody sacrifice or complete spiritual devotion, it is quickly disappearing into the realm of the archaic. Let's hope we don't also misplace the concept itself, because nothing could possibly be more important to a new marriage.

I Consecrate My Life to You. To consecrate something is to devote it to a sacred purpose, to dedicate it fully to God. We begin by consecrating ourselves to God. We consecrate our homes and careers to His glory. But we also consecrate a marriage to Him.

In another sense, we consecrate our lives to each other in marriage. We devote ourselves to godly service of one another. We make a vow in the wedding service to devote our lives to the other in this way. The key idea behind this kind of consecration is another c-word: *commitment*. If you've been married, you gave a great deal of thought to that word, because when you agreed to marry, you were making the most solid commitment of everyday life. You were saying, "This person will be my partner for the rest of my life." As we know, of course, that commitment is ultimately broken nearly half the time today, even in Christian marriages. But what does all this have to do with the following verses?

"Of the wood of Lebanon Solomon the King made himself a palanquin: He made its pillars of silver, its support of gold, its seat of purple" (3:9-10a).

The carriage in which Solomon brings Shulamith to the wedding is an exquisitely beautiful thing to behold. It is built out of the expensive cedar wood that is grown in Shulamith's Lebanon to this very day. The Lebanon Cedar is still depicted in the center of the country's national flag. Any builder will tell you that cedar is a fine wood, and Solomon will use a good bit of it in constructing the Temple in Jerusalem. Cedar has an aroma that people love and moths hate; therefore, we often line closets with it.

The carriage has posts of silver, a base of gold, and a seat that is the royal color of purple. Every detail makes a splendid impression as the carriage bears the king across his countryside. It now tells everyone that the new life of Shulamith is one built on quality details. In this way, Solomon symbolically consecrates the best that he has to his wife. The unspoken message: "It is all yours, my best for the best."

But what about our concept of marriage today? Stop and consider the modern idea of the prenuptial agreement—a plan for failure any way you spin it. Instead of saying, "All this is yours," we are saying, "Here are the things I am protecting from you." Is that a good message for the beginning of a marriage? Prenuptial agreements lay detailed groundwork for divorce, and therefore can be self-fulfilling prophecies. As for the event of the death of a spouse, we have wills to take care of things like that. There should be nothing about a marriage commitment that sits on the fence. You're either one flesh or you're still two free agents. By hedging your bet, you'll never experience that oneness, and a breakup is likely to follow.

I Consecrate My Love to You. The consecration of love is also involved here. Notice the end of verse ten: "Its interior paved with love by the Daughters of Jerusalem."

Solomon, as we've seen, has his sixty elite warriors, swords drawn. Shulamith has her bridesmaids, known in this book as the Daughters of Jerusalem. They may not have functioned in the role of bridesmaids as we think of it, but the point is that each member of the couple had a kind of "wedding entourage" from the appropriate gender.

What does "paved with love" mean? We speak figuratively of doing things with love today, but the meaning here could be more literal. Some scholars believe the interior of the chariot was paved with mosaic love scenes. Various theories have been floated, but I like Paige Patterson's best:

> *The best view of this is to suppose that the Daughters of Jerusalem, lacking the craftsmanship necessary to prepare the exterior of the palanquin, nevertheless skillfully modeled its interior into a delightful place for the shepherdess to ride as she approached her moment of destiny in Jerusalem.*[14]

It makes sense. The men would tinker with the platform and the rods and the exterior trappings; the women would be concerned about the comfort of the interior, where Shulamith would sit. It always seems to be a woman who adds the touches to make an interior "homey." In any case, love is included in the full commitment of Solomon to his bride. I need not elaborate that it must be so in any marriage.

A TIME OF CONFIRMATION

Song of Solomon 3:11

Finally, a wedding is a time of confirmation. But what exactly are we confirming?

Sociologist and marriage researcher Barbara Dafoe Whitehead has written: "Kiss love and marriage goodbye. . . . Courtship is dying; lasting marriage is in crisis." She explains her claim that we are witnessing a new mating regime that is far more temporary. "It consists of: hook-up, break-up, and get even. Is everybody happy?"

Whitehead goes on to answer that question with some definitions. "The hook-up is a brief sexual relationship with no strings or rings attached. It may be shorter than a one-night stand or longer than a fling . . . But sooner or later (usually sooner), the hook-up ends in betrayal and abandonment and thus leads to break-up . . . leaving behind regret and resentment."[15] What a grim description of modern "love."

Meanwhile, the book industry is promoting a new genre of self-help resources devoted to the art of female revenge. They're calling it "dump literature"; basically it perpetuates the theme, "Get a grip on yourself, girl. Get over him by getting even."[16]

What has happened to our society? Are there still any adults out there? We've lost our bearings when it comes to giving ourselves to another person with integrity, commitment, and consecration because the idea of being unselfish has become totally foreign. The

irresponsibility of cohabitation has undermined the very idea of lifelong devotion and the rewards that it brings. Our traditional biblical
ideas seem to come from another planet when love and marriage are
now discussed in this culture; they're laughed off as outdated or naïve.
Our new world is politically correct and practically miserable.

Therefore let's confirm exactly what it is we believe about marriage—
exactly what we want it to accomplish. The essential cannot be taken
for granted. In that light, the following are good questions we should
ask ourselves when contemplating marriage. And by the way, here is
who the questions are *not* for: those who are already married.

I've been asked, "How do I know if I'm married to the right person?"
It's nice to have a simple answer sometimes: If you're married, that's the
right person. It's your duty to make that marriage the best it can be.

"What if I catch someone's eye in an elevator, and there's chemistry
between us?" I was taught not to play with chemistry sets. The old
rhyme goes: Johnny was a chemist's son, but Johnny is no more, for
what he thought was H_2O was H_2SO_4. Walk away before the explosion,
my friend. Chemistry is not love.

If you're married, your only real question is, "How can I make this
marriage better?" This book gives you plenty of guidance on that, I
hope. But if you're single, the following questions might help you contemplate marriage to a particular mate.

Are Your Friends in Favor of This Marriage? Love can create a
self-contained world with a population of two. Who cares what friends
think? Both of you should.

"Go forth, O daughters of Zion, and see King Solomon with the
crown" (3:11). The young women of Zion have come out to join in the
celebration of Solomon's wedding. They seem to show up throughout
these chapters, don't they?

We believe the daughters of Zion are the friends Shulamith has met through her relationship with Solomon. They have approved of the relationship, and feel that each one makes the other one a better person. They're around at various times, and they have the opportunity to see how this romance works.

Have you ever had a close friend who suddenly went away and married someone you hadn't met? You probably felt uneasy about it. It's good and wise for friends to "vet" a new love interest for a friend. It doesn't mean these friends serve as some kind of board of directors that can vote "yay" or "nay," but good friends provide solid input. They know us well, they can be more objective from the outside, and hopefully they're willing to tell us what we might need to hear.

Therefore when you're seriously considering marriage, you should ask, "What do my friends think? What do my love's friends think?" If there's a significant amount of friction on one side or the other, that's a sign to stop, investigate, and think things through at the very least. These friends deserve their say; it could be that they have good reasons to be doubtful about your intentions.

I've seen too many cases in which someone ignored good advice, stubbornly went through with the wedding, and repented of the decision when it was too late to avoid a great deal of pain. We all need friends to hold us accountable, particularly in the great decisions of life.

Is Your Family in Favor of This Marriage? When we place families into the equation, matters can become sensitive. But we can't effectively start a new family without the love and support of the existing one.

"Go forth, O daughters of Zion, and see King Solomon with which his mother crowned him on the day of his wedding, the day of the gladness of his heart" (3:11). We can assume from verse 4 that Shulamith's mother has signed off on this merger, so this final verse of the chapter probably refers to Bathsheba, Solomon's own mother and the beloved wife of David. The verse tells us that she has created a special wedding crown for the occasion. It's not the royal crown that signifies that her son is the King of Israel; this is a specialized creation that is her way of saying, "We approve of your choice! We stand behind you and fully accept Shulamith as our daughter. Let this souvenir always remind you of our blessing on your wedding."

What happens when Mom and Dad don't approve of a potential mate? It's a very difficult situation with much at stake for their child. There is the obvious risk of making one of life's biggest choices without parental support and approval. That will create ongoing difficulties for the future: a damaged relationship with the parents and a precarious and unfair position for the new spouse.

On the other hand, Mom and Dad have a difficult role as well. They must provide guidance for their child and speak out if they think the child is making an unwise decision. Yet they want to speak the truth in love, keeping the channels of communication as free and clear as possible. In the end, their child probably has the legal right (wise or foolish) to follow his or her own will. If a mistake is being made, Mom and Dad want to be there to help redeem a poor decision.

The bottom line is that it's critically important that we marry with the approval of our parents. We are commanded by Scripture, from the Ten Commandments onward, to honor and obey them as long as they live. They are a precious resource in helping us make big decisions, and they often have a perspective that younger people lack. We love them, we have gratitude for all they've done, and we want an even richer relationship as we bring them grandchildren. If they have problems with a choice of mate, that should be viewed as a critical obstacle in the decision we've been planning; and we need to put aside our emotions and listen carefully.

DESTINY AND DESERVING

David McCullough wrote a bestselling and award-winning biography of John Adams, one of our country's founders. He describes a letter written by Adams to his wife Abigail in the days leading up to the Revolutionary War. Three factions divided America: British loyalists, American patriots, and the undecided who were driven by fear. Adams used a line from a theatrical hit of the day (a quotation Washington also used): "We cannot ensure success, but we can deserve it."[17]

In other words, we have only so much control over our destiny. We can't guarantee a happy ending for some enterprise, but we can do all we can to tilt the odds in our favor. If you start a business, its fate ultimately lies in the hands of God. But that doesn't mean you sit on your hands. There are a great many things you can do to make your business deserving of success.

The same is absolutely true of marriage. As couples line up for divorces today, they speak as if none of it was in their hands. Love just came, then love just left; who knew? Yet there are nearly infinite opportunities to extend an effort and make marriage better. It's true that one spouse cannot control another. She cannot make him desire a good marriage in the same way she does and vice-versa. He cannot change what is inside her. We cannot go into marriage knowing what the future holds, nor can we create the happy ending we yearn for. But we can deserve success. We "can act in such a way that transformation is most likely," as writer Gary Thomas puts it.[18]

For example, we can do all in our power to truly know the heart of someone before marrying them. That will require patience. We can make a decision as a couple to never let any obstacle come between us. That will require commitment. We can commit our marriage completely to God's glory. That will require consecration. And, should problems arise somewhere—as they surely will, and maybe already have in your case—we can be strong, wise, and willing to enlist the help of others. That will require courage.

You may not succeed. Anyone who promises a simple fix for your marriage isn't telling you the truth. But in fighting with all your might and prayer for a marriage, *you can deserve to succeed.* At the end of the day, that's all any of us can do. It's a worthy enough goal, and by no means an easy one. At any given time, there is always something else that can be done to make us more deserving.

Let me add one final word of hope for those who are truly struggling or who have already experienced the failure of a marriage. Should the marriage finally end, your life is not over—far from it. This may come as a surprise to some people, but marriage is not the sole purpose for which we were created. It is a wonderful and special gift, but it's not our deepest purpose. We were created to know, love, and serve God, and throughout history some of the greatest service has come from unmarried people and those who have experienced deep pain.

When a marriage fails, we have the opportunity to realize that there is a deeper and more profound marriage which is the one between Christ and His Church, including you. By no means will you ever hear me glorify or endorse the grief and disappointment of divorce—my prayer is that you can avoid that heartbreaking experience of life. On the other hand, you will certainly hear me say that we serve a God who always has a hope and a future for us no matter how much we have suffered.

At the end of your pain, you may find a new freedom to serve God. There will be more time to take up new interests, to do things such as short-term mission trips that prove difficult for married people. You will find new energy to replace the effort you poured into your recent struggles. Again, this is a promise from God if you will simply wait upon Him: "But those who wait on the Lord shall renew their strength; they shall mount up with wings like eagles, they shall run and not be weary, they shall walk and not faint" (Isaiah 40:31). In suffering, we feel we can't even get on our feet again. But God gives us strength to walk, then run, then fly. I have seen many wounded people miraculously take off and take wing to glorify God through their lives.

I want to say again that the greatest goal is always to let God heal a troubled marriage. That is invariably His will, so you need not pray about whether to leave. Sometimes the other may leave, however, and the matter is out of your control. At that point we need to be strengthened by the hope that our deepest fulfillment comes not from one's spouse but a perfect and loving God.

In her book *Creative Counterpoint,* Linda Dillow explains this thought further: "I can promise you that if you are living according to your purpose and calling as a Christian, you are obeying the will of God and there is peace in this obedience. The first reason you are to respond this way is not so that you can secure a hopeful change in your mate, but because it is God's desire that you make this kind of response."[19] A marriage just may die, but you are eternal. Whatever may happen in this world, you are a citizen of heaven, and God has a will for your life. I hope you find that thought as exciting as I do.

Your greatest strategy as a married person is to grow in Christ, to be all that He wants you to be. Devote yourself to marriage, but don't let marriage—at its best or worst—become your god. There is no substitute for the true, living Lord whom we serve. Nothing and no one else can bring us real peace and purpose but Him. Wait upon the Lord, trust in Him whether your marriage is wonderful, heavenly, and hitting on all cylinders, or going through a painful crisis. The unlimited power of God can make the best marriages even better, resurrect a dying relationship, or bring us new life and hope at the end of the greatest pain we have ever faced. As Corrie ten Boom once said, "No pit is so deep that God's love is not deeper still."

Never let your marriage obscure the face of God, but seek His face first so that your marriage will be more deserving of success. Simply trust in Him, serve Him in every way you know, and you will be surprised and delighted by what happens. ◆

1   Suze Orman, *Money Matters*, "When Walking Down the Aisle, Don't Trip Over Finances," 10 March 2006, http://finance.yahoo.com/expert/article/moneymatters/2890 (accessed 19 September 2008).
2   http://in.ibtimes.com/articles/20060828/mittal-vanisha-trump-forbes-billionaire-dubai-france-lvmh-arnault-wedding.htm].
3   http://trulyweddingblog.com/news/20-million-wedding-cake.
4   "$12 Million Wedding Gown Video," http://www.cbsnews.com/video/watch/?id=1332134n, 22 February 2006 (accessed 19 September 2008).
5   www.forbes.com/media/2007/07/12/celebrity-media-weddings-biz-media-cz_lg_ts_0712celebweddings_slide_2.html?thisSpeed=20000 (accessed 19 September 2008).
6   Nature Bulletin, No. 548, "Frankincense and Myrrh," Forest Preserve District of Cook County (Illinois), 13 December 1958, www.newton.dep.anl.gov/natbltn/500-599/nb548.htm (accessed 29 September 2008).
7   Walter A. Elwell, Philip Wesley Comfort, *Tyndale Bible Dictionary* (Carol Stream, IL: Tyndale House Publishers 2001), 633.
8   "Frankincense/Olibanum," www.scents-of-earth.com/frankincense1.html.(accessed 19 November 2008.
9   Ibid; Nature Bulletin, No. 548.
10 Cathy Lynn Grossman, "Couples Take Their Vows in a New Direction," USA Today (5-30-01).
11 Don Melvin, "Queen's U.S. Visit: Gowns, Crowns and Three Tons of Luggage," Cox Washington Bureau, 29 April 2007, www.coxwashington.com/news/content/reporters/stories/2007/04/29/BC_QUEEN_VISIT29_COX.html?cxtype=rss&cxsvc=7&cxcat=0 (accessed 19 November 2008).
12 Tian Dayton, *Keeping Love Alive* (Deerfield Beach, FL: Health Communications, Inc, 1993), 51.
13 Tommy Nelson, *The Book of Romance* (Nashville, TN: Thomas Nelson Publishers, 1998), 76.
14 Paige Patterson, *Song of Solomon*, *Everyman's Bible Commentary* (Chicago, Ill: Moody Press, 1986), 65.
15 Barbara Dafoe Whitehead, "How We Mate," *City Journal*, Manhattan Institutes City Journal, Summer, 1999, www.cit-journal.org/html/9_3_how_we_mate.html (accessed 19 September 2008).
16 Ibid; Whitehead.
17 David McCullough, *John Adams* (New York, NY: Simon & Schuster, 2001), 91.
18 Gary Thomas, *Sacred Influence: How God Uses Wives to Shape the Souls of Their Husbands* (Grand Rapids: Zondervan, 2007), 37.
19 Linda Dillow, *Creative Counterpart: Becoming the Woman, Wife, and Mother You Have Longed to Be* (Nashville, TN: Nelson, 2003), 155.

7

What God Thinks of Sex

Song of Solomon 4:1-5:1

In 1992, John Gray wrote a book called *Men Are from Mars, Women Are from Venus*. The book became an enormous best-seller almost immediately. The title itself entered popular culture as a catch-phrase, and the author was elevated to the status of expert on the differences between men and women—even after *Newsweek* magazine reported three years later that Gray had spent nine years as a celibate monk and secretary to New Age cult leader Maharishi Mahesh Yogi.

Whatever one thinks about his credentials, John Gray obviously touched a nerve. Everyone agrees that men and women seem to come from two different places. A couple of friends of mine, Bill and Pam Farrell, hit the target when they wrote their own opus on gender relationships: *Men Are Like Waffles, Women Are Like Spaghetti*. I've never been to Mars or Venus, but food metaphors speak my language! And by the way, we're going to see some of them in this chapter.

Bill and Pam nailed the difference between men and women in one extended illustration:

The His and Her Guide to Automatic, Drive-Through Cash Machines

HIS:

> *1. Pull up to automatic, drive-through cash machine.*
>
> *2. Insert card.*
>
> *3. Enter PIN number.*
>
> *4. Take cash, card, and receipt.*

HERS:

> *(#1-41) Pull up to automatic drive-through cash machine, check makeup in rearview mirror, shut off engine, put keys in handbag, get out of car because it's pulled up too far from the machine, hunt for ATM card in handbag, insert card, hunt in handbag for scrap of paper that has the PIN number on it, enter the PIN number, hit cancel, re-enter the correct PIN number, check balance, look for a deposit slip, sign checks, make deposit, make cash withdrawal, get back in car, check makeup in rearview mirror, start car, start pulling away, stop, back up, get out of car, take credit card and receipt from machine, get back in car, put card in wallet, put receipt in checkbook, put car in drive, drive away from machine, travel three miles, release handbrake.*[1]

We know the authors are stretching a point, but we also know they've earned a laugh because there's an undeniable element of truth in their example, right? Men and women simply have different ways of achieving the same goal. If only we could understand this, we would stand at the beginning point of wisdom in building a strong marriage. Nothing a man can do will make the woman think and act as a man would; nothing she can do will make him more like a woman. And you know what? I suspect we would be unhappy with the results if we could make each other over as clones of ourselves.

As humorous as the Farrell's comparison of the sexes may be, it begins to make sense when we see it in terms of God's intention, beginning with His plan for human sexuality. Consider how the world understands and defines sexual intimacy these days. (Actually, there's nothing very intimate about our culture's view.) The secular model sees the sexual drive as an animal instinct, something placed in us by "nature" to motivate reproduction of the species. If you happen to feel pleasure in it, that's something of an illusion in that it's only there to make you fulfill your procreative duty in replenishing the world.

Dennis McCallum and Gary Delashmutt discuss the grace and beauty of the biblical understanding. Yes, reproduction is an important part of God's mandate for us. But the Word of God reveals that our sexuality is an integral part of who we are, right down to the soul. We are made in the image of our Creator. Physical reproduction is one wonderful and miraculous by-product of something wonderful and miraculous already: the true fulfillment of a lasting love relationship. "If we pick a wildflower and take it from its natural environment, it wilts quickly. So, too, the satisfaction of sex is short lived when it is torn from the setting for which God designed it." [2]

Another writer put it this way: "Monogamy may not sound like much fun; certainly not in comparison to its alternative. Monogamy sounds an awful lot like monotony, doesn't it? Or monopoly? Do I hear mahogany? Yet we dare not relate monogamy to tedium, an endless board game, or a great aunt's table. True happiness—the deep, sustaining contentment we seek—lies somewhere down the 'Monogamy Road.'"[3] Those whose lifestyles are entrenched in the spirit of the age preach the gospel of one-night stands. They declare themselves liberated from the "baggage" of lifelong relationships that may grow tedious. They say that we can have sex with no strings attached. But it turns out that the strings tie us to our only chance for true joy in marriage—and the no-attachments approach is the real imprisonment.

The Song of Solomon is the Bible's case study of a plan for all seasons: courting, dating, engagement, the wedding, and life together for the rest of our days. Chapter 4 brings us to the honeymoon.

Warning: The deepest joys of sexual intimacy are detailed here—accent on the word *detailed*. This is Bible study for mature readers. We pastors tend to gravitate away from such passages as this one. But it's time to stop letting a confused world carry the dominant voice on such an important issue. It's time to take back the beauty of sexuality for God's people just as He intended it.

Let's discover what we can learn from a biblical honeymoon.

PREPARING FOR SEXUAL INTIMACY

Song of Solomon 4:1-7

Your Wife Is Prepared by What You Say. Verses one through seven of chapter four tell us about the preparation for intimacy. There is so much for us to learn here about the differences between men and women, and how we think and feel.

Solomon says to Shulamith, "Behold, you *are* fair, my love! Behold, you *are* fair!" (4:1). Then we peek ahead a few verses to find another declaration from the new husband: "You *are* all fair, my love, and *there is* no spot in you" (verse 7).

Men are designed by God in such a way that, when the time comes, they are more than ready to take care of business. Unfortunately, men tend not to realize that the wife is not as emotionally prepared. The husband is eager and excited; the wife is hesitant and needs the grace of time. She is designed in such a way that requires preparation, including mental stimulation. Her mind and imagination are the important trigger points, and a man needs to use language to motivate her thoughts.

Herein lies the problem for the proverbial man of few words. He needs a few good ones right now! He needs to choose his words wisely and thoughtfully. These things may not play to his innate gifts and skills, but for the love of his beautiful wife, he needs to give his best.

Solomon, of course, had no problems when it came to eloquence. He wrote some of the most beautiful and compelling verses of the Old Testament. He had, "the wisdom of Solomon." He was the very template for this kind of thing. But if we men can't duplicate his poetry, we can follow his example. He knows the way to a woman's heart is through her ears.

He speaks in simple words about her beauty. If you think it's necessary to memorize the love sonnets of Shakespeare, you're wrong. Notice that Solomon tells his bride she is beautiful. He does so in very simple language, but initially does it twice. Then in verse 7, he adds a third declaration of her beauty and adds that he finds her perfect in every way. None of this is beyond the simple eloquence available to any loving husband.

In Hebrew literature, when something is said three times the intended effect is strong and intense. Therefore the words alone may not capture the power of Solomon's feelings and expression. He is saying, "You are unbelievably lovely! You are an eleven on a scale of ten!" Then he tells her that her beauty is flawless—perfect in every way.

It's true, of course, that Eve was the last perfect woman; we can be certain that Shulamith was no more "perfect" in the literal sense than any other woman. The honeymoon isn't a time for being overly literal, is it? It's not a time for a critique by an artist—just the opinion from a loving husband. And that's precisely what Solomon proceeds to do. He declares her perfection, in his eyes, and then gives a detailed tour guide.

Your Husband Is Prepared by What He Sees. If women are prepared by what they hear, men are prepared by what they see. I realize this is not breaking news, but it deserves repeating: Men are visually stimulated by the beauty of women, and that gives the loving wife a role to play in preparation for sexual love. As men, we don't always listen well. But there's nothing wrong with our eyesight! We see the beauty of our wives and we are ready to act; we simply need to understand what it is that makes them match our readiness. We need to follow Solomon's verbal example.

Notice how visual these six verses are. This is a man on his wedding night, and you can be more than certain that his eyes are wide open. He takes inventory of all the beauty he can see, so much of it hidden by modest attire before this moment. I realize some readers want to scrawl TMI ("too much information") in the margins of their Bibles—do we really need a play-by-play account of a man's wedding night? We do, and here is why: We really need to know that the Word of God endorses the wholesomeness of sexual love within marriage. And before this chapter is over, you'll be delighted by the surprise guest who appears at Solomon's honeymoon. Let's keep reading.

Solomon expresses his delight over eight different physical features of his bride:

1. Her Eyes: What would be a better starting point than the eyes? At the beginning of our study, we discussed the ways in which the eyes are the windows to the soul, the most expressive feature we have. A woman's eyes are the focal point of her beauty.

Solomon says, "You *have* dove's eyes behind your veil" (4:1). Brides wore facial coverings then as now in that part of the world. This passage would suggest that at this particular time the veil stayed on until the couple entered the privacy of the bridal chamber. Solomon suggests here that his bride's eyes shine right through the veil. The literal meaning is that the veil highlights Shulamith's eyes, but perhaps the

most likely meaning is that Solomon sees the twinkle in her eye even
before he sees her whole face. On her wedding day, a bride has shining
eyes. Solomon's own eyes are filled with the lovely sight of his beautiful bride. Those in my generation may recall the popular song, "I Only
Have Eyes for You," when considering how Solomon's eyes were focused
on Shulamith's eyes behind her veil.

2. Her Hair: Think of Solomon reaching for Shulamith's face and
softly removing her veil. As he does so, her hair tumbles freely about
her shoulders. Once again we're puzzled by these ancient word pictures that seem out of place to modern Western sensibilities: "Your
hair *is* like a flock of goats, going down from Mount Gilead" (4:1).
While a guy today might earn an incredulous look from his bride
with that line, Solomon uses it on his wedding night—he knew
Shulamith would understand it as a compliment. Ever the naturalist,
Solomon constantly thinks of the beauty of the great outdoors—
animals, plants, geographical features. You and I may not see much
loveliness in a goat, but when we stop to consider the creative hand
of God in all the variety of His works, we realize there is beauty in
everything He made.

In this case, the imagery is particularly well-chosen. The sight of a
woman's long, silky tresses cascading about the neck and shoulders
is one that delights a man's eye. In Palestine goats have long, wavy
black hair. Solomon mentions Gilead, a place that is more than 3,300
feet above sea level with a magnificent view of the Sea of Galilee.
There is also fine grazing for cattle. At dusk, the shepherd guides
his flocks down the slopes and into a shelter. If you and I stood at a
distance watching the flock descend, the mountainside might seem
alive with a shimmering, moving wave of black hair cascading down
the mountain.

Solomon's declaration might not be the right sentiment for a modern Hallmark card, but for his own time and culture it is glorious poetry—a line that would delight a girl from the hill country.

3. Her Teeth: Solomon says, "Your teeth *are* like a flock of shorn *sheep* which have come up from the washing, every one of which bears twins, and none *is* barren among them" (4:2). Now we have teeth as twin-bearing sheep. In modern life, the mood would be totally ruined by this time. But hang in there—we figured out the goat reference, and we'll get a handle on this one, too.

We all know that sheep are sheared. The outer wool is removed, and the observer sees a transformation: a sparkling white sheep stepping away from the lining of mud and dirt that has been its outer coating. You see the connection? The flock is shining white like the teeth of Shulamith.

Think of the next part of the verse from an orthodontist's view: "Every one of which bears twins." Each tooth, if you think about it, has a "twin" on the other side of the mouth. In other words, Shulamith has a perfectly even set of teeth—something to be admired in the ancient world.

4. Her Lips: Solomon's roving eye moves from the fine teeth to the lips, and he describes these as a "strand of scarlet" (4:3). It is generally felt that Shulamith used some form of lip coloring, and of course red was their natural color. Cosmetics are no modern innovation.

The color scarlet is mentioned fifty-two times in the Bible. Scarlet lips complemented a tanned complexion.

5. Her Mouth: Remaining in the general vicinity, Solomon turns his attention to the mouth itself. He tells his beloved, "And your mouth is lovely" (4:3b). As one writer has put it, "this is kissing talk."[4] Paige Patterson, however, isn't so certain. In his commentary, he argues that this compliment really referred to Shulamith's speech; she spoke with grace. The point would be that a person's true beauty is measured in more than physical attributes. Beauty is as beauty talks.[5]

When you fell in love, weren't you attracted to the way your spouse spoke? On the other hand, have you ever been at a public gathering when you noticed an exceedingly beautiful woman, then revised your opinion the second she opened her mouth and words came out? Patterson's observation rings true, because the voice is one of the most important factors in making someone attractive or not.

6. Her Temples: "Your temples behind your veil *are* like a piece of pomegranate" (4:36). When was the last time you complimented your spouse on that feature? This is defined as the part of the face between eye and ear, but particularly in ancient literature, this Hebrew word referred to the cheeks. Now it begins to make sense. With less creativity than Solomon, we would say, "You have rosy-red cheeks."

Women's cheeks are an important part of the facial features. Ask any woman who is skilled with cosmetics. The cheek is thought to be "the gentlest part of the whole female body."[6] It can tell us something of a person's emotions when we observe a blush, or when the cheek loses its color during fear or aggression. The blush in particular has long been viewed as a sign of innocence in sexual matters, a token of virginity.[7]

Now, about the fruit factor. We find plenty of juicy, red pomegranates in our California grocery stores in the late fall. But at certain times and places they have been a rare delicacy. Obviously Solomon is thinking about the rosy color of the fruit, but there is another angle just as we've suspected with the mouth and speaking. In the ancient world, pomegranates were associated with sexuality. They were considered an aphrodisiac and a kind of natural fertility supplement. Solomon may be drawing on some of these associations.

One thing is certain: Shulamith's blush is indicative of the combination of shyness and passion on the wedding night: the true "blushing bride."

7. Her Neck: You do see where this is going, don't you? I hope I don't need to draw you a map to show what direction we're moving from the eyes to the hair, teeth, lips, mouth, cheeks, and now the neck.

"Your neck *is* like the tower of David, built for an armory, on which hang a thousand bucklers, all shields of mighty men" (4:4). A long, majestic neck has always been considered beautiful in a woman. In Shulamith's case, it is adorned with exquisite jewelry that her groom has bought for her. Solomon removes each jewel as he praises his bride for her grace and elegance. She, of course, is the crown jewel. Remember what is really happening here: the stimulation of a woman's passion through loving words.

8. Her Breasts: Given the manner in which our culture has vulgarized sexuality by reducing it to the quest for perfect body parts, this section is more delicate for today's readers. For Solomon and his times, the connotation was entirely proper—especially, of course, in the context of a wedding night. The groom says, "Your two breasts are like two fawns, twins of a gazelle, which feed among the lilies" (4:5).

Until now, Solomon has given Shulamith his commentary from the neck up. Now his eyes have come to the slim, youthful body of his bride. The image he chooses is one of grace and softness—twin fawns. These are nimble animals, easily frightened and rapid to flee. When we encounter young deer in a park, we are in awe of their grace, and we would love to caress them—but we know that one hasty move will scatter them into the brush. In much the same way, Solomon wants to be gentle with a loving but apprehensive bride. As a man with physical drives, he feels a sense of urgency. For her sake, he is soft and soothing with her using words rather than force.

Men can learn a great deal from this example. We certainly do reap what we sow, even in the bedroom. Speak to your wife in the language she understands—loving, appreciative tones—and her own passion will kindle into flame. Approach her selfishly according to your own needs and impulses, and you will drive her away as surely as the gazelle hurdles the hedge.

The physical inventory comes to an end with the sixth verse: "Until the day breaks and the shadows flee away, I will go my way to the mountain of myrrh and to the hill of frankincense." Compare this verse to Song of Solomon 2:17, which is very close in wording. The subject is desire, and the meaning is fairly obvious. Solomon looks forward to a very enjoyable evening, and sleep doesn't figure much into his plans. The reference to myrrh and frankincense reminds us that this is a wealthy man surrounded by the finer things in life, but the finest of all, to him, cannot be bought for any sum. This evening of passionate love is priceless for him.

As I look back over this section, I would choose two words to summarize all this excitement: time and tenderness. Love doesn't hurry, but stops and smells the roses. It isn't selfish, but dedicated to the pleasure of a partner. It isn't forceful, but gentle, and adoringly passionate. The preparation for intimacy is everything when it comes to connecting as God desires us to do.

Isn't it wonderful to see how the ancient truths of Scripture are unchanging across thousands of years, seismic cultural changes, and even intensely personal issues such as this one? His Word is eternal. His plan is liberating. And His rewards are joyful.

ANTICIPATING SEXUAL INTIMACY

Song of Solomon 4:8-11

The Excitement of Intimacy. Solomon says: "Come with me from Lebanon, *my* spouse, with me from Lebanon. Look from the top of

Amana, from the top of Senir and Hermon, from the lions' dens, from the mountains of the leopards" (verse 8).

Sometimes we can find out significant information by parsing the grammar. For example, in the seven verses we've just examined, only one personal pronoun is present: *you*. This is unique to The Song; Solomon is entirely the observer, completely wrapped up in the adoration of his bride. Now, however, there is a shift in pronoun from *you* to the possessive pronoun, *my*. He calls her, "my bride," (NIV) and will do so a total of five times in this next section.

The courting is complete, the wedding is accomplished, and the first evening begins. Solomon looks upon Shulamith now as his own and not as a separate individual. The eighth verse is a loving invitation to the excitement of intimacy that they can share together. The crucial point here is that true intimacy involves the loss of self and the devotion to the other.

Selflessness is the most neglected art in all of humanity. Genuine emotional maturity and spiritual commitment are required. Sacrifice is a constant theme. Therefore we shrink back from the biblical passages that instruct us to deny ourselves.

For example, Paul writes to the Corinthians about the foundation of godly marriage: "The wife does not have authority over her own body, but the husband *does*. And likewise the husband does not have authority over his own body, but the wife *does*" (1 Corinthians 7:4). No idea could offer such a sharp contrast with the spirit of the age in which we live. Ours is a *me* and *mine* society even within the bounds of marriage. We can't experience the greatest joys in life in knowing Christ or in loving our spouse without the required element of self-denial.

Solomon is telling his wife, "From now on, I devote myself to your joy and pleasure." And he invites Shulamith to come and see mountaintops and dens of leopards with him. Life is spectacular when we enjoy it

together. Have you ever noticed the emptiness that can be felt when you
see some incredible sight—a sunset, for example—and suddenly feel
that pang of regret that your spouse isn't there, too? Everything feels
richer and fuller when you have someone to share it with. When we feel
the absence of that person during special moments, that's the proof of
the passion that we share with one another.

"Come with me!" shouts Solomon. He already has an exciting life; he
can travel to all those mountains and zoos anyway. But now it's going to
be fun with Shulamith by his side!

The Expression of Intimacy. We can't help but express ourselves over
the things that excite us. It's the overflow of our joy. Solomon communicates how he feels in the next three verses:

> You have ravished my heart, my sister, my spouse; you have ravished
> my heart with one look of your eyes, with one link of your necklace.
> How fair is your love, my sister, my spouse! How much better than
> wine is your love, and the scent of your perfumes than all spices!
> Your lips, O my spouse, drip as the honeycomb; honey and milk are
> under your tongue; and the fragrance of your garments is like the
> fragrance of Lebanon (4:9-11).

The word for *ravished* means "stole." Shulamith has stolen his heart.
What he is saying in these verses is that he has lost the control of his own
feelings; she owns them now, and he belongs to her. She reestablishes that
ownership every time she gives him one look with those eyes. Why, even a
single link on her necklace is too much for him to handle! In other words,
everything that concerns Shulamith sends him into a state of ecstasy.

But why would he call her his "sister" in this passage? Five times
in the course of this book, Solomon calls Shulamith "my sister." We

wouldn't do that in our culture, but it was quite normal in the Israel of that time period. This was a term of endearment that implied respect and companionship not incompatible with romantic love. As a matter of fact, even in the midst of honeymoon passion, we should never forget that we are with a lifelong partner, best friend, and soul mate.

In the long run, deep and intimate companionship will mean much more than the physical pleasures of youth. The flesh, of course, is subject to age. One day we find that our get-up-and-go got-up-and-went. The beauty of friendship, especially Christ-centered friendship, is that it only matures and becomes richer. As a matter of fact, love is eternal.

Those of us who have had long marriages can affirm that there's nothing more precious than having that person to whom we can tell anything and everything. As a matter of fact, I sat down with my wife and talked with her about an item or two I was considering writing about in this book. She gave me wise counsel which I embraced without hesitation. The longer we are together, the more valuable to me her counsel becomes. Thus we help each other along and make each other stronger and smarter. Each of us knows we can expect complete honesty from the other. Don't you think everyone needs someone to tell them the truth and to listen to everything else that needs to be said? I cannot imagine living any other way.

In verse ten, fragrance reenters the discussion. Her love is better than wine, he says, and her scent better than spices. We've already seen that sight is the most important element in sparking a man's passion. Did you know that smell ranks second? Somebody has figured it out, because perfume companies accounted for $2.3 billion last year.[8] Women know that looks are paramount to their attraction, but when that little dab of fragrance is added, the results can be powerful.

Then comes a not-so-subtle hint that the time for action is approaching. Solomon says, "Your lips, O *my* spouse, drip as the honeycomb;

honey and milk *are* under your tongue; and the fragrance of your gar-ments *is* like the fragrance of Lebanon" (4:11). I hesitate to become too detailed with this verse, especially when Danny Akin will do so for me: "The idea that a particular kind of kissing began in France is put to rest by this verse! Deep, wet, sweet, and passionate kissing is at least as old as this Song." [9] I think we can agree that in The Song, nothing is done in a half-hearted way.

Finally we learn that Shulamith has perfumed her clothing as well as her body. In every way she has become a "Solomon trap" for the evening, a gourmet feast for his sight, sound, taste, touch, and smell—every bodily channel of sensory communication. The more we take advantage of the "good senses" God gave us, the more joy we'll find in physical love with our mate.[10]

APPRECIATING SEXUAL INTIMACY

Song of Solomon 4:12-5:1

Finally, right there in your Bible and mine, we come to the main event of the evening. It's about time, right?

Solomon says, "A garden enclosed *is* my sister, *my* spouse, a spring shut up, a fountain sealed" (4:12). We quickly recognize the reference to Shulamith's purity—her virginity. Solomon uses three metaphors to make the idea more than clear: a walled garden, a blocked spring, and a sealed fountain. Why use three? We'd get the idea with one analogy. The point is that these are three separate images of natural beauty: a colorful garden to nourish the eyes, the cool spring to quench one's thirst, and the majestic fountain for grace and beauty. All of these things can be closed off until the proper time; Shulamith has saved her-self for her husband in love.

He also says, "Your plants *are* an orchard of pomegranates with pleasant fruits, fragrant henna with spikenard, spikenard and saffron, calamus and cinnamon, with all trees of frankincense, myrrh and aloes, with all the chief spices" (4:13-14). He lingers in the garden metaphor because it is perfectly apt. The garden is beautiful, natural, and supplies a delicious feast from its fruit and comfortable shade from its trees. Again, a bride supplies all these wonderful gifts to her husband. She delights his eye, she nourishes his soul, and she provides him shelter from the heat and storms.

I must ask the female portion of my readers: How would you respond to being praised in such ways by your husband? I must ask the men: Wouldn't you like to find out?

Then, in verse 15, Solomon comes back to the water imagery: "A fountain of gardens, a well of living waters, and streams from Lebanon." Shulamith now stands before her husband for his loving delight, and his only. The blocked fountain is unblocked, and the waters can flow. Since water is the physical basis of life on our planet, no symbol could be more powerful. Solomon can now take a refreshing drink from this private stream. He can be cooled from the desert heat by bathing in it, and these "living waters" will rinse away the dust of daily living. He will be baptized into the newness of his marriage identity.

With the final act of becoming one flesh, all these things occur. As Shulamith hears the words, she must feel complete indeed—not to mention sparked to passion. Her husband not only adores her, but appreciates her profoundly. How could her feelings take any other course than to reciprocate?

The Satisfaction of Sexual Intimacy. I find the following item to be one more fascinating element in an amazing book of the Bible. We've seen how the Song of Solomon is divided into sections: dating, courtship, wedding, and finally the marriage of Solomon and Shulamith. But if we study this passage in its original Hebrew language, we see that these next two verses stand at the precise center of this lyric poem. There are one hundred eleven lines from 1:2 to 4:15, and there are one hundred eleven lines from 5:2 to 8:14. Those two central verses are the final one in chapter 4 and the first in chapter 5.

Now why should we find that amazing? We find that this book is so carefully, so artfully constructed that these verses are not only the "geographical" center—they are the center of its meaning. The book is one hundred eleven lines, central thought, one hundred eleven lines. Right between the two central verses, everything changes. Two individuals are gone, and one flesh replaces them. There's nothing coincidental about any of this, of course.[11]

The book itself forms a grand tour of the love between men and women—from meeting to mating to maturing. And right at the center, as in the center of the marriage itself, we find the culmination of the relationship that this book concerns. In the first of the two verses, Shulamith invites her husband to enter the garden and sample its many delights. In the second, Solomon has done so, and the lovers lie in each other's arms in blissful satisfaction as the wedding party continues to feast outside. This is a perfect image, a kind of momentary paradise at the center of the book and the center of marriage. It even hints symbolically of eternity in which Christ and His bride have finally been united in the ultimate paradise.

I find that so beautiful, so perfect, that no poet but God Himself could have devised it. The Song is all about beauty and passion, and there's a unique beauty and passion in its perfect construction. This is one of the countless signatures of our Creator that turns up repeatedly in Scripture. No man or woman could have written this Book of Books.

Expressing Desire for Intimacy. We recall Shulamith's delayed gratification policy cited twice in 2:7 and 3:5: "Do not stir up nor awaken love until it pleases." She has spoken the words to her friends and in all probability to herself. Wait for the moment of God's choosing. This is true not only of sexual expression but everything else in life—quite a difficult lesson for the microwave oven, fast food, try-now-buy-later generation. Reading The Song helps us understand why waiting is worth it. Could the wedding night have been so blissful with a casual-sex beginning? Of course not. Good things come to those who wait, and the things themselves are far better for the wait. "Awake, O north *wind*, and come, O south!" invokes Shulamith. "Blow upon my garden, *that* its spices may flow out. Let my beloved come to his garden and eat its pleasant fruits" (4:16). Shulamith has waited in purity for this moment. Here at the center of the book and of her life, she is ready to become a woman and a wife.

Experiencing Delight in Intimacy. And just now, we fade out on the fourth chapter and begin the fifth. In a time when Hollywood was more discreet, directors did the same with love scenes; fade-to-black just as things heat up.

Solomon speaks once again and catches us up on what happened while we were turning the page: "I have come to my garden, my sister, *my* spouse; I have gathered my myrrh with my spice; I have eaten my honeycomb with my honey; I have drunk my wine with my milk" (5:1). Isn't that something? After four chapters of build-up, Solomon closed the curtain at the moment of truth! I think we're just as happy to give the lovers their privacy.

In one verse, Solomon uses the word *my* an amazing nine times. It's hard to miss the emphasis. Shulamith would talk about her husband the same way now. This couple belongs to one another. Notice how all the roles of Shulamith come together in this wonderful verse:

"my garden, my sister, *my* spouse." She is his all-in-all, and a marriage is born.

But wait. There is a final postscript to the wedding night found in the latter part of 5:1: "Eat, O friends! Drink, yes, drink deeply, O beloved ones!" The eating and drinking, scholars agree, is simply more sexual poetry. But who is speaking? This is the special guest appearance with which I teased you earlier.

Actually it's a compelling mystery. Who would turn up at the very center of the verse to top off the wedding night and begin the final portion of the book? It's not the friends, for they wouldn't be present at this moment. It doesn't seem to be either Solomon or Shulamith, who wouldn't be addressing visitors at such a moment.

Craig Glickman has an interesting suggestion. He invites us to do a little detective work and consider who would have means, motive, and opportunity. Who, other than the couple, would be present on the wedding night? Who is the one other entity Who would be intimate with bride and groom, and could encourage the pleasure they've enjoyed? Perhaps most important, Who deserves pride of place at the epicenter of this book? I think you've guessed by now.[12]

Here at the core of sexuality, you see, the voice of God can be heard. Many scholars have come to the conclusion that these are in fact His words, His blessing, His delight in our delight. He endorses the pleasure between man and wife, because it comes to us courtesy of His creative art. Again, Craig Glickman from *A Song for Lovers*:

> [God] is glad they have drunk deeply of the fountain of love. Two
> of His own have experienced love in all of the beauty, and fervor,
> and purity that He intended for them. In fact, He urges them on to
> more . . . [This] is His attitude toward the giving of their love to each
> other. And by the way, this is His attitude toward couples today.[13]

I am persuaded by this argument. Who but God is at the center of this book, this Bible, this marriage, our marriage? How beautiful that we have His endorsement of sexual passion in marriage, and not only His endorsement but His exhortation to go to it!

Now we know the truth of what God thinks about sex. How could anything be so joyful, so essential, so life-giving and not have His approval? After all, "Every good gift and every perfect gift is from above, and comes down from the Father of lights, with whom there is no variation or shadow of turning" (James 1:17). I don't know of a more perfect gift than this one. I can certainly tell you that when I think of the depth and satisfaction of my marriage, I hear God speak. I feel His delight.

I also confess that it's gratifying to write this chapter knowing that so many Christians have grown up in churches where *sex* was the ultimate dirty word; where it was never mentioned in any positive light whatsoever. Yes, of course, we know it's an easy gift to misuse. We realize those springs aren't to flow, and those gardens aren't to be opened outside of marriage. But to never mention its wonderful essential nature is like never acknowledging the beauty of a sunset (only the air pollution it reveals), the power of the assembled body of Christ (only the hypocrisy that sometimes lurks there), or the appeal of a newborn child (only that it will cry and soil its diapers).

There is no gift from God that cannot be twisted by the evil one. What a tragedy when we allow the enemy to keep us from realizing the essential goodness of such a foundational gift for this life.

I hope that somehow I have helped you see with fresh eyes the amazing beauty of physical sexuality as God designed it for His children and revealed it through His Word. I know that the more I study the Song of Solomon, the more profoundly I appreciate what God has given us, and the more I learn about how better to love and nurture my wonderful wife.

Now let me leave you with this thought to ponder. Don't you think it's fantastic that we've discovered the greatest sex manual ever written, and that God's people have had it in their hands all along? It turns out to be hidden in the Bible, the last place on earth your Aunt Edna would look for it! And aren't you sorry you didn't carefully study the Song of Solomon a long time ago? The secret of perfect sex is now yours, for a limited time only. The offer runs out at the end of this life. So act now. Find a Christian husband or wife, and devote yourself to that person's pleasure. Study the whole Word of God and serve Him as a couple. Join a church and get involved in modeling and mentoring others in the principles of marital love done God's way.

But wait! There's more. Accept this offer now, and God Himself will be present with you to cheer you on, in life, and even in sex. Look for Him at the very center of all you do. There's no way your marriage is going to end up any other way than happily ever after. ◆

1   Bill and Pam Farrell, *Men Are Like Waffles, Women Are Like Spaghetti: Understanding & Delighting in Your Differences* (Eugene, OR: Harvest House Publishers, 2001), 123-124.
2   Adapted from Dennis McCallum and Gary Delashmutt, *The Myth of Romance – Marriage Choices that Last a Lifetime* (Minneapolis, MN: Bethany House Publishers, 1996), 101.
3   Hugh O'Neill and Greg Gutfield, "Your Honey or Your Wife," *Men's Health*, January-February, 1996, 72.
4   Tommy Nelson; 91.
5   Paige Patterson; 69.
6   Desmond Morris, *The Naked Woman: A Study of the Female Body* (New York: Thomas Dunne Books, 2005), 71.
7   Ibid; Morris, 72.
8   International Flavors and Fragrances, Inc, Press Release, 30 January 2008, http://pressreleases .iff.biz/phoenix.zhtml?c=65743&p=irol-newscenterArticle&ID=1101715&highligh= (accessed 20 November 2008).
9   Daniel Akin; *God on Sex*; 146.
10 Ibid Akin; 146-147.
11 Adapted from G. Lloyd Carr, *The Song of Solomon* (Downers Grove, IL: InterVarsity Press, 1984), 127.
12 Craig Glickman, *Solomon's Song of Love* (West Monroe, LA: Howard Publishing, 2004), 36.
13 Craig Glickman, *A Song for Lovers* (IVP Press, 1976), 25.

8

Love at Life Speed

Song of Solomon 5:2-8

John Lennon, the Beatle who was shot down in 1980, had a gem of a line in one of his songs: "Life is what happens while you're busy making other plans." That sentence beautifully crystallizes what a lot of people are thinking these days.

Sometimes we feel like tiny ants riding on a log that is floating rapidly down the river. One of them stays right up front for most of the trip, with a look of self-importance on his face. When a fellow insect asks what he's doing, the ant says, "Steering."

Every now and then we get the impression that we're only passengers on this thing called life—that it is bigger than we are and moving at warp speed. To what extent are we really holding the steering wheel?

Every New Year's Day, many of us make a neat list of resolutions. We're going to exercise more, be better husbands or wives, spend more time with our children, cut down on unhealthy foods, read through the Bible, and spend time with God daily—the list goes on. Then, on January 2, life resumes. The log starts drifting again, and before you know it, everything is sailing downstream. Life trumps the best-laid plans, including that sacred part of life called love.

At the honeymoon stage, the world is your oyster. Everything is beautiful, and there's no reason to think it will change. Then again, you're on a beach somewhere, you have a nice tan, and the rest of the world is an airplane ticket away. Reality sets in as soon as you come home and get busy. *Business*—busy-ness—is the great home-wrecker.

Consider the case of Lionel Rothschild. Does the name ring any bells? There was a time when Rothschild signified wealth and power to anyone who heard the word. There is a song called "If I Were a Rich Man" that substitutes in one verse, "If I were a Rothschild." The family founded an international banking dynasty beginning in the late eighteenth century. To keep the fortune under full-family control, intermarriage was arranged at certain points—this was before the genetic dangers of that policy were understood.

So it was that Charlotte von Rothschild of the German branch of the family found herself married, two days after her seventeenth birthday in 1836. The groom was her older first cousin, Lionel de Rothschild, of the English branch.

They met briefly when Charlotte was sixteen, and they seem to have sincerely fallen in love. As for many young lovers of the time, letter-writing was their chief mode of courting. Lionel, a shy and serious young man, wrote that he had "no amusement nor occupation, but that of preparing for and thinking of the happy times when I can call you Dearest Charlotte mine and mine forever." Solomon would have heartily approved of his wooing words. In another letter he offered "a thousand kisses and the assurance of my forever devoted attachment and love."

His teenage German bride, of course, was expected to leave her affectionate parents, all her friends, and her homeland to begin a new life in England. All this she was willing to do in order to be with the man she loved.

But there were problems from the beginning—the greatest being loneliness. When you leave everyone and everything to which you're accustomed, your husband has quite a void to fill. Yet Lionel was often consumed by his work. Charlotte would later write, "Lionel was never with me between the hours of tea in the morning and six in the evening." Her husband, unskilled in relationships, didn't comprehend the unhappiness of his young wife; he was too consumed in the demands of the family banking business.[1]

It happens all too often. Having procured his bride, the pleased husband turns his attention fully to his work. As a man, this is his specialty. He is all about action and achievement. He took care of that marriage thing, and he's checked it off his "to do" list. Now it's time to provide for his new family.

Yet a wife sees things differently. There are no checklists where love is concerned; she yearns for the companionship of her mate. As a woman, she is relational. She would rather be smothered in affection than possessions.

So what happened with Charlotte and Lionel? Stay tuned! We'll get to it, I promise. For now, however, I need to bring you up to speed on our other newlyweds, Solomon and Shulamith. They, too, have just gotten married and begun their new life. How long will the honeymoon last?

You'll remember that we now stand at the beginning of the second half of the Song of Solomon. Meeting, dating, marrying, and mating have all come before. Now follows that thing called life—that thing with an accelerator, but no brake.

With one hundred eleven lines and the two midpoint verses behind us, one hundred eleven verses will take us to the conclusion of this love story. Of those verses, it's significant to observe that eighty-eight of them are spoken by Shulamith—nearly eighty percent of this half. It is as if the courtship era belongs to the man and his assertiveness;

the marriage era belongs to the woman and her relational skills. Once marriage begins, the home is so often built around her personality. Shulamith will become our primary narrator from here onward.

REAL WORLD MARRIAGE

Song of Solomon 5:2

This half of the book begins with dreaming. The wedding night is in the past now, and the honeymoon seems to be over. As we're about to see, there has been a slight shift in the love relationship.

Shulamith speaks: "I sleep, but my heart is awake; *it is* the voice of my beloved! He knocks, *saying*, 'Open for me, my sister, my love, my dove, my perfect one; for my head is covered with dew, my locks with the drops of the night'" (5:2).

We've all been in this stage of half-sleep, where the mind has a tenuous grasp on its surroundings as the body drifts into slumber. Perhaps Shulamith has been waiting up for her husband and has begun to doze off. It's also just possible that she has moved from the passionate excitement of the wedding night to dull complacency, waiting for her busy husband to spare her some time.[2] That seems like a jolting change from the adoring verses we've just completed, but we don't know how much time has passed. Whether it's been a day or a month or a year, the "little foxes" (2:15) are already coming after the grapes.

This topic of complacency is an important one in marriage. In the beginning, we do all the little things to make ourselves as desirable as possible for a marriage partner. After the wedding we settle into a bit of a routine; and you can't spell routine without *r-u-t*.

It's inevitable, of course. We could never maintain the full-court-press energy and creativity of courting when we were absolutely single-minded about pursuing one another. But there's a moment when one or both of us sigh and say, "We've lost some of the magic." She feels she has been displaced for the top position in his heart by the widescreen television, or he is discouraged that she doesn't take as many pains with her appearance.

We need to recognize that many people go into marriage with unrealistic expectations. They anticipate it to be a regular theme park of pleasure and delight, a honeymoon everlasting. They need to make the transition from romantic to realistic; dating is a Hollywood movie starring Bogart and Bacall, but marriage is—well, dirty underwear, sour milk on the cereal, dull sessions of balancing the checkbook. Don't get me wrong, there is still a place for joy and romance at every stage of marriage, but now we're talking about real world romance. There's a difference. The challenge is to avoid giving in to complacency just because the initial fireworks show is over.

The verse indicates that Solomon is coming home late at night. Shulamith has been waiting for him and fallen half asleep. We're about to find out that she harbors a mix of desire, anxiety, and resentment.

Sometimes Responsibility Overtakes Romance. How do we know Solomon is slipping in late? He tells us himself: "My head is covered with dew, my locks with the drops of the night." This is a unique biblical expression, and it points to the weather conditions particular to Israel. Especially in late summer, heavy dew descends around midnight. Things are a bit similar in my neck of the woods, the California coast. Our meteorologists call it "night and morning low clouds." With Israel's short rainy season, the late night dew provides the only other refreshment for the vegetation.

We know from a later verse that Solomon has long, curly hair. What seems to have happened here in verse 2 is that his hair has become drenched in the dew. His tardiness, of course, is a logical explanation for Shulamith's disappointment. He has a kingdom to run, but she wants him to know his marriage needs him, too.

There's no way to get around this problem. Sometimes we have to take care of business. The boss wants us to fly across the country for a week, or some customer crisis demands late hours on the job. The ordinary stresses of life become an obstacle to a love relationship. Surely we have the maturity to put up with a few of these demands knowing that the mortgage and the car payments are coming due. But what if it becomes less of an occasional thing and more of a lifestyle? What if she comes to believe that he is married to his job?

Of course, in our times, it can work the other way as well. Many women are addicted to their careers just as many men have been all along. Therefore the challenge can come from either side or both sides. The threat to a strong marriage can become very serious.

Sometimes Words Aren't Enough. We all know about Solomon, son of a poet and musician, author of Proverbs, Ecclesiastes, and many of the greatest lines in The Song before us. What would you expect from him as an instinctive response when his wife is irritated with him? Words, of course. He is deceptively persuasive with the lexicon in his mind. He could probably have sold an encyclopedia to a Philistine.

Solomon makes a nice try, but when a spouse is on the warpath, eloquence is irrelevance. Words fall flat. Solomon uses the same kind of language that worked so well for him in the first four chapters: "Open for me, my sister, my love, my dove, my perfect one"(5:2)—four separate terms of endearment; he's a regular Sweet Talk Express.

It's important to understand here that in the culture of this ancient time and place, husbands and wives kept separate rooms. Solomon is in the house. He's tired after a hard day of ruling, but not too tired to knock on his wife's bedroom door.

Two of his four pet names are old standbys of his—*my love* is used nine times—but he tries two new ones on this occasion: *my dove* and *my perfect one*. That last one is somewhat of a *tour de force* of passionate endearment. In other words, Solomon knows he is in trouble with his wife. He has probably been working on his speech while on his way home, starting with the platonic *my sister* and building up to what he feels is the irresistible *my perfect one*. If that one won't open bedroom doors nothing will.

Not that Solomon is being insincere. I believe he means every single word; if he didn't, he wouldn't want to be with his wife so desperately. His words are heartfelt but insufficient. Where he excels in eloquence, he is lacking in timing. That will soon be made clear.

Bob and Yvonne Turnbull weigh in here with some terrific advice for husbands like Solomon. They instruct us that our wives need four things from us if we're going to keep the vitality in our marriage. The first of these is time. No matter what life demands of us, we must protect the right amount of time to devote to her.

Next in importance is talk. You can refer to our earlier discussion of the importance of verbal communication. Your wife needs to hear words of admiration and approval, not just desire. We also need to give our wives tenderness, which feeds her soul. Fourth and finally, she needs touch. That doesn't necessarily mean touching in a sexual context—loving, affectionate touch is an everyday requirement.[3] Time, talk, tenderness, and touch are incredible gifts from husband to wife.

If only the Turnbulls had been there to give Solomon a clue in this particular case. He had done just fine in the courtship stage up through the wedding night, but the hour is late and he's a little off his game. Perhaps his greatest priority these days is a stable and powerful Israel, but he also needs a stable and powerful marriage.

Mere words are not enough.

FROM RESENTMENT TO RETALIATION

Song of Solomon 5:3

Shulamith rejects the advance. She says, "I have taken off my robe; how can I put it on *again*? I have washed my feet; how can I defile them?" (5:3).

Contrast this response with her pre-wedding dream, when she awakened to find Solomon missing and went in search of him. We've come full circle. Now the bed is empty, he is the one who comes seeking, and yet the lock remains on the door.

At this point the modern advocates of cohabitation might suggest that Solomon and Shulamith had a good thing going, and marriage has ruined it. Wasn't the couple deeply in love before tying the knot? Isn't this proof that marriage takes the romance out of a relationship?

The truth, we would reply, is that the romantic heat often cools even before the ceremony. It cools, in fact, for those who live together for enough time. So marriage itself isn't the culprit. But let's not be fatalistic about this. We need to uphold the truth that passion need not die in a marriage. As a matter of fact, it won't if both spouses are committed to making their marriage a top-level priority.

What this scene is really about is not the ravages of time or the doom of a wedding license. The truth is that Shulamith is upset. The first words of her reply are "How can I?" As if the answer is not fairly simple. She has disrobed, washed her feet, and gotten settled in bed. How, she asks, can she possibly get dirt on her feet again? When we come right down to it, sleeping with her husband isn't worth a second foot cleaning. When we come *really* down to it, Shulamith is miffed. A contemporary paraphrase of her words might be, "Not tonight. I have a headache."

Yet this ambivalence doesn't seem to have been present just earlier when she was falling asleep. Shulamith was listening for her husband's voice, apparently eager to have him by her side. But she has waited. And waited. If he doesn't care enough to be there on time for her, she doesn't care to get her feet dirty for him.

There is an expression: "Hurt people hurt people." She is wounded, so she inflicts a wound. I think we can all recognize the emotions here. People haven't changed much since Old Testament days—not in matters of the heart.

I've heard how this same thing happened to a man and a wife who had been bickering until they stopped speaking to one another. The husband realized he needed his wife to wake him in time to make an early flight from the airport. On a piece of paper he scribbled a note that said, "Please wake me at five a.m." He left it by her night table where she couldn't miss it, then went off to sleep. The next morning he awoke and looked at the clock: nine a.m.! Not only that, a note was taped onto the clock. It read, "It's five a.m. Wake up."[4] Touché. When we've had all we can take, we tend to give back in kind.

The problem with retaliation is that it can start an endless cycle. No law says we have to strike back. As a matter of fact, God's law says we cannot. God tells us that vengeance belongs solely to Him, and He isn't loaning it out. (See Deuteronomy 32:35.) Paul tells us not to owe anyone anything except love. (See Romans 13:8.) Paul also tells us how love behaves: It "does not behave rudely, does not seek its own, is not provoked, thinks no evil . . . bears all things, believes all things, hopes all things, endures all things" (1 Corinthians 13:5-7). That is the recipe for one powerful helping of love, isn't it? It takes a good deal of strength to love with such discipline.

In real life, of course, the best of us fail to be so strong every single time. Solomon and Shulamith have an obstacle to their relationship, and it's more than the locked door. Shulamith is saying, "So sad, too bad. If you can't get home at a decent hour, don't expect any special attention from me,"[5] and it appears she is willing to sleep on her anger. Daniel Akin writes that the evening once held such promise for romance. Now it's gone in the opposite direction.[6]

Who can say which party is at fault? Solomon is a king, and there may have been a true crisis that delayed his homecoming. On the other hand, maybe he has been irresponsible in taking his wife for granted. We do know he has come home with love on his mind, but has forgotten what he taught us in a previous chapter: that for the woman, love needs the right preparation.

As for Shulamith, maybe she has been engaging in a pity party for one. She has had a lot of time to sit and simmer. But maybe it's not the first time this has happened. We don't have enough information to assign blame, but that's not our objective in this study. What is important is to learn what we can from the biblical narrative. It's important that we see ourselves in this couple because we, too, have our pity parties. We, too, let each other down, throw out cutting remarks, and lock the doors of openness that marriage requires.

In her book *Capture His Heart*, Lysa TerKeurst tells of boarding a shuttle bus at the airport and striking up a conversation with the sixty-year-old driver. She commented to him, "People must love to see the shuttle bus pull up because it means they're going home."

The driver laughed, "Yeah, everyone's excited to see me pull up to the curb. That's why I like my job so much. People get on the bus and they smile so big. They've just been waiting for me. And when I finally arrive, they're happy I'm here. I've often wished I had a video camera to tape people as they get on my bus with the smiling faces and the glad-to-see you comments. I'd love for my wife to see that tape. That's the way I've always wanted her to look when I come home from work."[7]

Family experts tell us that this is a crucial moment in traditional families—when a husband arrives home from a day at the office. The couple has been apart for eight or nine hours; they've followed separate schedules. Neither spouse knows what the other's day has been like. We need to be ready for that moment, choosing words and moods very carefully, using the moment to reunite and regroup spiritually. The husband in a foul mood can create a bad moment that becomes a "little fox." The unresponsive wife can do the same.

Earlier I quoted four key factors for husbands to remember. Here, again, courtesy of the Turnbulls, are four for the wives.

First, be his cheerleader. A man thrives on his wife's approval and praise. It's so important for a woman to understand this need in a man. He may be proud and incapable of expressing his need for it, but believe me—your husband wants you cheering him on. Let me offer you my own example. As pastor of a large church, and one who speaks on the radio and television, I get a lot of nice remarks from people. I'm grateful for every single one, but they all pale in comparison to a good word from Donna, my wife. She's the one person I'd rather please than anyone else because she knows me best, and because pleasing her pleases me.

Second, be his champion. Defend and promote him; carry his banner high. Third, be his companion. A man wants his wife to be his best friend. And fourth, be his complement. He wants you to complete him, to fill in all the blanks and take up where his personal gifts and abilities leave off.

If I could convince men and women to each follow their respective four goals, think of the difference it would make in our marriages.

FROM RETALIATION TO REGRET

Song of Solomon 5:4-6

So what happens with Solomon and Shulamith? Do they have a knock-down, drag-out argument? Is there door-slamming, vase-throwing, and an exchange of bitter recriminations? Does Solomon retract all the compliments he has paid her in the first few chapters?

What happens is that we come to the sadness that follows every conflict. How do you feel in the calm after an upsetting altercation? There are few circumstances in life that knock us more off our stride than to have something come between two close friends—when it's a marriage, the pain is even more acute.

Reconsideration. The psychology of these next verses is fascinating. Shulamith says: "My beloved put his hand by the latch *of the door*, and my heart yearned for him" (5:4).

Solomon is still in hopes of entering the room and completing his evening in a more pleasant way. He tries the latch on the door. Isn't it interesting, and even a little touching, for Shulamith to admit that her heart yearned for him to succeed in lifting the latch and coming inside? Despite her prideful resolve, she finds herself rooting for him to get through a door she has locked against him. She loves him. We know that she has yearned for him earlier in the evening. Why not just open the door and get what she wants?

Perhaps there is an inner struggle within Shulamith. Have you ever willed yourself to be angry with someone even though what you really wanted, deep in your heart, was to put things right with them? Have you ever let pride become the boss of you?

Shulamith has pretended she didn't really care whether he came or went; she didn't want to get any dust on her feet. Sorry, but she simply wasn't up to draping a robe over herself and climbing out of bed.

But that's not what she's really feeling.

Resolve. "I arose to open for my beloved, and my hands dripped *with* myrrh, my fingers with liquid myrrh, on the handles of the lock" (5:5).

She has been frustrated and impatient with Solomon, yes. But in the end, of course, he is *her* Solomon. Love is triumphant. He is out there uttering sweet nothings to her, and he is fumbling desperately with the latch. Just his own desire is enough to rekindle desire in Shulamith; it feels good to know someone wants you so badly.

She overrules her previous decision. Now she intends to get out of bed to let her husband in. Her hands are dripping with myrrh. Perhaps to signal her change of heart and to refresh his memories of the night in the bridal chamber, she takes time to apply a bit of sweet-smelling stuff before she goes to open the door.

Regret. It's sad, even heartbreaking, to read what happens next. Shulamith has had a change of heart. She has added fresh scent, and the evening looks as if it can have a happy ending after all. She feels the load of petty resentment fall off her shoulders, and she's eager to have Solomon in her arms again. But then she gets to the door, throws it open eagerly—and the smile leaves her face. The passageway yawns before her, empty. "I opened for my beloved, but my beloved had turned away *and* was gone. My heart leaped up when he spoke. I sought him, but I could not find him; I called him, but he gave me no answer" (5:6).

Now we can imagine that she feels the sting of regret. She has been a little drowsy, a little irritated, and she has said words that must have hurt Solomon's pride a little. At least he hasn't engaged her in argument, but has silently slunk away. There's nothing like the silence after a storm to make us see things in a new light and to say, "Oh, what a fool I've been!"

Shulamith and Solomon love one another. What's the point in pretending she doesn't want him, late hours and all? Didn't the Daughters of Jerusalem warn her there would be days like this? In our mind's eye, we can see Shulamith standing silently at that door, the myrrh on her fingers, all dressed up and nowhere to go. Like daggers to her soul, sorrow over her initial attitude mixes with panic at the hurt she has caused Solomon. Ultimately these emotions all combine to form a thick stew of confusion.[8] She is no longer in control of the situation or of herself. A moment ago, she had him right where she wanted him. Now she doesn't have him at all.

Timing can be pretty important. When he was willing, she was not. When she was willing, he was not there. It happens just this way for couples sometimes; one gets frisky while the other gets a headache. One feels romantic, the other feels like watching football. It can be difficult to get on the same page at the same moment. Shulamith has twice commented that love should not be awakened before its time. She could now add that love shouldn't miss its moment, either; if it can come too early, sometimes it can come too late.

FROM REGRET TO RENEWAL

Song of Solomon 5:8

I'm truly happy this is the Word of God rather than a contemporary film. The next scene could be in a divorce court with a momentous showdown between high-priced lawyers. Instead, there is redemption, love, truth, and all the wonderful things that go with being people of God.

Our brand of marriage is resilient. It can take the blows and actually get stronger from them like tempered steel. Solomon and Shulamith have had a silly little set-to. What pair of newlyweds has not? Now it's time for them to learn from this tempest-in-a-teapot and move on.

The eighth verse reminds us of the earlier dream in which Shulamith has walked the night streets in search of Solomon. It's almost as if that dream foreshadowed this moment, for now she is on the lookout for her husband again. She feels a certain degree of panic having rebuffed him in the way she did. He may be angry somewhere; she doesn't want the incident to blow up into a major storm.

In her excited state, she doesn't stop to think. Instead, she goes to her girlfriends, the Daughters of Jerusalem, who always seem to turn up at odd moments in this book. Shulamith mobilizes the DOJ and sends them out on a search-and-recover mission, posse-style. Here is the mission:

1. Find Solomon.
2. Tell him I'm lovesick!

I'm not making this up. Shulamith says, "I charge you, O daughters of Jerusalem, if you find my beloved, that you tell him I *am* lovesick!" (5:8).

It should be obvious by now that the marriage of Solomon and Shulamith is in no jeopardy at all. The biblical text offers convincing evidence that each is deeply in love with the other—just not at the most corresponding moments.

If we can see how desperately in love Shulamith is, you can bet her husband realizes it too. She is willing to go out in the streets and form a search party. On the other hand, imagine how this story might have played out in many marriages today. Shulamith might have seen Solomon was gone and allowed pride to rear its ugly head once more. "Well, you must not have wanted to see me *that* bad!" she might have barked, slammed the door, and sulked.

Then she might have gone to bed and tossed and turned all night, getting herself more and more worked up. Her man stays out late, comes home with "dippity dew" on his hair and love on his mind, wakes her up, works her up, and then walks away. What?

Next day, having had little sleep, she might have been in a nasty frame of mind. She would have assembled the Daughters of Jerusalem, not to search for Solomon, but to listen to her vent. Then the Daughters might have given her all kinds of "You go, girl" advice, mostly intended to teach that arrogant husband a lesson.

None of that happens in this story, but it happens in other stories, in other households, in other centuries. Foxes still enjoy stealth-snacking on grapes. Little things lead to big problems.

I make this point because I wouldn't have you assume that any issues in your marriage will be as neatly resolved as they are with Solomon and Shulamith. Solomon is the wisest man in history, and he has chosen a worthy wife. They are smart enough to get through, and grow through, the misfortune of this particular evening. But what about your marriage? Have you ever let a few ill-timed words come between you? Have you gone on to let a succession of words and incidents accumulate?

We're going to see that Solomon and Shulamith will patch things up nicely. Is there any reason you can't take the initiative as Shulamith did when something goes awry? That's all it requires: humility instead of pride. Remember that you love your spouse, and that petty resentment is a dead-end street. Yes, he/she said something to hurt you. Yes, it's difficult to live with the pain of a relationship that isn't working right. But you need to talk about it rather than brood about it—then go do something about it. Do you really believe that God cannot heal your marriage? Far, far greater miracles occur every single day. One of you can stop the deterioration. Both of you can reverse the damage and make your marriage as exciting as it was when it began.

MEANWHILE, IN A LONDON MANSION

Have you forgotten the Rothschilds? The banking couple from the beginning of the chapter? We don't want to close this one without helping them out of their predicament.

If you'll remember, Lionel and Charlotte were suffering from the same problem we've been talking about. Lionel was all about his work, crunching numbers into the early evening at the bank, maintaining a financial dynasty. Charlotte was at home, hundreds of miles from her family and friends in Germany, lonely and disappointed at the age of seventeen. Husband and wife were both shy people, and neither had any idea how to make a marriage work.

The heartbreak she felt was clear in the letters she sent home. Her father must have felt some guilt, having sent his daughter abroad to marry a relative (literally) stranger. He urged her to be more outgoing, to begin building a life for herself in her new home. She needed brand new friends, brand new adventures. He told her to explore London, and to make social calls on Sundays as people did in those days. She should also redeem her value to her husband—become a useful companion rather than a merely decorative ornament in a fine home.

Charlotte would not give up. She had the spunk to take her father's advice, and within a few years she was the toast of London society—no small accomplishment in London at the height of its high society era in the Victorian age. She entertained the rich, the famous, and the powerful. And instead of resenting her husband's emotional distance, she met him halfway. Charlotte may not have found the perfect man, but she was resolved to be the perfect wife. She overcame the timidity with which she had arrived in London and became a full partner to Lionel in every way.[9]

Now think of this. When Solomon shrank away from her door, Shulamith went into the streets to bring him back. When Lionel wasn't certain how to be a good husband, Charlotte made up the difference by being a perfect companion for the kind of social and business identity her husband had. Do you see a theme here?

Today, we make a lot of demands on others when we could be making something more of ourselves. We moan about how unfair the boss is at work when we could reduce so many of the problems by becoming a more dynamic employee. We brood over the needs that aren't being met by our spouse, but we presumably have an issue or two that we ourselves could improve.

Marriage is teamwork. It takes two of us to make it work, but in the end, we can only be fully responsible for how we ourselves react and behave. There's so much that you have in your power to do, if you will simply be obedient to God. It's your choice to harbor resentment or to make peace. It's your call whether to go out after him or to stubbornly insist on waiting for him to come apologize to you. In my years of counseling, I've never heard anyone express regret that they were the one to take the high road.

The unity or "one-fleshness" of marriage doesn't apply merely to the physical realm. It applies to the entire realm of the relationship. Everything must be shared. If your spouse has had a bad day, it's not your duty to be resentful or even to go into hiding. It's your duty to share the burden, to lighten the load. If your spouse has a new hobby, you should try to share that passion—give him or her someone to pursue it with. Maybe she needs to try watching football with him, and then he should try watching HGTV with her.

The law of entropy says that things in this universe tend to fall apart. Houses get old and decay. Even suns and stars scatter into dust after a while. In a marriage, a husband and wife begin in blissful unity. If they are not vigilant, over the years they will drift in separate directions. One little instance of bad timing, such as the one in this chapter, can multiply, setting off others. A tiny crack in the foundation can become a canyon. Entropy says that a marriage will fall apart like anything else unless things happen to reverse the process. That's why marriage, like spiritual faith, is a dynamic thing—not an achievement, nor an attainment to be put in a trophy cabinet. Marriage is alive and must be fed and watered.

Marriage and faith are muscles that must be exercised. They either grow stronger or they ultimately deteriorate. Lift a barbell one time, and your bicep is stronger by a tiny increment. Do it several times every day, and you may be the strongest man in the world one day. Likewise, in marriage, say one nice word and your relationship is better by a tiny increment. Avoid one argument, same thing. Do this repeatedly and your marriage will slowly give way to something that can easily pass for heaven on earth. Not only will it fail to deteriorate, but it will be infinitely better than it was when you first married.

We often forget that Peter, Jesus' disciple, was a married man. He wrote some advice that addresses husbands but applies to both spouses: "Husbands, likewise, dwell with *them* with understanding, giving honor to the wife, as to the weaker vessel, and as *being* heirs together of the grace of life, that your prayers may not be hindered" (I Peter 3:7).

Key phrase: "Heirs together of the grace of life." Is there any more beautiful expression of a godly marriage? That's exactly what we are—heirs together. Two people sitting and holding hands in a room where a will is being read. The will states that these two have inherited a kingdom. Everything in it belongs to them. Their inheritance is the grace of life—a beautiful godliness that will shine in everything they do together. People will watch that couple walk by on the street and the onlookers will whisper, "What is it about those two? How can they be so in love after all these years? How can they be that joyful?"

Not that you two, as heirs to a spiritual fortune, won't have your difficulties. No marriage is without them, not even godly marriages. Relationships are only as perfect as the people who have them. We will struggle at times. But here's the good news. Gary Thomas reminds us, "Struggling successfully and profitably brings a deeper joy than even trouble-free living . . . A good marriage is not something you find, it's something you work for."[10] See what I mean? You really can't lose—even when things are bad, it's all good.

Good times, bad times—at all times, God is at the center, and the husband and wife both know it. As they grow closer to Him, they grow closer to each other. Both are being transformed daily—by small increments—to the image of Christ. Therefore, by definition, they're becoming more alike and more like-minded. As a matter of fact, Christ is the third party in your marriage. Maybe as those onlookers watch you pass, one of them says, "Who was that couple?" And another says, "I thought I counted three of them."

That's love at the speed of life. The world hurries along, and we find ourselves running to catch up. That's okay, because the point is that, even at this pace, we know exactly where we're going, and the journey is half the fun—as long as you have the right traveling partner. ◆

1   Stanley Weintraub, *Charlotte and Lionel: A Rothschild Love Story*, (New York: Free Press, 2003), passim.
2   Paige Patterson, *Song of Solomon, Everyman's Bible Commentary*, (Chicago, IL: Moody Press, 1986), 82.
3   Bob and Yvonne Turnbull, *Team Mates: Building Your Marriage to Complete not Compete* (Kansas City, MO: Beacon Hill Press of Kansas City, 1998), 67-83.
4   From Gary L. Crawford, *In Celebration of Love, Marriage, and Sex*, (Xulon Press, 2008), 143.
5   Daniel Akin, *God on Sex* (Nashville: B&H Books, 2003), 169.
6   Ibid; 169.
7   Lysa TerKeurst, *Capture His Heart*, (Chicago: Moody Press, 2002), 12-13.
8   Adapted from Ibid, 86.
9   Ibid Weintraub, 78; *xvii*.
10 Gary Thomas, *Sacred Marriage* (Grand Rapids, MI: Zondervan, 2000), 130,133.

9

Rekindling the Fire

Song of Solomon 5:9-6:10

Craig Barnes tells the story of counseling a man with the proverbial cold feet. This fellow had been dating one woman for years, and he couldn't bring himself to propose.

Barnes wanted to know what was stopping him from popping the question after so much time. "I don't think she makes me happy," the man replied.

Barnes asked him to state his reasons, and that question turned out to be a mistake. The man answered in great detail. He seemed to have made an inventory of everything necessary to his happiness, every item of which this woman lacked—even though he'd continued to date her for years.

Managing to slip another question in edgewise, Barnes said, "Well, then, what kind of wife *would* make you happy?"

Now the man offered his conception of the perfect wife, an angel incarnate. As Barnes listened, he tried to form a mental image of the mate being described. At first he thought that the best fit would be a golden retriever, with its silky hair and its unquestioning affection. But then he realized that even a dog will make certain emotional demands on its owner.

Finally Barnes settled on the idea of a goldfish, the kind with the long, swishy tail. That's what this man wanted. A goldfish: remains in its bowl, looks very nice, and never asks you to talk to it, nor does it care whether you know how its day has been. Barnes concluded, "The last thing he needed was a wife, because his whole understanding of why the world existed was to meet his needs."[1]

What do you want from marriage? What needs do you expect your mate to supply? Have you ever sat down and given a focused answer to that question? Have you ever discussed it as a couple? The issue is both crucial and complicated. One of the most confusing aspects about it is that men and women need different things—or they need things that seem the same at face value, but work out differently in practical terms. For example, both men and women want friendship from their marriage, but they may have very different ideas of how a friend acts.

The humorist Dave Barry attempted to expound on the perennial question of what men and women want. Here is his handy, concise summary:

> *What Women Want: To be loved, to be listened to, to be desired, to be respected, to be needed, to be trusted, and sometimes, just to be held.*

> *What Men Want: Tickets for the World Series.*[2]

Okay, maybe that's a tad unfair. I know men who don't even like baseball and would substitute Super Bowl tickets. Or maybe just a really good pizza. We'll all agree that it's a challenge to compare our wants and needs, meet those needs for one another, and get the whole thing balanced and practical. If you can make that happen, welcome to the realm of connubial bliss; if not, keep reading. As Socrates once said, men who find good wives will be happy; men who find bad ones will become philosophers.

There's a lot of marriage philosophy in the Song of Solomon. We have the privilege of learning from the relationship story of Solomon and Shulamith—what they did right, and in some cases, what they did wrong. We know they faced what every marriage must encounter: the challenge of stoking the dying embers of romance. Marriage at its inception is like a roaring fire in the hearth: strong, warm, and cheerful. It seems to bear a wonderful glow, and other people receive warmth just by being around it. But every fire, as we know, will wane at times. It needs to be poked a bit; it needs a bit of fresh kindling and a log or two. In other words, the vitality of marriage will settle into dry ashes if it isn't fed and maintained.

I've already given men and women four starting points each, courtesy of the marriage ministry of Bob and Yvonne Turnbull. Can you remember those two Fantastic Fours? Let's start with the husband, who needs his wife to be his cheerleader, his champion, his companion, and his complement.[3] Bob and Yvonne are onto something, because we'll see these very principles reflected in the next part of Song of Solomon, chapter 5.

Then, having explored the husband's needs, we'll turn to those of the wife.

WHAT A HUSBAND NEEDS FROM HIS WIFE
Song of Solomon 5:9-6:3

When we last saw poor Shulamith, she'd been having a bad night. First she drifted off to sleep while waiting anxiously for her husband. Then she became petulant and refused him entrance. But then, changing her mind, she threw open the door only to discover he was gone. Clearly upset, she has gone out into the streets searching for her missing husband, and she even enlisted the Daughters of Jerusalem to help her comb the city and find him.

Even though Shulamith is now a VIP, the wife of a king, the supporting cast is a bit tough on her. Who else but close friends could get away with these words? They say, "What *is* your beloved more than *another* beloved, O fairest among women? What *is* your beloved more than *another* beloved, that you so charge us?"(5:9).

"Why make such a big deal out of it?" they're asking. "Isn't he really just another man? Guys are a dime a dozen."

He isn't just another man, of course—not to Shulamith. He is the king of Israel and of her heart. He is her only true love, and she has been separated from him right in the midst of a rare conflict within their marriage. She won't be able to rest or relax until he has returned and reconciled to her. But now she must give the daughters an answer. She wants them to know what it is that makes him "more than another beloved" to her. And, just maybe, she needs to review these things for her own benefit.

Her answer is outstanding. Somewhere across town, Solomon's ears are burning. Most importantly, however, her reply gives us an excellent overview of the critical needs of a husband that only a wife can supply. What should a wife be to her husband? Shulamith says . . .

1. HIS CHEERLEADER AND CHAMPION

The following verses are somewhat unique to ancient manuscripts of the Near East. Descriptions of a woman's beauty, such as we've had in the fourth chapter, are actually quite common. But physical descriptions of the handsome male, such as we're about to encounter, are rare.

What emerges is a careful description of Solomon as seen by an ador-ing wife. Those criteria, of course, are highly subjective; perhaps, in some ways, they say more about the speaker's heart than the husband's physique.

Of course, we're talking about a woman in love, and how she sees her man through the eyes of love. Any male would be more than pleased to know his wife talked him up in this manner. In short, Shulamith is her husband's best public relations director—his cheerleader and cham-pion. She will be those two things by affirming his identity, his intelli-gence, and his individuality.

Affirm His Identity. In verse ten, Shulamith begins to lay out what is special about her husband. She begins, "My beloved *is* white and ruddy, chief among ten thousand" (5:10).

Shulamith's litany of compliments begins with a statement which at first glance seems to be contradictory. Ruddy generally means reddish, so how can this man be white and ruddy? A closer look at the original Hebrew term for *white* suggests that a more specific translation would be "dazzling, glowing, clear, bright."[4] Shulamith is telling us that her hus-band is dazzling— spectacular. As a matter of fact he is "chief among ten thousand"—not quite one in a million mathematically, but close to it.

These are the first words from Shulamith's mouth when asked what makes her husband so special, and what sets him apart from other "beloveds." She is quick to tell them he is dazzling, a shining light, a man among men.

Is she exaggerating? Actually, no. All we have to do is read the his-torical narratives of the Old Testament to know that his wealth and wisdom exceeded those of any king in the world (1 Kings 10:23). In fact, his wealth and wisdom were greater than that of any mortal king throughout history itself (1 Kings 3:12-13; 2 Chronicles 1:12).

This is where I anticipate my female readers saying, "Well duh! Give me the wisest and richest man in the world, and I'll be a pretty good wife, too!"

This is beside the point. Yes, Solomon was unique, but so is the man to whom you are married. He was made by God, whose work is uniformly wonderful. In the eyes of his wife, every man should be special and worth cheering for.

Affirm His Intelligence. In the following verse, Shulamith says, "His head *is like* the finest gold; his locks *are* wavy, *and* black as a raven" (5:11). Solomon was unique and special, but he did not have a head of solid gold. What he did have was a head of incredible wisdom, and that's what Shulamith is talking about here. She is affirming his intelligence. Again, there are no other men out there who can match up to Solomon in this category, but our point remains: Make your husband feel smart. At all costs, avoid any remark that makes him feel ignorant or foolish. This happens sometimes in marriages, and it does terrible damage—whether it is the husband or wife who offers the disparaging words. A man can be smart in different ways. If not "book smart," for example, he might be good at working on cars. If that's not his thing, he is probably good at his job, which requires its own kind of training and understanding. A wife should find the areas in which her husband is intelligent, and give him positive affirmation and praise.

Affirm His Individuality. A wife should also point out the things that set her husband apart. No two people are exactly alike; your husband is truly unique in certain ways. Shulamith's answer is going to be highly detailed here. Like the counseling subject at the beginning of this chapter, Shulamith is going to tell the daughters more than they'll ever want to know on this subject. Most of the time, when we answer a question so definitively, it suggests we're highly passionate about the matter. That's the very attitude we should have about someone to whom we're married—we speak as if he or she is our favorite conversation topic in the world. Shulamith wants everyone to know she has the best husband in the world, because there is no one like him. She discusses Solomon from the angle of his personal appearance and covers nine different parts of his body.

His Hair is Black and Wavy. Shulamith takes it from the top, just as Solomon did when detailing the aspects of her beauty. "His locks *are* wavy, *and* black as a raven" (verse 11). As we've seen, Shulamith actually shares this trait with her husband. To this day, many natives of the region have black hair with plenty of curls. We also remember how this feature figured into the episode in the preceding chapter: Solomon's long, wavy hair was dew-drenched because he waited for the midnight hour.

His Eyes are Brilliant and Winsome. Shulamith next recalls how his eyes draw her interest. "His eyes *are* like doves by the rivers of waters, washed with milk, *and* fitly set" (5:12). Paige Patterson clarifies this analogy: She pictures the dark iris of Solomon's eyes surrounded by the white of his eyes.[5] She evokes the image of a dove bathing in milk. His eyes are perfect, being "fitly set" in his head in the way a diamond might be set perfectly into a ring. If eyes reveal the state of our health, Solomon was a healthy and vigorous young man. We remember that Solomon, in turn, described Shulamith as having dove's eyes. The two must have fully met each other's glances quite often—the sign of a couple that communicates well.

His Cheeks are Bearded and Fragrant. Shulamith takes her listeners an inch or so downward and tells them that "his cheeks *are* like a bed of spices, banks of scented herbs" (5:13). The root of the Hebrew word in the phrase *banks of scented herbs* also means "to grow." His full beard is sweet smelling to Shulamith. Beards can be unpleasant to women, when men don't care for them well. Solomon seems to be fastidious in maintaining his facial hair, including the use of colognes for a manly fragrance.

His Lips are Bright and Red. What about his mouth? "His lips *are* lilies, dripping liquid myrrh" (5:13). By the way, this is not the Easter lily but a generic term for a flower that grows from a bulb. It is probably more like a lotus flower or water lily; she has a dark pink or red flower in mind. His lips are also sweet. You'll remember that Solomon makes the same observation about Shulamith's lips, and we believe the implication of sweetness is that the words proceeding from them are positive and pleasing.

His Arms are Bronzed and Strong. Like Solomon, Shulamith eventually comes to the body itself in her praise-filled tour of a man and what makes him unique. "His hands are rods of gold set with beryl" (5:14). The word translated here as "hands" could be used to describe any part of the arm. It is most likely a description of the strong and well-proportioned arms of Solomon. If she were speaking in twenty-first century lingo, we might hear her say that he had "guns"—toned and muscular arms. Solomon was a physically powerful man. The use of the color gold probably describes his skin tone or perhaps his golden tan.

His Torso is Built and Chiseled. "His body *is* carved ivory inlaid *with* sapphires" (verse 14). Staying with contemporary slang, Solomon not only had "guns" but a "six-pack." We see a lot of men at the local health club who would like to hear their bodies described as of carved ivory. Today Shulamith would sigh, "What can I say? He has, like, killer abs, you know?" Solomon is clearly not the chubby, lazy variety of king who has servants to spoon his pudding into his mouth. This is a man who loves the outdoors, who hunts, who climbs mountains, who travels and corresponds with other monarchs as he inspects materials that will go into the construction of the temple for Jerusalem. He is also a man who is wildly popular with his people. We get the idea that Solomon doesn't have to be the most powerful man in the nation to be a "catch" for Shulamith. Any daughter of Jerusalem he chose might have been his for the asking. As Shulamith describes his body, he is handsome and strong indeed. And by the way, one Old Testament commentator suggests that the phrase *inlaid with sapphires* signifies "branching blue veins under white skin."[6] Sapphires are usually a deep blue. In other words, this is an individual so muscular that the veins show through his skin.

His Legs are Big and Powerful. Now for the limbs: "His legs *are* pillars of marble set on bases of fine gold" (5:15). Clearly an active, mobile man such as Solomon will have powerful legs, thighs, and calves. His feet are the "bases of fine gold." Pillars, of course, are columns that may or may not be set in golden bases. Solomon is supported by these two pillars of marble—the finest of stones—and set into golden bases, or beautiful feet.

His Face is Bold and Handsome. Interestingly, having reached the floor, Shulamith takes it from the top once again—just as if she can't quite get enough of the subject. It's like a child describing the circus. She comes to the last act and starts over again in the telling of the adventure, because she's too excited to stop talking! Shulamith says, "His countenance is like Lebanon, excellent as the cedars." The first word in grandeur during this era was the famous cedar of Lebanon from Shulamith's home. These trees could live two thousand years, and therefore grew to magnificent sizes. How could Solomon's face justify such a comparison? In her eyes, it can. She can think of no other way to explain its beauty, its uniqueness—so she compares it to the most incredible spectacle from the places she has lived. This is how love speaks.

His Mouth Is Beautiful and Sweet. "His mouth *is* most sweet" (5:16). Again, she seems to speak of what proceeds from Solomon's mouth. Having read this far in The Song, who would argue that the man wasn't a sweet-talker? On the other hand, let's not forget that this couple has well-documented kissing skills. Eugene Peterson, in his paraphrase *The Message*, gets it just right: "His words are kisses, his kisses are words." [7]

By now Shulamith has described her love from head to toe and back to head again. Having presented her argument to the court, she offers her closing statement: "Yes, he *is* altogether lovely." Solomon is surely more than the sum of his parts, regardless of how fine those parts are: gold, ivory, cedar, and all the rest. She has rebuilt him for her audience using the finest ingredients in the known world, much as Solomon would build the temple. But the end of the matter is that he is "altogether lovely"—as is this precious passage of our Bible.

All of this description is, of course, to answer a simple question— what's so special about this guy? What makes him any better than your garden-variety "beloved"? Now the Daughters of Jerusalem have their answer, and they're ready to ask where they can go looking for him. (Judging from their eagerness, perhaps Shulamith has made him sound a little *too* altogether lovely to a female audience!)

She is Solomon's cheerleader and his champion, his one-woman fan club. We read her words and say, "Wow! Too bad he's not there to hear them." But you can be certain he will ultimately know what has been said. Indirect compliments are powerful and guaranteed to reach their final destination by courier. Say something bad about someone and it will get back to them—we all know that. It's too bad we tend to forget that we can cast our bread on the water in a positive way, too. Women, if you champion your husband to friends, he will hear about it, and you will endear yourself to him in a unique way. Knowing you love him enough to praise him even when he isn't listening, will score bonus points for you. Trust me on this.

Whether you compliment him behind his back, or "in front of" his back, you need to compliment him regularly. A husband craves the respect and admiration of his wife.

2. HIS COMPANION AND COMPLEMENT

In some ways, this is the most exciting verse in the chapter. In completing her verbal essay, Shulamith says, "Yes, he *is* altogether lovely," as we have seen; then she adds, "This *is* my beloved, and this *is* my friend, O Daughters of Jerusalem!" (5:16)

If you can read that verse without being emotionally moved, you might want to check your pulse. Just consider the picture we have here—a woman on the streets, long after midnight, searching for a husband with whom she has quarreled. The unhappiness of that exchange has caused an equal and opposite reaction, so that now she wants him desperately.

She stands before her close friends, who basically say, "You would be out here on the streets looking for him like this? At this time of night? What is it about him that does this to you?" And the young lady begins to talk about her man. She goes into great detail describing him, using all the colors of a Lebanese rainbow—all the strong and beautiful and priceless things she can think of from her world, and concludes (for herself as much as for her listeners) that he is altogether lovely. Finally she concludes, "He is the love of my life, and he is my best friend."

Isn't it interesting that after a litany of pillars, rods of gold, beds of spices, cedars of Lebanon, and various premium ingredients, these two things—my lover, my friend—seem to surpass all that came before? She is his cheerleader and his champion, and why? Because he is her companion and complement, as she is for him. Romance and friendship: put the two together and you have a marriage for the ages.

Those who know me know I love the Bible. I love reading it, I love studying it, and I love teaching it. There is nothing about the inspired Word of God that I don't love. And one of the reasons is this: After digging into it for most of my life, poring through its treasures, reading and re-reading all sixty-six books and countless commentaries thereon, the surprises just keep coming. Just when I think I've seen it all, the Bible has some *new*/ancient surprise for me. "Where did this come from? How have I missed that?"

I had another one of those moments right here in the Song of Solomon, fifth chapter and sixteenth verse. I came to the words we've just examined: "This *is* my beloved, and this *is* my friend," and then 6:3, just a few verses later, caught my eye. Shulamith is speaking to those same daughters, and listen to what she says: "I *am* my beloved's, and my beloved *is* mine." She has said, "He *is* my beloved," and now reverses the equation to "I *am* his beloved." It was once said that in Hollywood musicals the actress Ginger Rogers could do every step Fred Astaire did, but do it backwards—meaning, of course, that they danced facing each other. Shulamith and Solomon are doing the dance of marriage facing one another. Each describes the other's features, each declares absolute love and adoration, and now we have the great statement "he is my beloved," forward and backward. And to top it all off, "this is my friend."

I've known married couples who were not friends. Just about all they had in common, after years of marriage, was a house, a bedroom, and a last name. They may not have divorced, but each of them would rather spend time with any of several other people than their spouse.

How would you answer that question—the person you would rather spend time with than anyone else? I'm being honest when I tell you that my wife is and always has been my answer for that question from the day I met her. And I hope she feels the same way about me. (I believe her when she tells me she does.)

Sex is wonderful, but it's not more wonderful than the ability to walk through life with a best friend, share everything with that person, and enjoy the simple pleasure of being together. As the years go by there is a special delight in the sharing of memories. We've had forty good years of marriage, so I've known Donna for the vast majority of my life. Whatever has happened to one of us has basically happened to both of us so our very minds and memories are shared possessions. I can't describe to you what a comfort that is in traveling through life. We enjoy reminiscing about all the people we've known, places we've gone, and adventures we've had over the years. And if I can't quite recall a detail, Donna can. If she missed something, I'll usually remember it. Life is simply richer when we use the buddy system.

Solomon understood this. Elsewhere he has written:

> *Two are better than one, because they have a good reward for their labor. For if they fall, one will lift up his companion. But woe to him who is alone when he falls, for he has no one to help him up. Again, if two lie down together, they will keep warm; but how can one be warm alone? Though one may be overpowered by another, two can withstand him. And a threefold cord is not quickly broken* (Ecclesiastes 4:9–12).

That about sums it up—the life of two friends. Working, the results are better; stumbling, the rising easier; slumbering, the bed warmer; struggling, the victory more sure. Love is wonderful, but it's friendship that does all these things. It's friendship that speaks to the practicalities of life.

For this reason, a lasting marriage is worth fighting for. When things aren't going well, I know it may not feel that way. Right now you might be saying, "We have no reward for our labor. We don't lift each other when we fall. When we lie down together, there is only coldness. And as for the struggle, we seem to be fighting each other, not some other force."

Please think about this point. There are countless couples who have come within a hair of giving up, but remained together for one reason or another. Time passed, the disagreements seemed to smooth out, and they came to a place of profound gratitude that they stuck it out. In the wisdom of advanced years, they were the one and only best friend each could have found.

I have seen this happen over and over. You may think that a bad marriage is the worst pain there can be, but I can tell you that separation and divorce are no picnic. Doesn't it make so much more sense, in obedience to God's Word and for the love you once enjoyed with your spouse, to go to work on a damaged relationship? Don't you believe God wants you to have that victory and that He will help you?

FOLLOW-UP QUESTION

The first question asked of Shulamith by the Daughters of Jerusalem had an edge to it, a "why should we care" quality. Shulamith gives an epic answer, and all the Daughters of Jerusalem can do is go to the next question, which introduces the sixth chapter of The Song. Their question: "Where has your beloved gone, O fairest among women? Where has your beloved turned aside, that we may seek him with you?" (6:1)

It may not be the most intelligent question—She says, "Find my husband," and they answer, "Where is he?"—but at least Shulamith seems to have driven away their doubts that this man is worth finding. Indeed, "that we may seek him with you" suggests she has won them over and convinced them of Solomon's worth.

What the daughters are really asking is where Shulamith thinks they should look for the missing husband. Again, the wife's answer is a revealing one. She has a pretty good idea where he has gone, because she knows him so well and understands how he thinks. In fact, Solomon has a place of refuge where he likes to go when he is troubled. There he can reflect in solitude. Even though it's a private and personal sanctuary for him, she knows its whereabouts—again, a good sign when a couple keeps no secrets from one another.

If Shulamith knew all along where he was, why stop and ask the Daughters of Jerusalem? It seems she was confused and upset. When we feel that way we need someone to listen. She needed to pour out the emotions she was feeling. Having done this, having reestablished her deep love for Solomon, she is able to focus on his likely location and go there.

Solomon has a garden, a fact which isn't surprising when we consider his many scientific and botanical interests. I found the following clue in a statement from Solomon in Ecclesiastes 2:5: "I made myself gardens and orchards, and I planted all *kinds* of fruit trees in them." I've mentioned in an earlier chapter that all of Solomon's works abound with references to natural details—plants, animals, geography.

"My beloved has gone to his garden," replies Shulamith. "To the beds of spices to feed *his flock* in the gardens, and to gather lilies" (6:2).

I wonder how many wives would know exactly where to look for a husband in a situation like this one? Would he flee to the golf course? The fishing pond? To the garage to tinker with his car? Shulamith knew where to find Solomon, because she was his friend as well as his lover.

How about you, husbands? Would you know where to find your wife? The Bible says we are to live with our wives "according to knowledge" (1 Peter 3:7, KJV). In other words, "with understanding" (NKJV). How well do you understand your wife? It takes genuine listening for that to happen. Have you found out her innermost thoughts, dreams, fears, and hopes?

We need to keep a kind of mental notebook on the things we discover. Sometimes we learn something the hard way. I'll give you a painful personal example.

Several years ago, before my knees started to give me grief, I was into running, and my greatest desire was to have my wife as a running partner. We were working toward that goal with fast walking and a little running. When Donna's birthday came, I bought her a pair of high-end running shoes—the trendiest thing for track fanatics.

That was a mistake! The present wasn't particularly romantic, but more importantly, it reflected what I was interested in instead of what she was interested in. I regretted that purchase for a long time. Now we can laugh about it, but I'm here to tell you it wasn't funny at the time.

That's okay—live and learn, right? That's one mistake out of my system that I'm unlikely to repeat. If you really love someone, you want to know everything about them, and even the blunders are good in the long run. Get to know your spouse—understanding what gift to give will make her feel loved and is a good indication you're on the right track (wait, maybe I should rephrase that).

WHAT A WIFE NEEDS FROM HER HUSBAND

Song of Solomon 6:4-10

Solomon, then, is found in the garden. The only good thing about a marital spat is the fun you can have in making up. Here in chapter 6, Solomon is going to repeat many of the words he has used in the fourth chapter. His speech here is nearly identical. Is he broadcasting a rerun instead of a fresh new episode, or is he repeating a classic performance by popular demand? I'll leave you to decide that. I think we can all agree that it's usually all a man can do to state something well once; sooner or later the well of great quotations is going to run dry, even if you are Solomon himself.

At the same time, the words of the wedding night are precious. Repeating them is something like repeating wedding vows, as some couples do. Why not try to recreate the atmosphere of the honeymoon? Everything old in the marriage becomes new again.

Solomon does add some new thoughts, and they help us to understand what a wife needs from her husband.

Your Wife Needs Time and Talk. "O my love," Solomon says, "you *are as* beautiful as Tirzah, lovely as Jerusalem, awesome as *an army* with banners!" (6:4).

Allow me to annotate. Tirzah was an agricultural city, just an ordinary town that would later develop great importance. Israel would become a divided kingdom after Solomon's life, and Tirzah would briefly be one of the capitals. At the time when Solomon says these words, no two towns could have been more different. One represents the country, one the city. Shulamith's beauty is as lovely as the pastoral plains of Tirzah, and as impressive as the mighty walls of Jerusalem. She takes all of it in—the simple and the grand.

Then Solomon tells his wife she is as "awesome as an army of banners." He feels strongly about this, because he repeats the sentiment in verse 10. No one but Solomon could have brought together all this diverse imagery; no one else was a world-class naturalist and a triumphant military leader at the same time. A millennium and a half later, he would have been called a Renaissance man—someone

skilled and educated in multiple areas—much like Leonardo or
Michelangelo. But he accomplished this within the limits of ancient
Mediterranean civilization simply by asking God for wisdom as a
young man.

Solomon knew the sight of an army of banners advancing across
hostile borders into enemy territory. For a general, such a sight was
overwhelming, emotionally moving, rousing, and thrilling. This was
the effect of Shulamith's beauty on his spirits. All of this, now—quiet
country town, bustling city capital, rousing battle flag—in one verse! So
rich is this imagery that we can easily forgive him for reusing some of
his better stuff from earlier in the other verses.

While we admire his word wizardry, however, let us also draw a
cautionary note from his later life. This man, intoxicated by beauty as
by banners, was capable of being intoxicated by women forbidden by
God—women who marched in under foreign banners in obedience
to other gods. Our strengths often carry within them the seeds of our
weaknesses, and we see this so often with the great men of the Bible.

Solomon had a tremendous capacity to love—that much is clear. In
this book, we see how it glorified God. In biblical history, we see how it
led to tragedy for Solomon's nation. He was warned about the danger,
but gave in to temptation and followed after these other women until
he found himself worshipping their pagan idols. The man with the
greatest wisdom was also capable of the deepest foolishness. We have
so much to learn from this, don't we?

We can only wonder, seeing Solomon's incredible joy here with
one woman, one soul mate—could he possibly have matched such
pleasure when he had seven hundred wives and three hundred
concubines? At the later time when he had wives he hardly recognized, was he happier than when he shared such deep soul intimacy
with one woman, Shulamith? He could describe every line of her

body. Somewhere along the line, Solomon lost his way in the truth of intimacy.

In most cases, age brings wisdom and discernment. Solomon lived that out in reverse. He began his career with incredible wisdom, beauty, strength, and accomplishment—all from God. He built an empire, then slowly squandered the wealth of precious gifts from heaven. The nation of Israel paid the price through the loss of his spiritual leadership, and civil war followed. We realize that to whom much is given, much is expected—and the magnitude of the fall, from such heights, can be devastating.

All of that, however, is still in the future. For now, we see a simpler moment of love between the younger Solomon and his one true love. This is the place where Solomon can teach us, and here he teaches us to offer time and talk.

Your Wife Needs Tenderness and Touch. Another intriguing remark: "There are sixty queens and eighty concubines, and virgins without number. My dove, my perfect one, is the only one, the only one of her mother, the favorite of the one who bore her. The daughters saw her and called her blessed, the queens and the concubines, and they praised her" (6:8-9).

Throughout this book, Solomon has spoken of Shulamith's beauty in the vocabulary of the natural world. We know that the centerpiece of all God's creation, however, is humanity. Everything God made bears His stamp, but nothing else bears His image. Therefore it's fitting that Solomon now compares Shulamith to other beautiful women. In particular, he compares her to the other women who resided in or near the palace. She is the favorite of her mother. She is cherished by the Daughters of Jerusalem. She is called blessed by all the women of the palace.

A natural question arises from this passage. What are all these other queens and concubines to Solomon? Didn't we understand that they came later—that at this time, he was a one-woman man?

This matter requires a bit of detective work into the life and loves of Solomon. As a matter of fact, we must go back to the life of David, Solomon's father and royal predecessor. At the time of his death, David had a number of surviving wives, including Bathsheba, who was Solomon's mother. These women were tied into the aristocracy of the day, an intricate system as it tends to be in all other times and cultures. Women could even become political capital.

This system was well in place during the early period of Solomon's rule, even though it's doubtful Solomon had become a polygamist. Certainly nothing else in this book has been consistent with the idea of him having other wives. The best explanation is that these women are carryovers from the latter part of David's reign.

At any rate, Solomon says that Shulamith is more beautiful than any of them. She is his queen among queens.

In verse 10, Solomon continues, "Who is she who looks forth as the morning, fair as the moon, clear as the sun, awesome as *an army* with banners?" As usual, Eugene Peterson renders these words beautifully in his paraphrase: "Has anyone ever seen anything like this— dawn-fresh, moon-lovely, sun-radiant, ravishing as the night sky with its galaxy of stars?"[8]

I have to tell you that I think Peterson has something there. I'm not about to tell my wife that her hair is like a flock of mountain goats, but this paraphrase of verse 10 is something I think I could tell my wife: "Honey, have I ever told you that you are dawn-fresh, moon-lovely, sun-radiant, and ravishing as a galaxy of stars?" Okay, maybe not. But Solomon is definitely encouraging me to praise my wife in more creative ways.

HOW TO START A ROARING BONFIRE

So there we have it. In short, men have needs that women must meet.
Women have needs that men must meet. All of us have needs that only
God can meet. A strong, loving marriage is not a given for anybody. It
takes a lot of wisdom and perseverance to keep the flame burning. You
have to know when to stoke that fire, which spots to stoke, and whether
to add fresh kindling (maybe a romantic vacation or a new mutual
hobby). Whatever needs to be done, we have to watch the fire at all
times and keep the sparks flying in a healthy way.

The good news is that there are so many pleasing, delightful things
we can do to make that an enjoyable and fulfilling process. I hope you've
sensed that as you've read this chapter. For example, men, your wife
needs your time and she needs to talk. Who says that should be drudgery? If you love your wife you'll enjoy both. Men who aren't natural
talkers invariably find that it feels good to open up a little bit. As for
time, there's nothing on television that will leave you with a better feeling than taking a walk with your wife, or volunteering to help her with a
household chore.

And women, you've learned that you should be your husband's companion and complement. You're going to like doing that. Let's say he
has a career in a certain field. Ask him to educate you about it. What
are the best parts and the hardest parts of his job? How's that industry doing right now? Learning the lingo will allow you to share in his
experience.

You can be his companion even in the work that is his passion, and
you can be his complement by finding those areas where his skills end
and yours begin. God designed the process to give us deep satisfaction.
And the fact is, it's fun.

Also, if you come to an impasse and can't seem to get things going
in your marriage, review that concept from Revelation 2:4-5 that we

discussed earlier: Remember your first love, and return to the things you were doing before. Court one another as you once did, and put the time into your relationship that you did when you were first getting to know each other. No couple is incompatible if it truly wants to be otherwise.

Most of all, read the directions. Where do you find those? All through the Bible. Ephesians 5:25 commands husbands to love their wives as Christ loved the church. If a husband says, "Well, I don't feel like doing that," I would remind you again that it's not about your feelings; it's about your will to be obedient. You go to work when you don't feel like it. Go to work on your marriage. Give it your best effort, and I can assure you that before you know it, your feelings will catch up with your actions. It's always easier to act your way into feeling than to feel your way into acting.

As we've seen, Shulamith didn't wait on her feelings; she went after her husband. She reviewed a checklist of everything that was wonderful about her husband—when is the last time you did that in your marriage? She counted her many blessings, and named them one by one. The next thing you know, she had found Solomon and he began doing exactly the same thing for her. Soon enough, the scene read like a repeat of their wedding night.

At this point, some would say, "That's all fine and good for newlyweds like those two in the Bible. It might be great advice for someone with less water under the bridge than we have. But by now, our marriage is what it is. It's just too late for us—too much time, too much hurt, too much bitterness."

To that objection I would reply that God has no statute of limitations when it comes to redemption and renewal. He is ready to begin when you are, and believe me, the size of the problem is nothing to Him. The greater the challenge, the greater He is glorified when He answers your prayer and restores your love. He specializes in the impossible, so never act as if it's all up to you and limited by your weaknesses.

Marriage is all about great demands and even greater rewards. I don't know about you, but I've found that everything that really matters is just like that. Getting through school was never easy, but the rewards were substantial. Building a career can be difficult and sometimes heavily discouraging, but isn't it worth it to provide for your family? Marriage is a fire that must be maintained, make no mistake. But if you do it right, it will roar into flame—it will create warmth and light that cuts through the darkness, casts out the cold, and draws in others to be nourished by the glow.

The older I get, the more I appreciate a glowing marital fire and a wonderful wife to share it with. ◆

1 Craig Barnes, "Learning to Speak Multiculturally," sermon preached at National Presbyterian Church, Washington, D.C., (10-3-99).
2 Dave Barry, *Dave Barry's Guide to Marriage and/or Sex* (Emmaus, PA: Rodale, 2000). v. (front matter)
3 Adapted from Bob and Yvonne Turnbull; 93-110.
4 http://www.blueletterbible.org/lang/lexicon/lexicon.cfm?Strongs=H6703&t=KJV.
5 Adapted from Paige Patterson, *Song of Solomon, Everyman's Bible Commentary*, (Chicago, IL: Moody Press, 1986), 90.
6 Quoted G. Lloyd Carr; 143.
7 Eugene Peterson, *The Message* (Colorado Springs, CO: NavPress, 2002), 1191.
8 Ibid; 1192.

10

The Romantic Husband

Song of Solomon 6:13-7:10

Bill Hybels is a friend of mine in ministry. He pastors one of the largest churches in America, the famous Willow Creek Church in Barrington, Illinois. A model of everything a pastor should be—Bill has built his church from mini to mega by helping thousands of unbelievers find new life in Christ. Bill is spiritually wise, personally likeable, physically in shape, and—the thing I like best about him—someone who is transparent and honest as a Christian leader. He has a very self-effacing brand of humor. I love listening to his sermon tapes.

Bill and his wife Lynne have written a great book about marriage with a clever title: *Fit to Be Tied: Making Marriage Last a Lifetime*. In it he offers an amusing glimpse into his own efforts to be that rare specimen known as a romantic husband. "Romance was never my strong suit," he confesses. "I proposed to my wife Lynne in her parents' garage; I took my Harley-Davidson on our honeymoon; I thought our best anniversary was the one we spent watching a video of *Rocky III*."

Realizing his deficiency, Bill knew he'd better elevate his game, but he had no clue what to do. Maybe flowers would be a start. So he started buying three-dollar bouquets from the florist who worked out of his car trunk on the street corner opposite the church. Armed with a regular bouquet, Bill figured he was officially on his way to being a certified romantic husband.

Yet Lynne seemed unimpressed. "Gee, thanks," she would say. "Where'd you get these?" Bill would remind her about the guy with the flowers in his trunk, and explained he was now a volume buyer. "I get a buck off for stopping there so often and two bucks off if they're a little wilted," he grinned, pleased with himself.

The flower gifts trailed off when Lynne continued to seem unmoved by this romantic outburst. It seemed odd to Bill until the truth finally came out at the couple's regular date night. Bill and Lynne occasionally had a session for clearing the air, a time for mentioning the kind of little grievances that could eventually become a problem if not nipped in the bud. On this particular evening at a cheap restaurant, they were having one of those sessions.

Lynne brought out a carefully prepared list of complaints. Bill was checking them off with her: "Yep. Guilty as charged. Oops. Right again. Ouch! So true—I need to take care of that." At the end, he was a little dizzy but promised to make the requested changes.

Lynne said, "Thank you. Now, how about your list?"

Bill didn't have a list, but it seemed fitting to come up with something, since his wife had been so thorough. "Well," he said. "There is one thing. I've stopped the flowers lately, right?"

"Can't say I've noticed," said Lynne.

Bill couldn't believe his ears. "Well, there you go," he said. "That's the problem. Untold hordes of husbands pass that corner where

I buy the bouquets. Do they stop for flowers? *No*. Do I? *Yes!* What gives? Why don't you appreciate it?"

"The truth is, Bill, I'm not impressed when you give me half-dead flowers from some guy's trunk that happened to be on your way home. The flowers are cheap and the required effort is almost non-existent. So I put the same amount of effort into my response to you. You're not thinking about what would make me happy. You're thinking about what would be most convenient."

Bill still couldn't believe his ears. "So let me get this straight," he said. "You'd rather I got up from my desk in the middle of the day, broke into my study schedule, got into my car, drove into town, and paid *quadruple* the price just for the hoity-toity flower box? You'd want me to have less sermon prep and gym time, just so you could have more expensive flowers? Are you telling me that's what would make you happy?"

Lynne smiled, "Yes! That would make me happy."

"But . . . but . . . what you're asking for is neither practical, economical, nor an efficient use of time."

". . . Which is an excellent definition of romance, Bill. You're learning," she smiled.[1]

I think Bill acquired his romance education the hard way that evening. He can join the club—some among us never get it. We guys just think differently. We like sports because there are numbers to crunch, called stats. A football quarterback has an efficiency rating; a baseball hitter has a batting average as well as a slugging percentage. We like things you can measure. When it comes to the game of love, we're out of luck. Spreadsheets don't apply, and numbers don't fit anywhere. Romance has to do with this mysterious force that is largely unknown to the male gender, called *emotions*.

Substitute the concept of worship for romance (there is a relationship between the two) and you have the same concept. A woman
named Mary sat at Jesus' feet while her sister Martha ran hectically
around the house cooking and cleaning. When Martha complained
about Mary's lack of work, Jesus defended Mary for doing the "one
thing" that was appropriate. (See Luke 10:38-42.) Observe: Mary
was neither practical, nor economical, nor efficient in her use of
time. Worshipping Jesus is about heartfelt devotion, not those
other virtues.

Romantic love, like worship, is no time for coupon-clipping, and it
is measured less by the mind than by the heart. It is *extravagant*. This
is one reason Solomon and Shulamith deal in extravagances throughout this book—in their love metaphors, in their perfumes, in everything they share with each other. To the rest of the world, it's a little
crazy. Between those two, it's the most sensible thing imaginable.

Not that love can subsist permanently on hearts and flowers.
Romance must abide throughout marriage, and that's why this
chapter exists. It is here to help us clueless males learn to do that.
But marriage is going to feel unromantic at times. It is going to hit
its rough spots. A former editor of *Time* magazine, Ernest Haveman,
once wrote: "The central truth is that the tide of happiness in any
marriage ebbs and flows. The marriage is ecstatically happy at times,
excruciatingly painful at other times, a mixture of good and bad in
between . . . Even the best marriage has its period of desperation." [2]

Dr. Robert Sternberg, a Yale psychologist, has done extensive
research on love relationships. He has actually attempted to create
strategies for making relationships work. Once we are married, he
cautions, there is the temptation to relax because it seems as if we
have "arrived." We've grabbed our partner, mission accomplished. As
action-oriented men, we turn (with some relief) to the more practical

realities of building the nest. Slowly, usually without being noticed, the romance leaks out of the relationship.

We are like Mary in dating and Martha in marriage. In dating, we sit at one another's feet and adore back and forth. In marriage, we run around getting things done, forgetting to stop and do that "one thing" that provides the joy—in this case, nurture and celebrate each other.

The danger, according to Sternberg, is that we don't even realize the romantic fuel tank is approaching empty. Children will squawk if they crave attention, but a spouse will not. There is no romance gauge with a big E for empty. "Relationships, like flower gardens, need to be nurtured. If they do not grow they will wither away sooner or later and die. Unfortunately, the price of taking a relationship for granted often does not show up for some time . . . The relationship needs constantly to be renewed and nurtured."[3] It's a bit like cracks slowly developing in the foundation of your house. The cracking happens so quietly you don't even hear it, until the foundation is suddenly in bad shape.

Here's my shocking statement for this chapter: I believe the husband should set the romantic tone in a marriage. I realize that we haven't done it that way in our culture. We've always associated the "touchy-feely stuff" (as men often imagine it) with that opposite gender. But as I read through the Bible, and particularly here in the Song of Solomon, I see that we've turned the whole idea upside down in our world.

Allow me to make my case as we look into Song of Solomon, chapter 7.

TAKING THE RIGHT LEAD

Song of Solomon 6:13

Before we move into the seventh chapter of The Song, we must deal with the final verse in chapter six. You'll remember that the original writers of the Bible didn't set those chapters and verses—these artificial divisions were added later to help us quickly identify where to find this or that among 66 books of Scripture. The numbers are not inspired, only the words of the original manuscripts.

Sometimes a new chapter was designated in an awkward way. In this particular instance, the last verse of chapter 6 should really be the first verse of chapter 7—just the way the original Hebrew documents had it. Idea-wise, this verse fits better with what follows it, and that's why we're studying it now instead of in the last chapter.

This verse is also the first time we find Shulamith's name. Solomon says, "Return, return, O Shulamite; return, return, that we may look upon you!" (6:13). We've referred to her all along by the derivation of that name, Shulamith, but it is here—and only here, for that matter—that she is identified.

The key word of the verse, however, is *return*, which occurs four times. The particular meaning is "Come home." Solomon is saying, "Come home, so we can look upon you"—not lustfully on Solomon's part, but because he misses her. This is a plea for reconciliation, for restored togetherness, and it comes from Solomon and his friends as well. Keep that thought about the friends in mind—we'll deal with it presently. Solomon longs to see his wife and have her by his side again.

Shulamith replies in the form of a question, and an initially puzzling question at that: "What would you see in the Shulamite—as it were, the dance of the two camps?" (6:13). I can't really improve on Gary Crawford's explanation of these odd words. He explains that there is a dance called *Mahanaim*, or "the dance of the two camps." Mahanaim is also a place—and the one where the angelic hosts appeared to Jacob in Genesis 32. Solomon thinks of Shulamith as an angel dancing before him—dancing being an expression of spiritual joy in the Old Testament.

The husband and wife know they have hurt each other; now they are ready for reconciliation. Crawford concludes that Shulamith "was dancing as an expression of joy and seduction before her husband, Solomon, there in the palace."[4]

But the key here is that Shulamith comes home at the heartfelt pleas of her husband, who takes the initiative and calls out to her. And he does so emphatically, judging by the four uses of *return*. Solomon takes the lead romantically, and Shulamith dances in joy for her husband's eyes only,[5] and, frankly, in a seductive fashion.[6] Yes, be prepared. We all know what is likely to happen when husband and wife are joyfully reunited.

Our premise is that the husband should take the lead in marital romance. That's exactly what happens here as Solomon calls his wife home. How often does the husband have the best chance to make things right after some kind of misunderstanding? How often does he have the opportunity to set a loving tone within marriage? If you'll think about it, you'll see how well it can work. If it's the wife who seems to step out in leadership for every need of the home, that doesn't mean it's the best system; it simply means we men aren't being proactive enough.

Sometimes we guys get the idea we are only to be workers and suppliers, with our main duties away from home in the workplace. It's a myth. We have the opportunity to stand up and do what's right in marriage and in parenting, to be the leaders God meant us to be. When something isn't right between Solomon and Shulamith, reconciliation begins with him. We'll soon see just how well that works.

SAYING THE RIGHT WORDS

Song of Solomon 7:1-5

Solomon takes the lead, and he does so with the right words. In marriage, it always begins with what we say and proceeds with what we do.

As we read this section, we learn more about how a husband can talk
the talk before walking the walk.

Praise Your Wife Publicly. Let's look again at what Solomon has said:
"Return, return, O Shulamite; return, return, that we may look upon
you!" (6:13).

Notice the word *we*—it seems a bit out of place, doesn't it? We would
think this exchange would be a private one between a husband and his
wife. As promised in the last section, we'll get to the bottom of that
question now.

The heading tips the reader off that others are involved in this
verse. In the translation I use, the New King James Version, the heading reads: "The Beloved and His friends." The implication is that it's
a group speaking, not a single individual. Just as Shulamith's friends,
the Daughters of Jerusalem, helped find Solomon that night, now
Solomon enlists his own friends. "I love my wife," he is telling them,
"and I want her back. Help me talk to her. Help me show her how
much we all miss her." For such an intimate book, friends seem to be
present a good deal. In The Song, we might say it takes a village to
raise a marriage.

Earlier in the book we mentioned that typical occasion when a husband speaks to his wife on the phone with friends all around. She says,
"I love you," and she wants him to say it back. He says, "You mean right
now?" He's a little hesitant to show actual emotions in public. Somehow
it goes against a perceived code of tough guy anti-transparency. We
have bought into the idea that John Wayne is the right model for real-
world husbands.

That kind of emotional facade is never shown in the Song of Solomon—by male nor female. These two spouses share their love verbally
in the town square. They let their friends know, and they take us, the

readers, into the warmth—and a few of the specifics—of their personal
and physical relationship.

But there's an important principle here, and we can't afford to miss
out on it. Affectionate public language is the norm in this book, and
it should be in our own lives. How do you and your spouse interact in
front of other people? Do you put on a little show of politeness that
doesn't match the private reality? Do you snap at each other in ways
that make others uncomfortable?

I'm not pleased to admit it, but I see the principle of public praise
violated more often than followed. It all begins when we enter the
comfort zone of marriage. We drop our guard; we ease up on the
maintenance of our best behavior. If we feel a little irritable, we let it
drift into our dialogue, and we make little cutting remarks we would
never have made in the early days—we rationalize it by disguising
the remarks as "humor." (Sarcasm, by the way, is a poor substitute
for humor.)

Then, having gotten into the habit of showing less respect and affection, we carry on the pattern in public. There's nothing that quite boils
my blood like seeing a husband put down his wife in the presence of
others. If you do that in front of others, I wonder just how bad your
treatment of her might be when we aren't watching. I hurt for her
because I know that no one's self-esteem can take the constant pound-
ing of such verbal disrespect.

And of course, it works the other way, too. I've also seen women
speak disrespectfully to their husbands in public. It shouldn't happen in
private, but when it's right out in the open something is terribly wrong.

Praise Your Wife Personally. The praise should be personal as well
as public. Solomon says, "How beautiful are your feet in sandals, O
prince's daughter" (7:1).

Those last three words have nothing to do with royal birth; we know that such doesn't apply to Shulamith, a country girl who has moved from obscurity to national prominence. She is "just folks," but to Solomon she is just perfect, with the air of royalty. Sandals were generally worn by nobles, and Shulamith now bears that distinction. But her queenly nature is in the eyes of her beholder, not the circumstances of her birth.

The Bible tells husbands that we should afford that kind of honor to our wives. (See 1 Peter 3:7.) There's nothing complicated about the idea of treating our wives like princesses. Like everything God commands us to do, it is doable if we will simply be obedient to Him. It's a matter of our willingness.

We need to start by seeing our wives as Solomon saw his beloved. Love has a way of making the one we love perfect in our eyes. Therefore we look upon them in an uplifted way, and we begin to treat them accordingly, in private and in public. If you are the husband, do you still hold the door for your wife? Do you pull out her chair before she sits down to eat, and do you rise when she enters a room? These are little gestures, behavioral pictures worth one thousand words. It's honor that everyone can see.

At home, do you often watch what she wants to see on television, just because you want to give her deference? Or do you insist on your show? Do you take her to the restaurant she chooses? In other words, these are all little things that every single husband can do as a matter of the will for the love of his wife. And you'll be surprised how genuine her gratitude will be.

Let's look ahead five verses to Solomon's summary statement in 7:6: "How fair and how pleasant you are, O love, with your delights!" One Rabbinic translation of this verse puts it this way: "In all the world there's no such delight for the spirit, and no other is as fair and pleasant as your love."

Eugene Peterson paraphrased it in *The Message* like this: "Your beauty, within and without, is absolute."[7] Powerful, personal praise.

Praise Your Wife Physically. Warning—this couple hasn't finished praising each other's bodies. It's clear that they like what they see when they look at one another. And they seem never to tire of talking about it.

Solomon praises his wife publicly, personally, and now physically. I think it's fair to assume that they're now in the privacy of their own home. Perhaps the friends of Solomon and the Daughters of Jerusalem have given each other a collective wink, made their excuses, and made themselves scarce so that the couple could be alone. Good friends know how to do that.

What follows is Solomon's most sensuous description of his wife. As on the first two occasions at 4:1-7 and 6:4-9, he praises his wife's body in very specific terms. Whereas he started with the head before, now he begins with the feet.

As I was preaching through this book to my congregation, I got some "not again!" looks when I came to this passage and informed everyone what was just ahead. There was a little bit of uncomfortable squirming in the pews, particularly since this is the most explicit portion of the book. As I explained in the introduction, most of us don't talk about these things in public at all, much less in church.

I thought about C. S. Lewis and his book *Mere Christianity*, which explains the essence of our faith and the logic behind it. At the time he wrote it, he was still a confirmed bachelor. Even so, he had some percep-tive words about Christian sexuality:

> *Christianity is almost the only one of the great religions which*
> *thoroughly approves of the body. . . . God Himself once took on a*

human body [and] some kind of body is going to be given to us even
in heaven. . . . Christianity has glorified marriage more than any
other religion: and nearly all the greatest love poetry in the world
has been produced by Christians. If anyone says that sex, in itself,
is bad, Christianity contradicts him at once.[8]

In other words, if you think that there is something ugly about the human body or sexuality, you didn't hear it from God. Over the centuries there have been cultural influences that brought that perspective into the church as an overreaction against public immorality. We stand firmly against the misuse of sex, of course, but that doesn't mean we stand firmly against its proper, God-designed place in things.

The human body is beautiful, and it was made by no one but God, who makes nothing that is ugly or "dirty." We are so shocked by Solomon, but he's the one that has it right. Perhaps he would be shocked by the modern church's denial of sexuality.

Having said all that, this next section was a little awkward to preach about on a Sunday morning! We are who we are partially as a result of cultural molding, and none of us are going to be comfortable standing up in the sanctuary and praising the different parts of our wife's body—and I don't think our wives would be okay with that either!

But it's exactly what Solomon does here. He reviews Shulamith's feet, thighs, navel, waist, breasts, neck, eyes, nose, head, and hair. From foot to hair, from toe to head, Shulamith gets the Solomon Seal of Excellence.

Now think about this. If these things are difficult to discuss in public, I imagine that for most people they're difficult to discuss in private, too. Yet our wives need physical praise. One aspect of a marriage is that it exists in time and we fear the ravages of age. A wife needs to know that her husband still finds her appealing after five years, fifteen years, twenty-five years, or more. She remembers how he used to respond to her—the way her body used to affect him—and she worries that she is now unattractive.

No loving husband wants his wife to live in the throes of those negative emotions. Who said we can only love the soul? That's not advanced spirituality, it's a non-Christian philosophy. Remember, our faith endorses the physical, sexual body. One minister clearly kept the fires of his marital love burning over the years. When he would attend a pastors' retreat, he would tell a couple of friends, "I can't wait to see my wife this weekend. When I get home, the *second* thing I'm going to do is put down my suitcase!" It was surprising and amusing, but he wasn't being rude, he was actually being godly, enjoying his wife, praising her publicly, and admitting he was a normal, healthy human being.

We husbands need to cherish the bodies of our wives, and let them know that we do. Embarrassment isn't called for, and apologies are unnecessary. And though this passage works through Solomon's perspective, we need to acknowledge that the principle is a two-way street. Men want to know that they're still attractive, too. Wives, take note.

Praise Your Wife Picturesquely. Most of us are really visual learners. That means that we take in new information most effectively through tangible images. Solomon shows here that it's not enough to make a broad, general statement. We need to draw somebody a picture with words rather than pencil. I can tell you from preaching that it's one thing to talk about a concept—let's say, righteousness. It's another to give a sermon illustration that shows what righteousness "looks like" when someone lives it out. Most listeners are visual learners, and they find the illustrations more memorable than the sermon points.

Solomon gives illustrations of his wife's beauty. And again, we are going to follow the concept, rather than the precise game plan. Your wife may not want to hear her body parts compared to some of the items in the following list. But she will certainly want to hear her beauty praised in an appropriately specific way. Solomon's words don't reflect our modern culture. Use your own good judgment when praising your wife.

Quick review of high school literature: A *metaphor* is a comparison saying that one thing "is" another, such as "Life is a rat race." The statement is not literal but is drawing a parallel. A simile is a comparison using *like* or *as*, such as "Life is like a baseball game" or "He is as sly as a fox." Solomon makes good use of these literary terms in this passage.

For example, "Your waist is a heap of wheat set about with lilies" (7:2). We're smart enough to know she doesn't have a waist made of wheat. It's a metaphor.

Likewise, "The curves of your thighs are like jewels" (7:1). That's a simile. Solomon takes common items of beauty from his time, and uses them to praise Shulamith's beauty.

Let me offer a summary of the passage:

> Her "thighs are like jewels, the work of the hands of a skillful workman."
> Her "navel is a rounded goblet."
> Her "waist is a heap of wheat set about with lilies."
> Her "breasts are like two fawns."
> Her "neck is like an ivory tower."
> Her "eyes [are] like the pools in Heshbon by the gate of Bath Rabbim."
> Her "nose is like the tower of Lebanon."
> Her "head crowns [her] like Mount Carmel."
> Her "hair of [her] head is like purple; a king is held captive by [her] tresses" (7:1-5).

Being literal here would cause a real problem. Think hard and use your imagination to put all those similes and metaphors together into one composite image. I don't know what the result would look like, but I doubt we would call her beautiful—in Solomon's culture or our own. I suppose it's the thought that counts. Solomon is thinking of beauty in a more abstract than literal way.

Gary Smalley's book *The Language of Love* is a brilliant work on the subject of communication. The author develops the concept of using word pictures to communicate the deepest feelings and emotions of our hearts. As I came to this passage of the Song of Solomon, I thought about Smalley's book and opened it again to see what he had to say. I was surprised to find that he employed this very passage from The Song as an example of effective communication through word pictures. He says that word pictures transmit ideas in extremely memorable ways.

Smalley defines a word picture as "a communication tool that uses a story or an object to activate simultaneously the emotions and intellect of a person. In so doing, it causes the person to experience the words, not just hear them."[9] For example, Romeo makes use of this principle with Juliet in Shakespeare's immortal play:

But soft! What light through yonder window breaks?
It is the east, and Juliet is the sun . . .
See, how she leans her cheek upon her hand!
O, that I were a glove upon that hand, that I might touch that
cheek![10]

In my far more primitive grasp of the English language, I can only say, "That's some good stuff!" From my own experience, I know that wives appreciate our efforts to communicate in word pictures.

My wife loves to read, and she especially loves a good mystery novel. As a matter of fact, she is so intrigued by that genre that she has been working on a mystery of her own, along with her best friend Peggy, over the last couple of years. I've known about the hours they've put into their big project, but Donna didn't allow me to read a single sentence. Donna's policy was: "You can read it when it's done."

I was curious, but she was a closed book. "Who are you basing your characters on?" I'd ask.

"You can read it when it's done."

"What about the plot? Where is it set?"

"You can read it when it's done."

Finally the book was complete, and Donna was as good as her word. I was allowed to read the book from cover to cover. It was riveting—a real page-turner! I couldn't put the book down, and that would have been true even if I weren't married to the co-author.

I wanted to tell her, as powerfully as possible, about the excellence of her work. I didn't rehearse a word of this or plan it out in any way. I instinctively drew on our mutual love of John Grisham's novels. I said, "Honey, this is a John Grisham mystery," and her face lit up! To her that was the ultimate compliment.

Now I could have simply said, "Honey, it's great." But the use of a word picture—one I knew would be effective, because I know her—was far more effective. It scored points with her and gave her the encouragement anyone needs when they're trying something new. Later, I heard her share my evaluation with a friend, and I knew I had done well.

We men tend to be businesslike in everything—straight to the point, no nonsense. And there's a virtue, a degree of integrity to that. We don't want to be hypocritical flatterers. On the other hand, we want to communicate our love with sincere eloquence and power. I was in no way insincere when I compared my wife's book to John Grisham;

I read her book with the same enjoyment as I would read one of his. But I knew I needed to find the best, most loving way to build her up. I needed to be specific.

If you truly love your wife, husbands, you will find those little touchstones from her world to praise her. You can call her a regular Martha Stewart in her cooking, or you can compare her eyes to those of some movie star. It doesn't have to be Shakespearean (we'd all be in trouble if it had to measure up to the Bard's standards). It simply needs to come from your heart and her world.

ENJOYING THE RIGHT RESULTS

Song of Solomon 7:6-10

Finally, we need to enjoy the results by demonstrating romantic love. As Ed and Gayle Wheat explain in one of the classic books about Christian sexuality, our wives want to hear the right words, but they also want to experience the right behavior that shows we want them as well as love them. Solomon and Shulamith know their bodies belong to one another.[11]

What is important here is that Solomon's words don't stop at conveying his wife's beauty; they demonstrate her desirability. He shows he yearns for her physically. Solomon says,

> *How fair and how pleasant you are, O love, with your delights! This stature of yours is like a palm tree, and your breasts like its clusters. I said, "I will go up to the palm tree, I will take hold of its branches." Let now your breasts be like clusters of the vine, the fragrance of your breath like apples, and the roof of your mouth like the best wine"* (7:6-9a).

Don't expect me to give you a precise explanation of those verses; I think they're fairly clear no matter what translation you're using.

Solomon is speaking passionately about consummating his love for his wife.

It is now that Shulamith, who has been silent, finally speaks. She has the last word: "The wine goes down smoothly for my beloved, moving gently the lips of sleepers. I am my beloved's, and his desire is toward me" (7:9b-10).

This is the third in a trilogy of statements that creates a kind of three-part thesis statement of the relationship of Solomon and Shulamith. These words tell us all that we need to know about this couple:

"My beloved is mine, and I am his" (2:16).
"I am my beloved's, and my beloved is mine" (6:3).
"I am my beloved's, and his desire is toward me" (7:10).

For the first time, we can put the three statements together and understand their beautiful symmetry. The first time she has emphasized her ownership of her beloved; the second time, her beloved's ownership of her; the third time, on a deeper level, she underlines the truth that she belongs to him, *and* that he desires her.

It's the final puzzle piece of marital intimacy. Many women are beautiful, but Shulamith is the one Solomon desires. During that evening when he came home too late, she had reason to wonder about that; it seemed he was caught up in other matters, whatever they may have been. Now she can have no doubt about her husband's passion, which she shares with no other woman.

No matter how long we have been married, it is wonderful for our wife to be confident that our sexual desire remains, and that it applies to no one in this world but her. We need to make that clear for two reasons. First, it is a beautiful and effective way to affirm her as a woman. Second, she can't read her husband's mind. She needs to know when her husband desires physical intimacy with her. Words, gentle touch, body language, even the eyes can carry the desired message.

Ed Young, Jr. has written about the meaning of marriage. He suggests that there are many purposes for which God instituted it. One is the ultimate expression of the companionship for which He wired us. Another is that the family is the foundation of human society. A third reason is procreation. But sex itself is about more than filling the earth with more of our kind. God made it *good*. He made it enjoyable, and that can only be because He desires our delight.

Yet that's still not the end of the matter. Young goes on to suggest that there may be a more profound spiritual meaning to marriage even than any of these things. The sacrament of marriage represents the bond between Christ and His Church. We are set apart for something greater than ourselves in marriage, even as we are in our church identity as believers.

In marriage the union is greater than the sum of its parts. The church, which becomes the body of Christ, is similarly a group of individuals who now becomes the presence in this world of the Lord Himself. In both marriage and ministry "God uses this relationship of giving and taking, sharing and caring, sickness and health, to help sanctify us to Himself, to make us pure, to make us holy."[12]

In other words, by the very nature of being married, we should find ourselves becoming transformed to the image of Christ. Together we are walking in the Spirit. Together we are walking toward the will of God. Every step of the way, we are helping each other, healing one another, encouraging one another toward the ultimate goal. And together we should find ourselves growing more like one another, and mutually more like Christ, that third party Who is more visible every day.

I was on the way out the door to preach one morning when my wife said to me, "Honey, your left pant's cuff is curled down."

I started to fix my cuff and she said, "You've got something white on the bottom of your pants." I had been oblivious to these imperfections, needless to say. My mind was sermon-bound.

Do you think she was finding fault with me? No, she pointed out these things because she loves me, she takes pride in me looking my best at church, and she wants every single listener to be hearing my words rather than puzzling over my wardrobe malfunctions.

There are times when she has pointed out more serious imperfections; she "has my back" in every way. I am a better man every single day of my life for being married to Donna. She lifts me up. She watches out for me. She counsels me when I need advice, consoles me when I need comfort, encourages me when I need bravery, and when I need humbling—well, she knows how to help me back to my rightful place with loving grace.

Among my deepest hopes is that she can say the same of me. It's not that we have a special marriage, although I hope and personally believe that we do. The point is that everyone should have a marriage that makes both members a little more like Christ. Ed Young, Jr. concludes the matter: "Marriage, I believe, is not so much for our happiness as it is for our holiness."[13]

The happiness, by the way, is a pretty nice by-product. ◆

1   Adapted from Bill Hybels, Lynne Hybels. *Fit to be Tied: Making Marriage Last a Lifetime*, (Grand Rapids: Zondervan, 1991), 61.

2   Ernest Havemann, "The Intricate Balance of A Happy Marriage," (*Life*, September 29, 1961,), 122.

3   Robert Sternberg, *The Triangle of Love: Intimacy, Passion, Commitment* (New York: Basic Books, 1987), 92, 273.

4   Gary L. Crawford, *In Celebration of Love, Marriage, and Sex—A Journey Through Song of Solomon* (Xulon Press, 2008), 175.

5   Patterson; 101.

6   Ibid; Crawford.

7 Eugene Peterson, *The Message*, 1193.
8 C.S. Lewis, *The Complete C. S. Lewis Signature Classics*, (New York: HarperCollins, 2002), 86.
9 Gary Smalley, *The Language of Love*, (Pomona, CA: Focus On The Family Publishing, 1988), 17.
10 *Romeo and Juliet*, Act 2; Scene 2.
11 Quoted in, Ed and Gayle Wheat, *Intended For Pleasure*, (Old Tappan, New Jersey: Fleming H. Revell Company, 1977), 142.
12 Ed Young, Jr., "Creative Leader Newsletter," March, 2008.
13 Ibid; Wheat, Jr.

11

The Great Escape

Song of Solomon 7:10-8:4

Ralph and Janice were approaching their fiftieth wedding anniversary. That's quite a milestone for any couple, and someone told the pastor. He happened to be preparing a sermon on making marriage work, so this seemed like a golden opportunity. The pastor decided to invite Ralph to the podium and interview him about what it meant to enjoy fifty good years of marriage.

As it was quite a large church, the pastor had never met Ralph. But he called him on the phone and shared his interview idea. Ralph said he didn't consider himself a better husband than anyone else, but he would be glad to help.

When Sunday came, the pastor came to the proper point in his sermon and introduced his guest: "Some of you may know that Ralph and Janice will be celebrating fifty years of marriage, their golden anniversary, in just a couple of weeks. What a wonderful illustration of all the principles we're exploring in today's message. We're fortunate to have Ralph come and share a few of his secrets with the rest of us today. Ralph, how have you managed it? What's your secret of staying the course with one woman for five decades?"

Ralph smiled and said, "Well, it's really not as hard as everybody seems to think. I've spent money on her when I needed to. But I think the most credit of all goes to our getaways."

"Aha!" exclaimed the pastor. "The marriage getaway! I have always believed it's one of the genuine secrets of a long-lasting relationship. Can you give us some examples of particularly successful ones for you and Janice?"

"Well," said Ralph, "The best one was probably the getaway for our twenty-fifth anniversary. I took her to Beijing, China."

There were plenty of impressed *oohs* and *ahs* from the congregation. What a generous husband Ralph was. The pastor nodded respectfully and began to wrap up his mini-interview: "Ralph, you are an example for all of us. We've enjoyed hearing from you! Tell us your plans for this even bigger anniversary coming up—fifty years. Where are you planning to go this time?"

Ralph replied, "I'm going back to Beijing to get her." [1]

The pastor was on the right track. Weekend getaways are one of the big secrets of good marriages. Every married couple needs to get away from it all every now and then. Hopefully, however, they need to get away *for* each other rather than *from* each other! I get the idea Ralph hasn't quite figured that out.

Couples have always needed an escape hatch in the compartments of their lives. Our study in the Song of Solomon surely proves it to be true. We've seen tensions over Solomon's schedule and his allotted time to spend with his wife. There was an early conversation with the Daughters of Jerusalem in which Shulamith worried over the demands on her husband, and she even wondered why she was reduced to following along in his entourage: "Why should I be as one who veils herself by the flocks of your companions?" (1:7)

Later, we followed with fascination as she sat up late, fighting drowsiness and resentfulness as she longed for her husband to come home and join her in the bedroom. Of the entire book, these are some of the passages in which Shulamith is the most recognizably human to us: a young wife who is restless and perhaps a tad naïve about the demands upon a king. She seems to have allowed her frustration to fester until that night when it came to a head, when Solomon finally appeared at her bedroom door unacceptably tardy—and was denied.

"Enough is enough," she seems to have been saying. "See how you like having to wait."

The demands of the real world were already coming between Shulamith and Solomon. But the crisis only drove them closer together, as crises should do with God's wiser children. The tiff simply made husband and wife realize how desperately they loved one another, and how unbearable it would be to turn away from the amazingly fulfilling relationship they had built.

We find ourselves now in a chapter that shows how Shulamith has grown up. She is learning to handle her role as "first lady" along with the demands of her husband's life. The events beginning at Song of Solomon 7:10 occur sometime later, and Shulamith has figured out that Solomon is never going to be a creature of leisure. If she wants Solomon, she will have to take him as she finds him—a man who belongs to a nation, and not just a wife.

Don't you love the way these narratives from the Bible have a delightful ring of truth about them? This is marriage as we really experience it, from naïve idealism to mature pragmatism. At first, the stars are in our eyes. We feel as if we're living in some kind of storybook, that we've married our true love, and everything to follow will be part of the happily- ever-after system. Life, of course, says differently. We experience our first reality checks, endure our first disagreements, survive a setback or two, and in time we find ourselves wiser and tougher as married adults. A couple of trips around the block, and we're no longer expecting life to be a fairy tale.

Instead, we're ready to be intentional about married life: roll up our sleeves, and work to make this relationship the best it can be. At least that's how it's supposed to work out—we're talking about *wise* couples.

And this is a wise couple. Somewhere between the chapters, Shulamith has learned this very lesson—probably quietly, by increments, just as you and I have learned it in life. Joseph Dillow has written:

> *Instead of sitting around resenting Solomon for his preoccupation with his job and his late night approach, she assumes responsibility for her behavior and changes the relationship. First of all, she is more aggressive to him sexually, as is illustrated by the dance of Mahanaim. Then she reveals she has planned a vacation in the Lebanon Mountains where they will walk, enjoy the springtime and make love. Furthermore, she builds his anticipation of the time together.* [2]

There we have the education of Shulamith in just seven brief biblical chapters. Bible narratives are complex yet concise. We would love to read more, and find out such things as the chronology of these events and how they interface with Solomon's political career—but the book gives us what we actually *need* to know: the essentials of a marriage relationship as modeled by one fascinating couple. What we will discover here is that we must be proactive in marriage. That means taking action to nurture and maintain the precious gift of marriage that we share.

One of the best ways to do that is through a weekend getaway adventure.

YOUR INVITATION

Song of Solomon 7:10-13

An Enamored Affirmation. A plan is afoot! Shulamith is going to get her husband out of town where she doesn't have to share him with all the officials and dignitaries. Once she wanted to do this permanently— now she's happy to steal a few days of undisturbed intimacy.

Our first point is that it helps to be creative in proposing a weekend getaway. First, Shulamith affirms the security of the relationship she and Solomon have: "I *am* my beloved's, and his desire *is* toward me" (verse 10).

As we saw in the last chapter, Shulamith danced provocatively for her husband. She knew exactly how to grab his attention, and now she is going to take advantage of that opportunity. His attraction to her enhances her feeling of personal security; as long as he so clearly adores her, she knows she has a place in his life. In our own time, the spirit of the age tells us that women should not find security in their men; they are to be fully independent. Man-based security for women is supposed to be an archaic and outmoded idea. But the point is actually a practical one: in plain terms, for women, security is sexy.

Rabbi Shumley Boteach is an immensely likeable radio and television host. His television show is called *Shalom in the Home.* In an article about women and their desires, he asks us the question of why women want to get married. After all, a woman loses her maiden name—some would say her independence. She endures pain in child-bearing. She will be expected to do housework, raise the kids, and support her husband in whatever direction he chooses. She will probably continue to carry the primary burden of homemaking even though she, too, will be in the workplace—the necessity for affording a house.

Why would a woman want these things? The rabbi's answer: "Because a man can give a woman the one thing her parents cannot.

Her parents love her, but only he can choose her. He can make her feel
special and unique."[3]

A man chooses a woman from the entire pool of women in this
world. For this reason, her wedding day is the happiest day of her life.
And at the wedding, all her bridesmaids will long for the day when they
will be chosen, too.[4]

Being singled out means receiving the gift of security—being loved
so much that a man will bond himself for life with her. Security, for that
reason, is sexy.

This is the foundation for many women, and therefore Shulamith
begins from that base and proceeds with her invitation: "His desire is
toward me." She realizes she is the one that he wants, and therefore she
can have the confidence to propose a large commitment like this one.

Her desire is a part of things, too. She has acknowledged her desire
previously. And in Genesis 3:16 God says to the first woman, "Your desire
shall be for your husband." When marriage works as it should, desire
is a two-way street. As a matter of fact, we remember that God had his
conversation with Adam and Eve in the context of their fall, that is, after
their disobedience to Him. God says that "your desire *shall be* for your
husband, and he shall rule over you." It's a discouraging picture of the toll
that sin has taken on our marriage relationship, and we see many marriages just like that. But Paige Patterson points out that "where a holy love
exists, the effects of the fall will, in fact, be minimized."[5]

What an exciting thought! In other words, we struggle in marriage,
and sometimes "rule over" each other because we are fallen creatures
who make our own lives difficult. While we'll remain sinful until Christ
returns, we have the opportunity to find a measure of holiness through
certain godly channels in life. One of these is marriage, and as we've
been saying throughout these chapters, its purpose is to make us more
like Christ—*holier*.

Solomon and Shulamith exemplify a holy marriage with mutual desire, just as God designed it to work. No one is "ruling over" anyone else. But how can we find such a wonderful balance? Tommy Nelson wrote of a getaway, a cruise, that he and his wife Teresa had planned:

> *Our luggage seemed to be misplaced at the outset of the voyage, and we faced the hard, cold fact that we might be several days on the ship with only the clothes we had on our backs. I tried to comfort Teresa by saying, "I've got enough money with me that we can buy the things we need once we stop at the first island." She could not be consoled. Finally, in tears, she said, "But I had a special red night-gown just for tonight." I went straight to the captain of that ship and said, "I want my baggage! Find it now!"* [6]

I laugh when I read that account, but I applaud, too. Here is a husband who is lovingly affirming his wife by showing his desire for her in a playful way as she shows her own desire through bringing the red nightgown.

An Enticing Invitation. These next three verses continue the invitation for the getaway in a provocatively appealing way. We know what's happening—Shulamith is giving her husband the old come-on!

The dance has secured her husband's full attention. She has those wheels turning inside his mind; she has just about closed the sale. Shulamith now says,

> *Come, my beloved, let us go forth to the field; let us lodge in the villages. Let us get up early to the vineyards; let us see if the vine has budded, whether the grape blossoms are open, and the pomegranates are in bloom. There I will give you my love. The mandrakes give*

off a fragrance, and at our gates are pleasant fruits, all manner,
new and old, which I have laid up for you, my beloved (7:11-13).

The references to the budding vines, the opening of the grape blos-
soms, the blooming of the pomegranates, and the pervasive fragrance
of the mandrakes give us the time reference for this getaway. It is the
springtime, when, as Tennyson wrote, "a young man's fancy lightly
turns to thoughts of love." [7]

Apparently a young woman's fancy can turn in the same direction,
and it is Shulamith who is making the first move. We have observed in
past chapters that she is a normal, healthy young woman with normal
and wholesome sexual desires. Now she is bringing creativity into the
equation by finding just the right setting for an unforgettable rendezvous. She invites him repeatedly, *Let's go! Let's go to the countryside, let's*
go to the villages, to the orchards!

This, of course, would give Shulamith the home field advantage. She is
a country girl through and through, just as Solomon has spent his life in
the booming metropolis of Jerusalem. This is a girl who has worked in the
sun, who can take Solomon on a walk through the gardens and identify
every flower and tree. She is the one initiating this plan because it gives
her the chance to take the lead in creating the perfect getaway vacation.

She knows what Solomon desires, and all her plans revolve around
pleasing him; but her own desires are factored into this equation, too.
The setting is one that she cares a great deal about, perhaps the one
place in all the world where she is happiest (as long as her husband
is with her). One way to fulfill Solomon's desire is to inflame her own
desire, and the countryside will help to do the trick. "You can take a girl
out of the country, but you can't take the country out of the girl."[8]

What about these villages? Shulamith is speaking of small, un-walled
clusters of homes that dotted the countryside in the homeland of her

youth. I can see these rolling hills and cottages in my mind because I've traveled in Israel and seen some of these locations that haven't changed in thousands of years.

She might have approached him like this: "Solomon, don't you think we need a little trip somewhere, maybe when you come to a stopping point in your schedule?" It wouldn't work, because that stopping point never quite arrives. For all of us who lead busy lives, the rat race never skips a lap. Shulamith knows this. Therefore she says instead, "Come on! Let's go!" And she paints him a mental picture of the destination. It's important to create a sense of urgency—*this is somewhere you want to be now, if not earlier!* Shulamith specifies getting free, getting up early, and getting away entirely because she knows that once Solomon checks into the office, it's all over. She might as well unpack the suitcases in the front hallway and forget the whole thing. The strategy is to escape with eyes fixed on the goal with no looking back.

It's also interesting to notice her suggestion to check the vineyards to see if they're blossoming. Why? Because this idea would appeal to Solomon as a way of taking care of business. It's probably how he met her in the first place. The vineyards are important to Solomon and the kingdom, producing grapes as a major export. Therefore Solomon now has an excuse to get out of town, and it just so happens that the vineyards are a little corner of his job description where she can be a key player, having been around orchards all her life. Shulamith knows her man, and she's crafted her plan. It's clear she has put a good deal of thought into this invitation.

Donna and I have had to learn the same lesson in our marriage. One month off in the summer is generally our only time to be away from ministry. A Sunday morning preacher can't indulge in frequent weekend getaways. What we've learned to do instead is to find joy and togetherness in the ministry opportunities we do have. I've learned, for example, that my wife likes to shop. That doesn't mean she makes many purchases, but she enjoys simply shopping. That's not me—it takes me a quarter of an hour to proceed through a shopping mall and realize there's nothing I want on the premises. But the first store Donna steps into is a destination for her. She could live in there for a month.

I've long since figured out how to make use of that fact. I have a secretary who manages all our travel itineraries. As part of her assignment, she researches the shopping opportunities for our travel destinations. She includes the directions in the packet of maps we receive at the time of the trip. I find out what Donna wants to do or see in that city, and we plan it right into the schedule. I preach and teach, and then we have an afternoon date for having some fun together. It's good for us to get away—even in the context of ministry responsibilities. If you're very organized and proactive about it, you can make work and leisure coexist in a well-crafted schedule.

That's exactly what Shulamith is doing here. She knows Solomon needs to travel up into the hill country and inspect the vineyards, and she finds a way to tie it into a romantic retreat for both of them.

At the end of verse eleven she briefly tantalizes Solomon just to make the invitation more compelling. The idea is that something good will be waiting for him under one of those trees, but she leaves the details to his vivid imagination. The mind has a way of filling in blanks more effectively than actual details could ever do. The promise is that if he thinks they've had a good sex life in the past, just wait until she gets him into that mountain air. Again, she entices him with the senses—the smell of mandrakes in season, the sight of colorful and delicious fruit, and of course, the thought of Shulamith herself in all her beauty and desirability.

Mandrakes, by the way, have an appropriate place in the conversation. In Hebrew the word for them means *love-apple*. They were considered an aphrodisiac and a stimulant for conception, so the simple mention of them could be provocative. Genesis 30:14-16 offers an example of mandrakes and their "love connection." The plant is poisonous, by the way, but the scent, similar to the apple, is still used in some perfumes.[9]

Finally, Shulamith promises that every variety of "pleasant fruits" awaits Solomon at the gates of this earthly heaven. By now we've noticed what she means when she speaks of these (see 4:13). Her own physical and sexual attractions are part of her reference.

In short, she makes him a little offer he can't refuse. Solomon is probably throwing a few clothes into a suitcase before she's finished the last sentence.

YOUR PREPARATION

Song of Solomon 8:1-2

After the invitation comes the preparation. If we want to maximize our time together, we can't afford to simply take off on a trip without thinking through what we hope to accomplish. We need to plan the specifics of a getaway, but we also need to plan the intangibles that affect our relationship. Shulamith will continue to show us the way.

Talk About Your Expectations for the Weekend. The next words from Shulamith are initially confusing to us: "Oh, that you were like my brother, who nursed at my mother's breasts! *If* I should find you outside, I would kiss you; I would not be despised" (8:1).

Having gotten Solomon all ready for love, what's she trying to do now? Spoil the mood? This doesn't seem like a brother-sister moment. That would certainly make no sense, so we quickly conclude that Shulamith's words have a different meaning.

It turns out that in Hebrew culture, there were bounds of propriety for public behavior. Out in the streets a Hebrew man could speak only to his sister or his mother, as opposed to other women. Nor could he display public affection to anyone other than those two. In other words, Shulamith will want to stop and kiss her husband as they walk through the marketplace or among the vines. She could only do that if she were his sister.

Of course, if that were the case and they were siblings, she wouldn't feel this kind of passion anyway. But that goes beyond the simple point that Shulamith is deeply in love with her husband, powerfully attracted to him, and frequently has the urge to pucker up and give him one on the lips—whether there are people around or not. Of course, Shulamith is still being quite the provocateur. By evoking that image of "forbidden public love" in Solomon's mind, she stokes his desire even further. Yes, it's going to be quite a weekend.

It's important to set the romantic tone long before leaving. Build up those expectations; it can't hurt. Anyone who has ever been a child will tell you that Christmas morning is thrilling, but not as wonderful as the long, drawn-out anticipation. The journey is as important as the destination. Therefore, how do you make a weekend getaway have an impact larger than the short time period? Get those thoughts churning now! Stoke the fire and keep it sizzling. Be primed to fully enjoy each other once you arrive.

Talk About Your Excitement for the Weekend. Shulamith also shares her excitement for the coming getaway: "I would lead you *and* bring you into the house of my mother, she *who* used to instruct me. I would cause you to drink of spiced wine, of the juice of my pomegranate" (8:2).

This is a continuation of the brother-sister metaphor, of course. In those days, there were no public schools giving sex education. It was the mother who instructed her daughter in the ways of love. As we all know, this is a teaching task that should be done with gentle wisdom and discernment in the home. Far too many of us learn the "facts of life" in inappropriate ways that send all the wrong signals about the nature of sex—something truly degrading and horrifying to a young person, rather than a wonderful gift of God reassuringly explained by mom or dad.

The meaning here is subtle, but the implication is that Shulamith would take Solomon to the place where she learned her introductory lessons, and expect Solomon to give her the advanced course. The "spiced wine and juice of my pomegranate" may speak of soft kisses. "In other words," Paige Patterson asserts, "she would depend on Solomon for instruction and enthusiastically return the physical intimacies he enjoyed."[10]

Obscure as the specific meanings may be, we can catch the general drift, can't we? This is going to be a weekend of physical love not a business trip, not a sight-seeing trip, not a visit with elderly relatives.

Shulamith is preparing her husband sexually and building his excitement.

YOUR CONSUMMATION

Song of Solomon 8:3-4

Finally will come the consummation of all the planning and dreaming—the weekend itself. A respite, a little piece of heaven in the midst of everyday drudgery.

Shulamith says, "His left hand *is* under my head, and his right hand embraces me" (8:3). Do you recognize the words? They are a reprise of 2:6, a sensuous expression indicating "a reclining posture on the part of both the king and his bride. Solomon's left hand supported Shulamith while his right hand embraced her. The word *embrace* means 'to enfold with the arms. . .'"[11] Finally the two are together and within each other's embrace.

The couple has come full circle from an upsetting misunderstanding to a kind of second honeymoon—every bit as romantic as the first. In this short book of the Bible we see the unpredictable roller coaster ride that marriage is for most of us. Some of our greatest joys come through that relationship and some of our most painful episodes as well. You can have the most perfect marriage in creation, and you're still guaranteed a few disagreements. Marriage may make us holier, it may make us better than we were individually, but it is still a challenging blend of two imperfect human beings.

As we read the early chapters of the Song of Solomon, we assume we're reading the greatest romance ever written. The passion is off the top of the scale, the words are sheer poetry, the man is the wisest and wealthiest in history, and the woman must surely be the most beautiful. And yet this is the entire point: Even *this* remarkable couple is going to struggle. Yet when they do, they will point us all the more surely toward the path of reconciliation. Solomon and Shulamith have built their marriage on the solid foundation of godliness, so they are going to endure. They are going to continue and even elevate the pleasure they've already enjoyed rather than see it slip from their grasp.

And this brings us to the third appearance of a familiar quotation: "I charge you, O Daughters of Jerusalem, do not stir up nor awaken love until it pleases" (8:4). We're reminded about the relationship between love and timing. This was all too easy to understand when Shulamith was unmarried and restricted in her responses. But what about now? Why can't love be stirred up whenever it pleases on the right side of the wedding day?

Well, for one thing, there is still a level of restraint that marriage requires. We've already seen that she wishes she could kiss her husband as a sister could, but propriety won't allow for that. Now, perhaps walking among the vineyards, she wishes that she and her man were in a private place where they could express their passion.

But also the repetition of this verse is a reminder that, as Solomon would say: to every time there is a season under heaven. There was a time when she had to wait. Now the waiting is over. Now is that time she was describing as "until it pleases." This is the culmination and consummation of all the waiting. There comes a time when every dream and desire is fulfilled. The full expression of passion between husband and wife is only a foretaste of the glory that awaits us in the next life. For then Christ and His bride will finally come together without the restraint of this world's fallen state.

YOUR RECREATION

God built season and cycle into the very fabric of creation. The world turns for us, summer becomes autumn becomes winter becomes spring, and a new cycle begins. Meanwhile, day becomes night becomes a fresh morning. What do you think God is trying to tell us about our identity as His creatures?

These cycles are our way of measuring time. In a manner of speaking, they're signposts that say, "Beware! Time is on the march. It never pauses, never stops." In most places, summertime is recognized as a kind of "cease fire" in the business world, when men and women are allowed, for a brief time, to catch their breath and restore their energy. At the end of the year, there is another holiday season, though we've done all we could to make it even more stressful than the rest of the calendar. Every civilization and culture builds in its own structures and customs for work and rest.

We need night for sleep at the end of a day. We need the weekend for rest at the end of a work cycle. We need to stop and be with family at the end of the year; because it's important to be reminded that time never pauses, and a new year is upon us. If we don't refresh ourselves, if we don't allow God to recreate us, we will let the time slip away. We will also burn down to the wick like so many wax candles.

All these rest cycles are built into our cultural lifestyle, but not into marriage. There is no culturally-endorsed time for a husband and wife to go aside and reconnect. Is it any wonder that so many of our marriages struggle today? Most of us never consider that marriage requires at least the same level of care and maintenance in life as everything else precious to us. I have known Christians who are quite disciplined about taking time for God on a daily basis, moving through a regular study of the Bible, praying with discipline—but it would never occur to them to show such loving care with the precious gift of a spouse and a marriage.

So what if you let that marriage deteriorate? Please realize that you can't compartmentalize these things; your marriage does not occur in a vacuum, but is woven into the fabric of your life. If your marriage hurts, you will hurt. If it fails to grow, so will you. Believe me, if it dies, a part of you invariably dies with it. These are strong words, but true ones.

Therefore I'm going to suggest something crazy, something you may never have thought about. What if you sat down with your spouse and became intentional about planning regular weekend getaways together—not "sometime," not "when we come to a stopping point," but on a definite and intentional schedule? And what if you took a leaf from Shulamith's book and did all the groundwork planning in advance—everything required to make it the weekend of a lifetime?

What if you continued to enjoy a summer vacation with the entire family, but at least two weekend getaways just for the two of you? You could go somewhere in the mountains every autumn, somewhere green and garden-ish in the springtime. Solomon and Shulamith seem to have enjoyed the best of both worlds—mountains and gardens—on their Lebanese vacation. But I'm not going to do your planning for you. Design it however you feel led, and for the purpose of mutual joy. Think about how thoughtfully, cleverly, and creatively Shulamith enticed her husband to get away, even get a little business done with love on the side.

Simple question: Is there any reason in the world you can't do this? If you find yourself hesitant, ask yourself why. Weekend getaways are very affordable; they need cost hardly anything at all, actually—remember though, romance is not about economy or efficiency.

If something in you makes you recoil from the idea of a focused time with your sweetheart, is that not in itself a leading indicator that you need this time together? Remember, we've spoken about how it's easier to act our way into feeling rather than feeling our way into acting. Therefore act on obedience, on the life commitment of love you've made to your spouse. The feelings are certainly going to come. That's the point of the whole exercise, at least in part.

I like to say that life was meant to be lived at eighty percent of our capacity, so that we have a margin of twenty percent left to deal with the unexpected issues that arise. Unfortunately, I live at something like ninety-five percent capacity, and I leave myself little margin to care for the unanticipated needs that sprout up. If I begin to sense that I need time alone with my wife, it's going to be difficult because I'm hemmed in by my own cluttered appointment book. I also know that this gets tougher as we get older. We just seem to have more and more commitments, and we become increasingly less free to take care of what's really important, rather than what seems urgent.

YOUR TRANSFORMATION

There is a story told about some Americans who went on an African safari. They were eager to take in as much as they could in the brief period they had before going home. They kept pushing their native guides to hurry, hurry, hurry. Finally, on the third morning, the travelers found the guides squatting under a tree and refusing to move. When asked why, the guides said, "We shall rest today to let our souls catch up with our bodies." [12]

There is so much truth in those words. Our bodies are flying around at the speed limit, and our souls can only move as fast as they can move. Pretty soon body and soul are no longer connected. This is why we feel so refreshed at a retreat or having a change of scenery—just getting away where we can leave the daily planner and the cell phone behind. Then we can actually open our eyes. We can smell roses. We can have focused conversations without all those anxieties dominating our thinking, and perhaps we can even enjoy love again.

I'm writing these words hoping I'll heed them myself. The truth is that I'm doing better at it. There was a time when I couldn't justify taking a month off from a church, a radio ministry, and a television ministry. Oh, we would go somewhere, but when Sunday came I would climb onto a plane and fly back to preach. Then I would rejoin my family and resume vacationing. Do you think I really experienced the rest and renewal that a getaway is supposed to bring? Do you think it was fair to my wife or children?

But I learned. You see, when I take the month of August off I find that for two weeks I'm still expecting the phone to ring. I'm still thinking through ministerial strategies. I'm not really "away" yet, because the little switch hasn't gone off inside me. This is why we talked about *preparation* for a getaway. It's not defined by being somewhere else. It's defined by letting your soul catch up with your body.

At least one of you in the marriage needs to be sensitive to this need and insist upon getting away together. In this narrative, Shulamith was the one to take the initiative. It often happens that when the man becomes consumed by his work the wife finds herself saying, "If I don't plan this thing, no one will." But men, you need to take the lead sometimes.

Believe it or not, I've done it myself. I knew my wife loved San Francisco, though she had only been there once. I wanted to surprise her—to take her there when she didn't even know she was leaving town. I knew I could make flight and hotel reservations. That part even I could handle. But of course I hadn't reckoned with packing a suitcase for Donna! When that realization dawned upon me, I turned white as a sheet. The right clothing, all her makeup and accessories—boy, I had gotten myself in deep. The closer the trip came, the more stressed I was because I was petrified of leaving out one of Donna's travel essentials. It was scary for me before the trip, and it was scary for her once we got there! But you know what? Those little details didn't matter at all. We had a great time, and we still laugh about the adventure. Donna loved it that I had taken the initiative to take her on a surprise trip to the City by the Bay.

We're learning that surprises can have a wonderful effect on marriage. And when we transform our marriage, we transform ourselves. You see, as we get away, we fall in love with each other all over again. And that's not a bad feeling at all; it's a little dip in the fountain of youth that transforms how we're going to function once we get back to the real world. But at the same time, we find ourselves reconnecting with God. We simply can't do that when we're sprinting all the time, and when our fellowship with each other in marriage is not what it should be.

Through the Old Testament sons of Korah, our Lord said, "Be still and know that I *am* God" (Psalm 46:10). Have you done it lately? Have you stopped to take a deep breath, maybe stepping outside to look at the stars and drink in the silence? Do that tonight—hand in hand with your beloved. Catch up with God, both of you together. You need to be still and know He is God, and you need to know your life partner, too.

Go ye, therefore! Go to the hills. Go to the sea. Go to the woods and camp out. It doesn't matter where you go, just so you go into the arms of one another and taste the twin joys of being a spouse and a child of God. ◆

1   Adapted from marriage illustration entry, www.preachingtoday.com, submitted by Brett Kays, Flat Rock, Michigan. (accessed 27 January 2009).
2   Joseph Dillow, *Solomon on Sex*, (Nashville, TN: Thomas Nelson Publishers, 1977), 143.
3   Rabbi Shumley Boteach, "What a Woman Wants," *World Net Daily*, worldnetdaily.com/news/article .asp?ARTICLE_JD=50735, 22 June 2006 (accessed 31 November 2008).
4   Mark Gungor, *Laugh Your Way to a Better Marriage*, (New York, NY: Atria Books, 1999), 94.
5   Paige Patterson, *Everyman's Bible Commentary*, Song of Solomon (Chicago, IL: Moody Press, 1986), 110.
6   Tommy Nelson, *The Book of Romance*, (Nashville, TN: Thomas Nelson Publishers, 1998), 177.
7   Alfred, Lord Tennyson, "Locksley Hall," *Poems*, (Boston, MA: J.R. Osgood, 1877), 82.
8   Lois Kerschen, *American Proverbs about Women* (Greenwood Publishing, 1998), 185.
9   Lise Manniche, Werner Forman, *Sacred Luxuries* (Cornell University Press, 1999), 102.
10 Paige Patterson; 114.
11 Paige Patterson; 115.
12 Og Mandino, *University of Success* (New York: Bantam Doubleday Dell, 1983), 424.

12

Staying in Love for Life

Song of Solomon 8:5-14

Imagine this: a husband and wife who haven't had an argument since 1946.

But wait. Even in '46, they had already been married for more than two decades. Add six decades plus to that. They've been married for eighty-three years, as of this writing. Clarence and Mayme Vail are getting pretty good at this thing.

When the couple married in 1925, Calvin Coolidge was president, Babe Ruth was all the rage, and movies had no sound. Clarence was eighteen that year, his bride only sixteen. They had been sweet on each other since eighth grade, and their parents gave them their blessing to go ahead and marry. No marriage in modern history has lasted longer. We might have to go back to Abraham and Sarah to find a better marriage story.

Like so many other couples with staying power, the Vails seem nonchalant when asked for their secret. There is no magic formula, they insist; they simply made a sacred vow at the altar, and they have regarded those vows quite seriously. As for the absence of arguments, Mayme credits her husband: he's the strong, silent type who by nature isn't given to bickering.

The Vails originally moved into a one-room home. Together they endured the Great Depression, the Second World War, several other wars, and unprecedented cultural and technological revolutions. The only true challenge, as they saw it, came in 1948 when Clarence came down with tuberculosis. Staunch Catholics, the couple prayed hard and clung together. Mayme made a vow to God that if her husband pulled through, she'd attend Mass every day for the rest of her life.

Clarence was spared, and Mayme was as good as her word for sixty years until her health made it impossible to attend church daily. Together the couple finally moved into a retirement home in 2007. From there, they try the best they can to follow the exploits of their one hundred and eighty-six descendants. That number was not a misprint. You see, the Vails have six children, thirty-nine grandchildren, one hundred and one great-grandchildren, and forty great-great-grandchildren. They are a one-couple family tree with deep roots. The Bible told them to be fruitful, and apparently they took that one pretty seriously, too.

Clarence naps frequently these days, but Mayme is said to look young for her age; she could easily pass for ninety. She makes quilts, as she's done all her life; she receives two Masses per week; and she continues to care for her beloved husband, eighty-three years into the wonderful, always surprising adventure of holy matrimony.[1]

Their commitment is inspiring, of course, but we know there is something more than simple commitment at work here. We are committed to many things without the obvious delight that the Vails have shown with each other. Honoring a commitment is a powerful concept, a question of obedience and integrity. But what about love? Isn't love truly the glue that holds a marriage together? Isn't it the reason why we get married in the first place? If commitment is the engine of a strong marriage, love is the fuel that makes it run so smoothly.

Let's think about love, the great mystery, the core emotion of this world.

In the late 1800s, Henry Drummond wrote a little essay called "The Greatest Thing in the World" that became a classic devotional book. Reviewing 1 Corinthians 13, he concluded that love is ultimately the secret of life, and that we cannot truly live until we truly love. Therefore love is "the greatest thing in the world," life's ultimate secret, given that God Himself is love (1 John 4:8). When we begin to take hold of His love *for* us, His love takes hold *of* us. We begin to love other people in His supernatural, humanly impossible manner. It is an awesome power the world can never reproduce, because this love doesn't come from earth.

That is the kind of love we read about in Scripture. But this four-letter word has become victimized by its careless use in a society that defines it as a feeling that comes and goes, something we "fall" in or out of, or even a generic fondness, as in "loving" pizza or "loving" a television show. How sad that we don't reserve a separate word for divine love, as New Testament Greek does: *agape* love. There is something more than a generic fondness about the kind of love Christ showed for us on the cross. The kind of gracious love God has stubbornly maintained for us through all our centuries of disobedience, even the kind of love we see in a godly couple that remains joyfully together through life. This love is powerful stuff!

The best definition I know of *agape* love is giving ourselves to someone with no strings attached and for no expected reward. If I can love you even if you do the worst and I gain the least, if I love you just because I love you—well, that's a supernatural love. It rises above human nature, because it is not our way but our Creator's.

If you think about it, every other emotion we have is turned inward. What makes love unique is that it shows the possibility of self-sacrifice, which is the image of God in us. This is at the very core of the kind of marriage we've described in this book. There is no response to love but to accept it, because it is a gift and not a transaction—except for the one case when it is reciprocated *in kind*, at which time it becomes something holy, a two-way relationship of self-sacrificial love. This is marriage, and it is indeed beautiful.

As we read the New Testament, we understand *agape* love in the person of Jesus Christ, the ultimate model of self-sacrificial, unconditional love. Then we begin to see it manifest itself in human relationships, particularly in that passage known as 1 Corinthians 13. In two hundred seventy-one words, Paul defines God's kind of love with poetry and precision. John Wesley and many other historic leaders of the church regard 1 Corinthians 13 as the greatest chapter in all of the Bible.

In reading that chapter, we discover Paul has written a kind of job description of *agape*—what love actually does. The chapter is filled with action verbs. Love is not a feeling or a reaction. It is not passive but active, a force to be reckoned with. Love gets busy.

Other emotions come naturally: fear, desire, sadness, and the rest. A small child will feel all of these things. But *agape* love must be adopted as an act of the will—ultimately it isn't an emotion at all, though it does involve emotions. Pulitzer Prize-winning writer Katherine Anne Porter has written: "Love is taught, always by precept, sometimes by example . . . Love must be learned, and learned again and again; there is no end to it. Hate needs no instruction, but waits only to be provoked."[2]

Gary Thomas adds, "Love is not a natural response that gushes out of us unbidden . . . but hate is always ready to naturally spring forth."[3] People don't love selflessly unless they are taught to walk in obedience to God.

We see it in the final verses of the Song of Solomon, the passage that completes our exploration of this fascinating book. Once again, I'm amazed at the things our Bible does that no other book can do. In this case, we find seven principles in this Old Testament chapter that correspond to the words Paul was to write centuries later in his letter to the Corinthians. I was amazed by the parallels, and I was left to wonder whether Paul actually reviewed The Song before he wrote the epistle. I do know this: The same Holy Spirit inspired both passages, so we shouldn't be surprised by how perfectly they dovetail.

THE STABILITY OF LOVE

Song of Solomon 8:5

"Who *is* this coming up from the wilderness, leaning upon her beloved? I awakened you under the apple tree. There your mother brought you forth; there she *who* bore you brought *you* forth" (8:5). Apparently the getaway rendezvous has ended. Solomon and Shulamith are in the royal chariot, hurrying through the desert on their way back to the palace, "coming up from the wilderness." The wife leans upon her husband in the closeness of intimacy. They may be talking casually, recalling the places they've been and the times they've enjoyed. They're refreshed by their escape from the world and their time together.

How about the apple tree reference? Earlier, Shulamith has spoken of Solomon as being "like an apple tree among the trees of the woods . . ." (2:3). In 8:5 we find another repetition of that motif. Love is something like a fruit tree, a gift that keeps giving: abundant, nourishing, and tasteful. What we think of when we see a tree, however, is sturdiness and stability. Solomon and Shulamith knew that a cedar from Lebanon could live for hundreds of years, while kings and kingdoms rose and fell. What living thing could be sturdier? The first Psalm speaks of the man who delights in God's law: "He shall be like a tree planted by the rivers of water, that brings forth its fruit in its season, whose leaf also shall not wither; and whatever he does shall prosper" (Psalm 1:3)—a tree used as a picture of endurance and consistency.

Now listen to Paul speak of one of the qualities of love: "Love never fails" (1 Corinthians 13:8). Don't you love those words? They sound lofty and magnificent—until you give them a little thought. Love is failing in every direction, wherever we look! Nearly every family has a broken relationship somewhere or other. Who says love never fails?

There is a difference, of course; no one said *marriage* never fails. Paul uses the word *ekpipto* which means "to collapse," or "to fall down," or "to be lowered in value." God's love doesn't collapse or fall down. The world's idea of love, a passing feeling, can and will collapse. Emotions aren't built on anything substantial, but agape love is eternal. Its leaf shall not wither; it never fails because God never fails.

What a marvelous job this poet has done in describing it:

> *When the last day is ended,*
> *And the nights are through;*
> *When the last sun is buried*
> *In its grave of blue;*
> *When the stars are snuffed like candles,*
> *And the seas no longer fret;*
> *When the winds unlearn their cunning,*
> *And the storms forget;*
> *When the last lip is palsied,*
> *And the last prayer is said;*
> *Love shall reign immortal*
> *While the worlds lie dead!* [4]

Would you like to have a love that reigns immortal? Such a love would not only hold your marriage together, it would make it powerful and fulfilling. Embrace Christ and you will know this love; follow Him and it will overflow into every relationship you have. That is a sturdy love, a love with stability.

THE SECURITY OF LOVE

Song of Solomon 8:6

Shulamith says: "Set me as a seal upon your heart, as a seal upon your arm" (8:6).

A seal in that day was not only a sign of ownership but a sign of great value. You would never set a seal upon something of little worth; you would carefully mark it as your property. Today, you wouldn't install an expensive burglar alarm on your garden shed, but you would on a fine home.

Shulamith wants to claim ownership of Solomon's heart, to have her name engraved upon his soul. As they ride back to Jerusalem in the chariot, she leans upon him, near to his heart where she feels secure. Back at the palace, he will undoubtedly be whisked away by chattering advisors. Shulamith wishes she could be set upon his heart, sealed in such a way that no one could come between them.

Security has proven to be a constant theme in this book, hasn't it? The idea has come up four different times. We don't think about the word very much, but a secure feeling is essential to marriage. It provides us peace that we need. Women in particular need to feel the security that a good marriage will bring. As one commentator has written, "The seal was two-fold: inner feelings and outer behavior. She didn't want any other woman to catch her husband's attention, and she didn't want her husband to be looking at any other woman."[5] It's about love, yes, but it is also about security.

Shulamith already knows she has his love, but she wants to reaffirm it. During their vacation, she has had him all to herself, and she doesn't want to let go of that sense of perfect belonging when the two are back in Jerusalem society and beautiful women are all around.

First Corinthians 13:7 tells us that love "endures all things." That means that in genuine love, we have true security. Ultimately, we find it in knowing God. Among human relationships, our greatest security is found in the partnership of marriage. At the altar, we vow that we will endure all things together: "in sickness and in health, for richer for poorer, 'til death do us part." Love endures all things, and what a comfort that is in the times in which we're living.

I've mentioned my friend Gary Smalley, a fine writer and speaker. He has also raised a fantastic son who, along with his wife Erin, is following in his dad's footsteps. Greg Smalley is willing to be transparent in sharing about his own life issues. This story from his marriage is a good example.

Greg tells how he and Erin had an issue related to his busy travel schedule. Greg would leave for a speaking tour, and while he was gone, all three kids would pile into the bed and sleep with their mother. Then, when he came back home, it was difficult to shoo them all back to their own rooms. It could often take days to break them of the habit again. Greg finally decided to lay down the law with his family. He gathered his kids and told them that, while he was gone, they could sleep in his room until one night prior to his return. Then they had to go back to their own beds.

Several weeks passed, and Greg was once again coming home from a trip. He was met at the airport by Erin and the children. Since this was before September of 2001, the group was able to proceed to the arrival gate. The plane had a late arrival, so there were hundreds of people standing around the tunnel from which Greg finally emerged. His son

Garrison came running toward him shouting at the top of his voice, "Hi Dad! I've got some good news! Nobody slept with Mommy while you were gone!"

Greg adds, "If only you could have seen the looks."[6]

I hear a story like that and know immediately that there's security in that marriage. They feel free to share such an amusing incident because they belong to one another, and there's solid trust. How many couples today really have absolute mutual trust in each other? If an atmosphere of suspicion or jealousy ever permeates a marriage, that marriage can't approach what it is designed to be. We need the security that Shulamith and Paul are describing.

THE STRENGTH OF LOVE

Song of Solomon 8:6

The next comment is a striking one, as powerful in its wording as anything in Scripture: "For love *is as* strong as death, jealousy *as* cruel as the grave; its flames *are* flames of fire, a most vehement flame" (8:6). Compare that one to a New Testament passage from Paul: "For I am persuaded that neither death nor life, nor angels nor principalities nor powers, nor things present nor things to come, nor height nor depth, nor any other created thing, shall be able to separate us from the love of God which is in Christ Jesus our Lord" (Romans 8:38-39). Shulamith says that love is as strong as death; Paul says that love is stronger. Christ, of course, spans the difference.

However, The Song 8:6 is also a perfect match with 1 Corinthians 13:13: "And now abide faith, hope, love, these three; but the greatest of these *is* love." In all three passages, we see the staying power of love.

Notice that Shulamith describes the strength of her love for Solomon using two similes and one metaphor. It is "*as* strong *as* death," "as cruel as the grave," and is "a most vehement flame."

"Strong as Death" is an interesting expression because it seems so
unlikely. Death is dreaded, love is desired. Death is an ending, while
love as described here is eternal—symbolized by the endless circle of
the wedding ring. But "just as death cannot be subdued," writes Patterson, "so love is also invincible and cannot be repressed."[7] Again, the
best example is God's love. That's an amazing picture of the unbreak-
able strength of the love of Christ, from which nothing can separate us.

But we can love with the love of Christ, too. *Agape* love never lets go.
It's unlike the kind of love the world advertises. In counseling married
couples over the years, I've probably heard this statement two dozen
times: "But Pastor, you don't understand. I just don't love her/him anymore." Those words are offered as the ultimate get-out-of-marriage-free
card. "The feeling is gone, so I will be, too." It's a far cry from the eternal thing Paul describes that is stronger than death, greater than faith
and hope.

I remember an occasion when someone played the "I don't love her
anymore" card and I chose to confront it squarely. I replied, "I see. So
you've chosen to disobey God."

"What did you say?"

"You've decided to disobey God."

He said, "What do you mean?"

I said, "It reads this way. Are you ready? *Husbands love your wives.*
Which part of that don't you understand?"

"Well, *you* don't understand. I just don't have any feeling for her."

I explained that feelings don't enter into this discussion for the reasons I've already offered in previous chapters. Love is not a feeling but
an act of joyful obedience. My friend said, "But let me tell you what my
wife did . . ."

"It won't change anything. It still says right here, *Husbands, love your
wives.* I don't see any loopholes."

Gary Thomas calls it both cruel and self-condemning when a husband admits he doesn't love his wife. The husband believes his declaration comes across as an indictment of her, as if it were her responsibility to somehow account for his loving feelings. Instead, "put in a Christian context, it's a confession of the man's utter failure to be a Christian."[8]

The solid truth is that God has given you your spouse *and* the love you need for that spouse. If you attempt to reject either or both of those precious gifts, then it's a simple matter of disobedience—no one can stop you from leaving, but don't try to describe it in terms of an emotion gone missing and a free option for walking away. Neither is relevant.

There was a time when this epidemic was a male-based thing. But we've seen it equal out a bit in recent years. Women are saying, "I don't love him anymore." The same concept of disobedience applies, and the same solution: Stay and start loving.

"Jealousy Is as Cruel as the Grave." This sounds initially like a negative statement. In truth, the Old Testament often describes a righteous kind of jealousy, as odd as that sounds. When God says he is a "jealous God," as He does often in the Old Testament, He is speaking of wanting every bit of our devotion, as He has every right to. The difference is in what you want and why you want it. Envy is unrighteous; this kind of jealousy is the desire to preserve what already belongs to you. Jealousy "is possessive and exclusive,"[9] and it is "a righteous concern and protective care."[10]

Don't get carried away with this new idea of "godly jealousy." Godly jealousy means that you do your utmost to keep your spouse's attention focused on you—to protect your spouse from any temptation to be unfaithful.

God is jealous for us. He's jealous for our purity, for our honesty, and for our obedience in marriage.

"Flames of Fire, a Most Vehement Flame." This metaphor is so designed as to emphasize the intensity of the flame. Think of a forest fire that rages out of control. Love is a powerful fire that burns in our hearts. Because it is supernatural, it is a compelling force to the degree by which it takes us by surprise. Daniel Akin observes: "The love God kindles in a marriage over which He is Lord is such a fervent and fiery flame that nothing on earth can extinguish it or put it out. . . . This is a passionate love, a red-hot flame."[11]

THE STUBBORNNESS OF LOVE
Song of Solomon 8:7

Love is stable, secure, and strong, but also a stubborn thing. This is another word we often use in a negative way, but we would all agree there is a time for rightful stubbornness, just as there is a righteous jealousy. We've already mentioned God's stubborn love for us over the centuries of our disobedience. Praise His name that He is willing to be stubborn rather than wishy-washy about that. Shulamith writes, "Many waters cannot quench love, nor can the floods drown it" (8:7). Staying with the metaphor of fire, imagine someone throwing bucket after bucket of water upon a campfire, but the flames keep leaping back into place. That's the image of stubborn love that will not be quenched, that suffers whatever comes its way but is never discouraged.

We know something about wildfires in California. Huge tankers are often employed to drop massive amounts of water on these fires. We're told that much of the time the fire wins out. The fire evaporates a good bit of the water before the water can envelop the flame.[12] Fire is a stubborn force, difficult to subdue.

Those of us in the ministry see our share of misery and hear more than our share of sad stories. But I will also tell you that we witness incredible demonstrations of the power of God's love. There are so many stories of spouses whose love was only heightened and enflamed by the misfortune a partner faced. When we fall in love, we don't count on a spouse to become a paraplegic after a tragic automobile accident. We don't count on our beloved to enter a long bout with cancer, or suffer some other life disaster. But love never abandons need; in fact, it proves itself by coming into its own in such times. I've told you about Mayme Vail, who walked to church every day for sixty years to thank God for letting her care for a husband stricken with tuberculosis. I have seen the love of God poured out to a spouse who could not respond in any way. We see these things and we know love is real; we know its Author is real, or to what could we attribute such a power?

Love is the eternal flame, a fire from heaven that never becomes ash. "Loving is not primarily what you receive but what you do—and do even when boredom, resentment, or hunger for novelty tells you life can be better somewhere else."[13]

THE SACRIFICE OF LOVE

Song of Solomon 8:7

Frederick Buechner has defined our next term in this way: "To sacrifice something is to make it holy by giving it away for love."[14]

He is describing one of the true secrets of godly love. Jesus described it, then demonstrated it: "Greater love has no one than this, than to lay down one's life for his friends" (John 15:13). In other words, to give what is difficult to give is a proof of love; to give one's life is the ultimate gift and the ultimate proof. In marriage, sacrificial love is the key to staying in love for a lifetime.

Listen to how the Song of Solomon makes use of this concept: "If a man would give for love all the wealth of his house, it would be utterly despised" (8:7). The idea is that a man would be laughed out of the neighborhood for trying to buy love with his possessions. We all know that love cannot be bought or sold, only given.

Craig Glickman adds one qualification: "But if you cannot give all the wealth of your house to gain love, is there anything you can give to attain it? There is. But it's much more costly than the sum of one's possessions. It is the gift of oneself. Solomon and Shulamith gained love only when he gave himself to her and she gave herself to him in return. Two priceless gifts made one priceless love."[15]

This concept is also covered by 1 Corinthians 13:3: "And though I bestow all my goods to feed *the poor*, and though I give my body to be burned, but have not love, it profits me nothing." We can actually sacrifice without love, but we cannot truly love without sacrifice.

Real love, then, is the giving of oneself, which is already a sacrifice. There will be more and more as love and commitment grow. There comes a time when sacrifice becomes the default position in a loving relationship. We are constantly willing to give up something in order to bless the one we love.

THE SELF-CONTROL OF LOVE

Song of Solomon 8:8-10

Marriage also includes the quality of self-control. As we read through our passage in The Song, we suspect there has been a change of scene. Solomon and Shulamith are no longer alone. Shulamith's brothers are on the scene. We can't be certain about the nature of the occasion— perhaps some kind of festival or reunion.

We remember how the brothers once made Shulamith work in the vineyard (see 1:6). Her father is never mentioned; he may have died earlier and left his sons to carry on the family work. Now the brothers are remembering the time when their sister was a little girl: "We have a little sister, and she has no breasts. What shall we do for our sister in the day when she is spoken for?" (8:8). Siblings are often playful together after they're grown, reminding each other of this or that amusing incident. Now, at a time when Shulamith has become a beautiful queen, perhaps they're recalling the girl at a time before puberty, when she roamed the orchards as a tomboy. Even then, they could foresee the beauty she would become. What would they do to protect a little sister's honor until the right man came along?

Her brothers observe that she will become either a "wall" or a "door" (8:9). A wall is stationary and represents moral strength; a door swings open and closed and represents moral laxity. The first option is the one for which loving brothers would hope. If she is a "wall," that is, if she guards her chastity, they will honor her with a battlement of silver. If she behaves as a "door," she will have to be shut behind boards of firm cedar—that is, locked away for safekeeping.

The brothers are acting as a good father would act then and now. What dad hasn't had a thought of putting his daughter somewhere safe from boys with dishonorable intentions?

Virginity is a delicate gift from God. If only young people could be allowed to hold onto that understanding without the world pushing them into decisions they'll regret. The norm today is that virginity is something to be cast off like baby teeth, and that waiting for marriage is abnormal behavior. The truth is that men and women who save themselves for marriage have something beautiful that their friends have denied themselves. A bride and groom with self-control can present their bodies to one another as gifts of purity. Isn't that worth the wait?

Shulamith's brothers are ready to affirm and celebrate good moral decisions on their sister's part. They're willing to take disciplinary measures if they note danger signals.

Now, after these two verses of nostalgic indulgence, Shulamith brings her brothers back to the present: "I *am* a wall, and my breasts like towers; then I became in his eyes as one who found peace" (8:10). She is no longer that little girl, but a mature, healthy, and morally pure young lady who has observed the discipline of delayed gratification. The latter part of the verse is particularly beautiful. As Solomon sees a virtuous young woman before him, she in turn sees the peace and joy in his eyes.

Lost virginity can never be recovered. But let us remember that it can be forgiven—by God and by a spouse. Once a couple is married, this factor of self-control is no less important. The husband and wife reserve themselves for each other exclusively. They maintain a kind of virginity in relation to the world as they give themselves joyfully to each other. From then on, self-control protects a faithful and devoted marriage.

THE SELFLESSNESS OF LOVE

Song of Solomon 8:11-12

Love is a challenge, and each of these attributes reflects that. But this final factor is perhaps the most difficult of all: the challenge of selflessness, which is the most familiar component of genuine, godly love. In one way or another, all the other attributes have this one at their core.

Our world, of course, cannot comprehend selflessness. In the 1970s, *Looking Out for Number 1* became a bestselling self-help book, and at the time the title provoked a bit of discussion and controversy. It would seem less shocking today because self-absorption is the way of the world. Again, it's not difficult to see the connection between this philosophy and the age of widespread divorce. Married love requires emotional maturity, disciplined perseverance, and a willingness to put the other person first. When two people "look out for number one," and number one happens to be the person in the mirror, there will be trouble. When number one is the other spouse, they're onto something.

Shulamith is still reminiscing with her brothers. She says, "Solomon had a vineyard at Baal Hamon; he leased the vineyard to keepers; everyone was to bring for its fruit a thousand silver coins. My own vineyard *is* before me. You, O Solomon, *may have* a thousand, and those who tend its fruit two hundred" (verses 11-12).

What is happening here? It seems likely that Solomon owned the vineyards in which Shulamith labored as a child. Her family had paid the annual rent of one thousand silver coins. Had the girl not been put to work outdoors—had they found reason to lock her away behind those boards of cedar—she and her future husband might never have met.

Shulamith reminds Solomon that he may have as many as a thousand vineyards, but she has only one. She is speaking of herself metaphorically, of course. Her vineyard is herself, kept pure for his delight all this time. In a teasing way, she is saying, "So where is my rent? Where are my thousand silver coins?"

"Those who tend its fruit," are, of course, her brothers who have cared for her until the day when her groom came to bear her away. She has forgiven her brothers, and she signals that by saying they're due two hundred coins for their watch-care over her life. They have brought Solomon a profit of fruit in his vineyards; they have brought him a precious gift in their protection of their sister. She comes to him now with character, integrity, and purity.

Solomon now whispers, "You who dwell in the gardens, the companions listen for your voice—let me hear it!" (v. 13) Craig Glickman observes: "Her voice is a song in the gardens, dovelike music in a paradise. When she sings from her heart, her words touch his heart, and the melody resonates through his soul."[16]

The Song of Solomon is thus coming to its ending with a song of Shulamith. Their love has come of age like the grapes in the vineyard, sweet, and full of life and health. Shulamith responds to her husband's invitation with one of her own: "Make haste, my beloved, and be like a gazelle or a young stag on the mountains of spices" (verse 14). It's not the first time she has compared him to a gazelle or a young stag. On their honeymoon, she has referred to mountains as places of delight, and she does so again. We see the selflessness in man and wife, not making demands on each other; both devoted to the pleasure of the other: each finding the true joy that can come only when we reach out to someone else rather than live in the self-imprisonment of self-absorption.

On the fateful night of their misunderstanding, we could see hints of selfishness in each of them. Shulamith was making demands on Solomon's priorities, while he was making demands on her patience and availability. Both were thinking of their own pleasure. It was almost a relief to see them stumble, because then we knew this was a human couple with a marriage set squarely in this world, not a fantasy one. We love the Bible because it is always about truth.

But then we watched the couple grow. It was their very stumbling that led to their leaps of maturity. This is how it goes in marriage. As single people, we have known how to live independently. As married people, we must learn to sacrifice that independence and the self-priority that goes with it.

Paul reminds us once again in 1 Corinthians 13:5: "[Love] does not seek its own."

We learn not to seek our own, but to live instead as loving fellow servants. Thus we find the truth at the heart of Jesus' paradoxes: the last shall be first, we must lose our souls to find them, and so on. In Matthew 16:24, Jesus invites us to deny ourselves, take up our crosses, and follow Him. Marriage is included in that process of self-denial. As with all things, it leads first to a cross, but ultimately to a crown.

If your marriage is in pain, remember that the reward is always still waiting ahead for you. Be strong and of good courage, and know that God will be with you. Keep following Him, beyond the cross, through all the difficulties, and you can reap the reward that comes to all those who persevere in His name. That means enjoying all the good things that come from a long marriage. Believe me—it's more than worth it, more than wonderful, more precious than gold.

TAMING THE FOXES

You could argue that in the long run, marriage is more about the little moments than the big ones. Early in the book we talked about the "little foxes," those little irritations that lead to big trouble. But there are so many wonderful little moments in marriage, opportunities for something to go wrong, when instead we find we've gained the skill to make them go right. I'll give you an example from my life with Donna.

I love watching basketball. Due to its lengthy season and my tight schedule, however, I simply don't have the luxury of enjoying many games. My compromise is to try and carve out a little extra time during the NBA playoffs during the spring and early summer. My wife and I have an agreement. She knows that when playoff time comes, I'll have the family room television set staked out. I don't watch a great deal of television otherwise, and when I'm away from home, Donna will use that set.

On this particular occasion, my team had an important game and I was thoroughly into it. Donna was upstairs watching her own show on the upstairs set. I was on the edge of my seat, watching a tense fourth quarter. Suddenly, with no warning, a graphic appeared across the screen. "A recording," it informed me in ominous writing, "will begin in one minute."

"*What* recording?" I demanded of the screen. But the television ignored my question and, sixty seconds later, carried out its warning. The channel changed by itself, and I found myself watching some other show I didn't even recognize.

I'm sure you're techno-savvy and two steps ahead of me, since I'm still catching up with digital watches and microwave ovens. I have only the vaguest conception of what a DVR is, but Donna had just installed one. She had set it to record a regular show in case we were out some week and she missed it.

Naturally I was oblivious to all that. All I could do was wail in my loudest, least pastoral voice, "Oh, NO!"

Donna came running in a panic, wondering if aliens from Mars were descending upon San Diego. It didn't take long for her to see my face, my television screen, and my evident problem. She attempted to quickly return me to the comforts of ESPN. The only problem was that she couldn't figure out how to stop the recording, and the DVR would not listen to her desperate pleas any more than me. This was a highly committed electronic component; it had its orders and was dedicated to carrying them out.

It took me only a couple of minutes to regain my composure and realize there would be a replay of the game. Then we looked at each other and began to chuckle over how ridiculous the whole scene was: the mysterious DVR, my lack of awareness of it, and her inability to save the day . . .

In a bad marriage, it could have been a bad moment. In a good marriage, all things work together for the good, because we've learned, by the grace and love of God, to *point* them in that direction. We know we are part of one another, and we are just as staunchly committed to one another as that DVR is to making me watch a show I don't care about.

It's a beautiful thing. I don't have to like Donna's show, and she doesn't have to become a basketball fan—although both of us would make those moves in a heartbeat if it was important to the marriage. When any point of tension arises, we know how to recognize the little foxes and tame them before they get to the grapes.

THE PERFECT SPOUSE

I wouldn't hold our marriage up as an example of perfection. We will have our moments, just like everyone else. But we are going and growing together on a journey we are very much enjoying. Love is no longer about what needs I want met, or what things I want done for me. It's not only more blessed to give than to receive, but in the end it's a lot more fun. It is truly important to me to please my wife, to be a part of her world, and to have her as a part of mine.

In *The Art of Understanding Yourself*, author Cecil Osborn tells about a couple receiving marriage counseling. In the presence of her husband, the woman told the counselor, "I'd like to have married a man who was very strong, yet very gentle. I'd like to have married a man who would have been strong enough to have put me in my place when I got out of line, but understanding and sensitive enough to know when I needed to have my own way. I'd like to have married a man who would be tolerant of my occasional outbursts and emotional tantrums, and wise enough to see that I need a good cry now and again. I would like to have married a man who would pat me and console me without bothering to argue with me."

On she went, describing the paragon of virtue that she felt she deserved as a husband. Meanwhile, the spouse in question simply sat and listened. At the end of the diatribe, he finally spoke: "You know,

I think there was someone like that once, but if I recall correctly, they crucified Him between two thieves."[17]

If we're honest, we all want the perfect spouse, but we can no more find one nor become one. We're bound to fall short of each other's unrealistic expectations unless we bring a third party into the marriage. Yes, this third party was indeed crucified between two thieves, but we all know that was not the end of the story. He rose again in order to help us rise again. If death itself is no match for Him, how much more can He help us toward victory in marriage? What is there that Christ cannot accomplish if we're willing to invite Him into our households, into our kitchen, into our bedroom?

The kind of godly marriage that Solomon and Shulamith had is not humanly possible. On the other hand, it is supernaturally possible. The question for you, my friend, is what you will do with that fact—what you will do with all the truths we've discussed in this book. The beleaguered husband in the previous story was right: the only one capable of perfection was crucified between two thieves a long time ago. The good news is that there is more to the story. He rose again so that we can all do the same—not just when we die, but when we experience any other kind of death in life. A dead friendship can always live again. A dead career can be resurrected. The death of hope is never final, *including* when that hope has been lost for marriage.

Yes, the Resurrection of Christ applies to your marriage. It applies to every single factor of your life, as a matter of fact. If only we could comprehend the incredible, infinite meaning of that concept, how different this life would be. Then we would never give up hope in anything, least of all marriage—such a beautiful and essential gift of God.

If your marriage has been through torment, think of the torment of Christ on Good Friday. If you are tempted to take the easy way out, take courage in the fact that He didn't, even knowing what kind of suffering was ahead for Him. And if you find it hard to believe that something new and lovely can arise from the ashes of a dead marriage, ask God to help your unbelief. Meanwhile, act on that hope. Start treating your spouse as the most wonderful person in your life and your marriage as the most important decision, other than your salvation. I believe your love can last a lifetime. Your Lord *knows* it is so.

Move forward in the faith of God, the love of Christ, and in devotion to your spouse. ◆

1   "Couple, married 83 years, share their secret," by Mike Celizic, published by TodayShow.com, 17 March 2008, http://www.msnbc.msn.com/id/23671580. (accessed 28 January 2009).
2   Katherine Anne Porter, *The Days Before* (New York: Arno Press, Inc., 1952), 181.
3   Gary Thomas, *Sacred Marriage*; 40.
4   Frederic Lawrence Knowles, "The Survivor," *Love Triumphant: A Book of Poems*, (Boston: Colonial Press, 1906), 36. http://books.google.com/books?id=bZYXAAAAYAAJ&pg=PA36&dq=%22love+sh all+reign+immortal+while+the+worlds+lie+dead%22&ei=hf0RSYabIovuMq-UsYYO.
5   Tommy Nelson; 188.
6   Adapted from Dr. Greg and Erin Smalley, *Before You Plan Your Wedding... Plan Your Marriage*, (West Monroe, LA: Howard Publishing, 2008), 50.
7   Paige Patterson; 116.
8   Gary Thomas; 40-41.
9   Daniel Akin; 256.
10 Tommy Nelson; 117.
11 Daniel Akin; 256-257.
12 Gillian Flaccus, "Unstoppable firefighters all but concede defeat to big, fast flames," Oakland Tribune, 24 October 2007, http://findarticles.com/p/articles/mi_qn4176/is_/ai_n21078645(accessed 5 November 2008).
13 David Sanford, "Learning to Love Means Staying When You Want to Leave," Marriage Support.com, http://www.marriagesupport.com/articles_advice/article.asp?articleNum=280&From=Col&ID=8& email=cthlrd@aol.com&orderid=1891(accessed 5 November 2008).
14 Frederick Buechner, *Wishful Thinking: A Seeker's ABC* (New York: HarperOne, 1993), 101.
15 Craig Glickman, *Solomon's Song of Love*; 151-152.
16 Craig Glickman, *Solomon's Song of Love*; 163.
17 Adapted from Cecil Osborn, *The Art of Understanding Yourself*, (Grand Rapids, MI: Zondervan Publishing House, 1967), 146.

Afterword

So whatever became of Solomon and the love of his life? The Bible leaves that question wide open.

We know a good bit about the king himself, of course—and not all of it constitutes a happy ending. As for this particular love relationship, however, God has chosen to withhold the details of its progress.

And you know what? That's very appropriate. For not only is that couple's success an open question, but it's the same for those of us who are married today. What does the future hold for your union? Will your love deepen gloriously, or will you allow it to slowly unravel?

I believe that every essential need for maintaining a fantastic marriage is detailed in the inspired Word of God. This book in particular, the Song of Solomon, has so much to teach us about loving for a lifetime. If you will follow your Lord down life's pathway, hand in hand with the mate He has given you, with His Word as the light for your path, there is no reason in the world that you can't experience the ultimate joy of marriage in true mind, body, and spirit. As we've discussed, there is nothing in this world or any world that can separate you from the love of Christ, and that love can, in turn, make the two of you inseparable. It can knit your hearts together so that you will cling joyfully to one another.

But I would be remiss if I didn't emphasize one critical fact. This wonderful power is only available to those who have become God's children through a saving relationship with Jesus Christ. And I'll tell you why that is, in a few paragraphs ahead. First, however, let's deal with this primary question—the most demanding one of your life, even more important than "will you marry me?"

The question is: If you were to die today, would you be certain that you are going to spend all of eternity in the presence of God, cleansed, and forgiven from all your earthly sins?

You see, the Bible tells us that there are none who are worth, on their own merits to enter heaven as an inheritor of eternal life. Every person who has ever lived, with the exception of God's own Son, has committed sin. That word is defined in the Bible as "missing the mark," or failing in any small way to be what God intended. Because He is a holy and perfect God, His standards are absolutely perfect. Just as darkness flees from light, the darkness in us can't stand in the presence of His perfect light. We would have to somehow be totally pure. And as far as we are concerned, that is impossible, unattainable, out of the question. Neither you nor I can live a single day without missing the mark, and for that matter, missing it over and over. This is simply the human condition and has been so ever since the rebellion of Adam and Eve.

Therefore our sin creates an unbridgeable gulf between God and His children. But wait—did you catch that word, *unbridgeable*? For there is one thing that can close the gap, and that is the cross. Since Christ is perfect, He can and did elect to die for our sins. The Bible tells the story of how He was nailed to the cross not for anything He did (He was sinless) but for everything *we* did. He was thinking about you as He suffered; He was thinking about all of us.

And because a sinless Man was willing to take on the full brunt of punishment for all the sin of the world, sinful people can take on His *perfection*. We can know that heaven awaits us, because Jesus Christ will stand before God and say, "This person is guiltless. I took his/her punishment as his/her substitute." Yes, we can now stand in His awesome and holy presence, pure and spotless.

But it's not all about heaven. Here comes the second part that I promised to explain above: why only those in Christ can experience all that marriage can be.

Part of salvation happens *right now*. You can be saved from so many tragic mistakes in life. You can be saved from foolishness. You can be saved from yourself. For the moment you accept God's free gift of salvation—the moment you say, "Yes, God, I want to know You, I want to walk with Christ"—a wonderful miracle occurs. God's Holy Spirit enters your heart once and for all. You may not feel any particular emotion or sensation. It may happen very quietly, but I assure you it happens. And you will never be the same.

From that moment on, the Lord Himself lives within you, counseling you, encouraging you, imparting to you at least one spiritual gift, and gently nudging you when you take the wrong road. This is why you must know Jesus Christ in order to experience the kind of marriage we're talking about. No one else has that incredible advantage of the Holy Spirit living within. I can tell you from years of marriage that the Holy Spirit is the third party that has made all the difference in the union of my wife and me. We serve Him together, and He helps us cherish and adore and serve one another.

YOUR DEFINING MOMENT

I've never shied away from asking people directly, "Have you prayed to receive Christ?" The question is just too critical, too momentous. It's not enough to simply *think* we're "spiritual" or "good people." We must, by a deliberate and conscious act of will, accept the offer that God is holding out. That offer may come during a sermon, during a friend's sharing of his faith, or in a book like this one. This very moment is such an example if you've never actually accepted Christ as your Savior. If that's the case, you'll never in your life read words more important than these.

So what about it? If this is your time, you need only do a couple of things. First, talk to God. Use your own words, by all means, but they should convey a message along these lines:

> *Lord, I am a sinner. I own up to the fact that I can never please you through my own efforts. Every day of my life I miss the mark. But I know that Your Son, Jesus Christ, died for me, in all His perfection, to pay the price of my sins. I accept His gift. I acknowledge His sacrifice on my behalf. And from this moment on, I identify with Him and will follow Him wholeheartedly, finding and doing His will for my life.*

Once you have prayed that prayer, you will be saved that very moment! Again, don't worry about your feelings. At first, nothing may seem to be very different at all. But in truth, everything is different. You are in Christ, and Christ is in you. From there, it's very important that you find a strong, Bible-believing church and begin to serve the Lord there. If you are married, serve Him together. But even if your spouse hasn't yet found Christ, continue to pray for your spouse; continue to serve God.

If you prayed to accept Christ today, know that the angels are singing in celebration (Luke 15:10). The RSVP list for heaven has grown by one, and that's a cause for rejoicing.

We also want to be certain that you get off to the best possible start in following your Lord and Savior. If you need guidance or have questions, let us know at Turning Point at www.DavidJeremiah.org or call us at 1-800-947-1993.

MY PRAYER FOR YOU

One final word about you and your love life. Please find the following paragraph that best fits you.

If you are single and hoping to be married, my prayer for you is that
you will take to heart our discussion about finding the right one; that,
having done so, you and your spouse will enter into marriage with
all the joy and unlimited possibilities that newlyweds can experience
under the Lordship of Christ.

If you are already in the early years of marriage, my prayer is that
you realize just how blessed you are that God has brought you a spouse,
and just how capable God is of taking hold of your marriage and trans-
forming it into a match for the ages, a union to bless the future. You can
begin today to devote yourselves to one another more selflessly than
ever, to listen to one another, to serve one another, to stoke the fire and
build the flames of your love higher and higher.

If you're a veteran at this pursuit called marriage, and you've been
together for years, my prayer is that you're willing to go back to work,
to do the things you did at first; that you and your spouse will recommit
yourselves to raising your joy and devotion to new levels. Don't think
it can't happen—I've seen stagnant relationships gloriously revitalized
too many times. Take a weekend getaway. Fall in love all over again, and
make sure Christ is a part of everything.

If you've been through the heartbreak of divorce, my prayer is
that you'll realize that your joy is not forever extinguished, and that
God most assuredly has great things ahead for you. The wisdom
you've gained through your pain can become a powerful gift that
you can help others who come behind you and that God has a hope
and a plan for your life. And if that pain has come through grief,
and you've been left behind by a spouse who has gone to be with the
Lord, know that you will be reunited someday. Best of all, be very
certain that the marriage you enjoyed was only a foretaste of the
deeper, more profound life that awaits all of us who serve the King.
Then one day we will be united in the perfect relationship of the

one final and ultimate marriage, that of Christ and His Bride, the Church.

That will be a great day of family reunion, won't it? But the good news is also about *right now.* There is so much joy to be savored even in this fallen world of ours—so much happiness, so many surprises. Solomon and Shulamith are the proof of that, but why take their word for it? Find out for yourself: from this day forward, for better or for worse, in sickness and in health, as long as you both shall live. ◆

STAY CONNECTED

to the teaching of Dr. David Jeremiah

Take advantage of two great ways to let Dr. David Jeremiah give you spiritual direction everyday! Both are absolutely FREE!

Turning Points Magazine and Devotional

Receive Dr. David Jeremiah's monthly magazine, *Turning Points* each month:

- Monthly Study Focus
- 52 pages of life-changing reading
- Relevant Articles
- Special Features
- Humor Section
- Family Section
- Daily devotional readings for each day of the month!
- Bible study resource offers!
- Live Event Schedule
- Radio & Television Information

Your Daily Turning Point E-Devotional

Start your day off right! Find words of inspiration and spiritual motivation waiting for you on your computer every morning! You can receive a daily e-devotion communication from David Jeremiah that will strengthen your walk with God and encourage you to live the authentic Christian life.

Sign up for these two free services by visiting us online at www.DavidJeremiah.org click on DEVOTIONALS to sign up for your monthly copy of *Turning Points* and your Daily Turning Point.